D1475364

My Parents Went Through the Holocaust and All I Got Was This Lousy T-shirt

A NEAR-LIFE EXPERIENCE

S. Hanala Stadner

Illustrations by S. Hanala Stadner

Mi
matter inc.
an imprint of Seven Locks Press

www.myparentswent.com
Contact: (800) 354-5348

Matter Inc. is an imprint of Seven Locks Press

Printed in the United States of America
Library of Congress Cataloging-in-Publication Data
is available from the publisher
ISBN 1-931643-76-8

Cover photos by J.P. Yim
Cover and content design by Heather Buchman

Some of the names have been changed because she wanted to.

For Kati: Thanks for the intensive psycho-dialysis.
I don't know where I'd be if not for you,
but I know it wouldn't be a good place.

For Pete: Who paid for Kati. And for everything else.
Thanks for being such a good sport about my portrayal
of you as a *shlemiel*. And thanks for your faith in my writing
(and for the FedEx-ing, office supplies, and spa treatments).

For Ma and Daddy:
You taught me I could survive anything—even you.

And for the six million Jews,
I'm sorry I can't go back in time and kill Hitler.
You are not forgotten.

Table of Contents

Acknowledgments

I want to thank you . . .

Sally, my yoga instructor, who said as I was hanging upside down, "What makes a person become a drug addict?"

Heather Buchman, the plastic surgeon of publishing. For a book designer, you made the perfect editor. And, if not for you, I— for your business—might still be re-writing. (p.s. I fought to keep this cover.)

Margaret Burk, my eighty-six-year-old editor from Georgia, who, in her lovely southern drawl said, "Honey, do you *have* to mention blowjobs so much?" Thanks for understanding that yes, I did. I had seventeen thousand sentences, you helped figure out what order they came in.

Jim Riordan, publisher, distributor, gentleman, for believing in the book and *going for it* even though the title scared you. We'll always have Manhattan (Book Expo 2005).

The sponsors who helped shape my little TV show, especially: Sports Club LA (The Sports Connection), Arthur's (Jewels) on Montana, Gilda Marx Athletic Wear, and most of all, National Promotions & Advertising.

The women and men in my twelve-step meetings. And you know who you are. I hope you do, because I'm not supposed to mention you by name. (And if you don't know who you are, you aren't working a good program.)

Bill Wilson and Dr. Bob, and the little group they formed in Akron—especially Bill, the least anonymous AA member in history—who said, "Please, if you can help it, don't let your anonymity stand between you and helping a fellow alcoholic."

David Rensin, author, who saw my public access show and wanted to write a book about me, but after reading my material said, "I'm not going to write it. You are."

Carrie Winston, my publicist, who said, "If you write a book, I can get you on TV." And who, by the time I finished writing it, retired.

Carl Reiner, for creating a wonderful home life. It wasn't mine, but it did more for me than you know.

And for your words of encouragement and advice: Eddie Van Halen, Valerie Bertinelli, Ann-Margret, Dennis Franz, Marlon Brando, Jerry "Chicago Seven" Ruben, Jess Walton, Leeza Gibbons, Beverly Sassoon, Buddy Hackett, Alec Baldwin, Dallas Raines, Herb Edleman, Barbara DeAngelis, Wink Martindale, Robert Evans, Marcus Allen, Peter Schindler, Bill Macy, Marvin Davis, Rabbi Steven Carr Reuben.

. . . Let me tell you, it didn't hurt.

Guilt—the Gift That Keeps On Giving

There were twelve million Jews in Europe before the Holocaust.
Hitler killed half.
That left six million feeling guilty.

My parents survived Hitler. I survived my parents. Ozzie and Harriet they weren't. Going through the Holocaust made them cranky.

I wasn't crammed in a boxcar headed for Auschwitz. I came later. I grew up in a bungalow in Canada watching *Captain Kangaroo* and eating Alphabits. Yet, if you and I were to speak for five minutes, I'd work into the conversation that my parents are Holocaust survivors.

I didn't go through the Holocaust; the Holocaust went through me. And it likes to talk about itself. I don't try to bring it up, it *comes* up. Like bad clams. Just the *sight* of a swastika gives me a hot flash. It's like swallowing horseradish.

My education began in the crib. I didn't know from *The Cat in the Hat*. My bedtime stories were *The Aunt in the Camp*. The bogeyman under the bed wore a Nazi uniform and spoke German.

Today, I strive to be spiritual, but I have intrusive thoughts. On vacation in Maui, I'm floating in the calm ocean and Adolf Hitler snorkels by. Water is seeping through his mustache into the dive mask. I'll give him a "final solution"! I push Hitler's head into the ocean floor with my flipper, reach into his Speedo, yank off his penis and feed it to the fish. They eat *dick*-tators.

My body's on vacation, my resentment's at work.

I have money. I have everything—including bouts of hysteria. Having everything doesn't take away the nothing. When I'm not crying, I look confident. People say, "*You* were an obese, alcoholic, drug addict with agoraphobia? Impossible! You're an aerobics instructor!" I take that as a challenge, like they don't believe me. I wasn't given credibility as a child, and now I'm not sure if *even I* believe me.

I had bad *heir conditioning*. My mother told me, "I'm mad and it's your fault." I had no reason to think she'd lie, so I assumed I was a bad girl. It's something I learned along with chewing, and like chewing, I do it automatically . . . and often. Food—I have issues. I floss before getting on the scale.

❖ ❖ ❖

I've always wanted people to know my story, and I also worry they won't be interested. I wormed my way out of the womb with an attitude—"*Hello!! Does anyone care what I just went through?!*"

People say I *feel* too much. I say, "That's what narcotics are for."

Drugs—I've done them with TV stars. And before appearing on game shows. And in limos with foreign men. I've had an amazing amount of adventures considering I spent most of my time butt-melding with the couch, remote in one hand, Fritos in the other. Best explanation I have is— you have more time when you don't cook.

I *need* people, and people suck. Meaning, I get sucked into them—the way *Star Trek's* ship, The Enterprise, got sucked into menacing planets by powerful tractor beams. I've been drawn to people who've vaporized me. Batterers. Blamers. Boozers. Bigamists. This is who I find, and I don't even know I'm looking. It's the Attractor Factor. Resist the pull? Like Scotty told Kirk, "I don't have the power!" My pattern of gravitating toward chaos was programmed in me when I was just a small enterprise with no protective force shield.

I formed a personality rather than a person. I try to figure out the *right* way to act, what's expected by the important people, the *real* people, like the ones on TV. Meanwhile, I don't focus on faces. Floors, yes. I can tell you about linoleum.

❖ ❖ ❖

It's perpetually Sunday night, half-past-*Disney*, and I haven't started my homework. A five-thousand-word essay on the French Revolution is due in the morning. Revolting peasants—I can relate. Textbooks lay scattered about on the kitchen table and my pencil keeps breaking. Where do I start?

Daddy's belt will come off when he sees the report card. I want to close my eyes and go to sleep until adulthood.

But I'm thirty-five. It's time to open my eyes.

Life screams, "BUZZZZ! Wake up!"

"No, it hurts, I have to keep my eyes shut."

"But people are all around. You're getting old. Stuff's happening. Get *up*!"

"Not yet . . . not yet . . . I'll start life soon, but not yet."

The years march on like Germans into Poland. My own war to wake up disturbs my sleep. But I can't risk waking up. Not yet . . . I'm nearly a person; I'm close to becoming real; I'm almost living. But really, I'm just having a *near-life experience*.

I have one question: Can I ever feel as good sober as I did on Quaaludes?

The Pre-Lude:
Heroine-Sheik

1979, I'm living with Lewis. Lewis goes to work, I go to work on my tan.

I meet a forty-year-old foreign man down at the pool. He's wearing a Speedo, no deodorant, and twenty gold chains around his neck—I'm thinking he better not jump in the deep end.

He doesn't. He takes the chaise next to mine and offers to shmear on my SPF-free, generic Bain du Soleil. Skin damage? Oh please, like I'm going to live long enough to wrinkle.

He tells me he was some prince in some country before some coup, and asks if I've ever tried Quaaludes.

"No," I say, "I haven't." He shows me a white pill (looks like an Altoid with *714* engraved on it). Wow—714—like Joe Friday's badge on *Dragnet!* Which came first?

He says, "Quaaludes are like a bottle of tequila in a pill." Hmmm . . . so, they don't make you throw up or get fat. It's an excellent pill!

My new friend says, "I have more at my place."

So we're at his place. He disappoints me by breaking a pill in half. "A whole one is too strong for you, my dear."

"Don't be silly." What kind of a wimp does he think I am? I grab both halves, bang 'em back with a glass of wine, and pass out on my way to sitting down. Good. All I ever wanted was *out*.

The next thing I know (and much of my life can be put that way), I'm watching flames dance in a gas fireplace that's done in a nautical theme. I don't think it works design-wise.

I hear wet, slapping noises. Somebody close by is having sex! When I'm able to focus, I realize it's the naked man on top of me. Logic dictates that if the man on top of me is having sex, so am I. But all I can think is—I wouldn't do that. I'm not promiscuous. Nevertheless, I feel sticky and there seems to be a bearskin rug under me. At least, I'm hoping it's a bearskin rug . . . he may have invited a friend. But since I couldn't cheat on Lewis, I have a problem figuring out what's going on. I push the hairy, damp body away. He reaches for something on the coffee table, cracks it, shoves it under my nose, and commands, "Sniff!"

I've been trying not to breathe in through my nose since we met. But I do what I'm told.

Sensations flood body parts I've been in denial of. Oh-my-God. The feeling? Take the biggest goose bumps you've ever had and put them in your pants. I want more, but I don't know what to ask for.

"That thingy I inhaled—"

Omar says, "They are poppers!" Paupers?

"Poor people?" He doesn't get the joke.

I keep popping up, and the next thing I know (*see?*), it's evening. I slither back home. Jeffrey Dahmer should have felt such guilt.

I never saw my prince and the poppers again, but I was a changed woman. I discovered my destiny. I would hunt down and marry a pharmacist.

*How does a nice Jewish girl from Canada
become a California coke-whore?*

PART ONE

Blueprints for Addiction

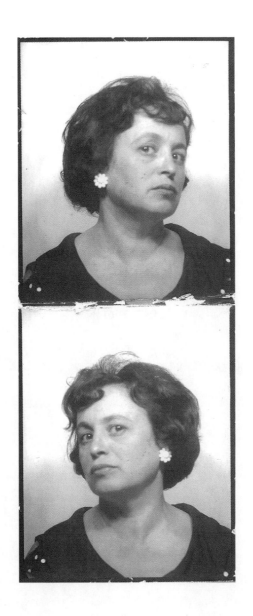

I Was Born Nervous—
Then My Mother Scared Me

Near the beginning . . .

World War II ended in 1945, but in our house the fight's still on. When Hitler stopped doing it to Ma and Daddy, they started doing it to each other. It's not their fault. People get good at what they do often, and they like doing what they're good at. Ma and Daddy are good at fighting. I want peace talks, but who listens? Nobody. That's the problem. I turn the TV up loud.

I want my family life to be a *Dick Van Dyke* episode. It's more like a psychotic episode. *Jerry Springer* in Yiddish. Yiddish is what Ma and Daddy speak. It's dramatic. Lively. It's the language that brought you, "*OY.*" It can make any bad situation seem worse. It can also be pissy. If Eskimos have ninety words for snow, Jews have a hundred for idiot. Jewish people can do contemptuous-snooty-disgust better than any other people in history. And like Jews throughout history, Ma and Daddy are always prepared for their next battle.

Ma and Daddy's English vocabulary is limited, "crazy," "on sale," "eat this." Daddy has always wanted Ma to call him "*Darling.*" She calls him an idiot. Actually, Ma strung you and idiot together. It comes out "*Y'idiot!*" She's a master of disgust. Her favorite word is—*FEH!*

Let me explain *feh. Feh* means "Get out of my face you stupid piece of *dreck*." And to explain *dreck*—"Everyone and everything that is different." If anyone says something that conflicts with what Ma knows is right, rather than think about it, she calls it *dreck*, and with an air of dismissive superiority she waves the *dreck* away like you'd wave off a bad odor.

Here in Canada, Ma and Daddy speak Jewbonics (see glossary), a mix of English words and Yiddish tone. It's a judgmental language loaded with shortcuts and devices to express emotion, mostly sarcasm. Indictments pose as inquiries.

For example, Ma says, "Tell me, vhy are you so crazy?" I try to answer, mistaking it for a question. Questioning is big. One question answers another.

For example, I say, "Ma, can we go to a movie?"

Ma says, "Vhat, I have time to go enjoy myself?" Again, I try to answer.

In Jewbonics, a statement is easily challenged by repeating it as a *question*, stressing one or two of the words.

For example, I say, "Ma, I get scared when you yell at Daddy."

Ma says, "You get *scared* vhen I yell at *Daddy*?!"

This is Jewbonic code for "You're stupid for being scared. Besides, you aren't *really* scared anyway."

But I *am* scared. And to express the fear—and subsequent frustration from being humiliated—I throw back at Ma and Pa Holocaust the words they taught me, "SHUT UP!" My words aren't heard, so I throw tantrums. I writhe on the ground like Gumby possessed. God forbid anyone in the house should say, "I'm sad" or "I'm scared" or "I'm hurt." How do you share a feeling you're not supposed to have?

◆ ◆ ◆

I have a special form of childhood Attention Deficit Disorder. I can't hold Ma and Daddy's attention. The Holocaust, dancing a polka in their heads, distracts them.

The *hora* is a Jewish dance done at bar mitzvahs and weddings. Dancers are locked onto each other, going round and round in a circle, ending back where they started. Always the same song and dance. Actually Ma and Daddy don't dance the *hora* as much as the *horror,* and they don't need a special occasion.

The Wailing Wall separates my room from the kitchen.

Ma and Daddy are carrying on a screamfest. It's been echoing in the kitchen since Daddy turned off Walter Cronkite. I crouch in my room and squish my ears to my head. I can still hear. (The Sony Walkman hasn't been invented yet; it's harder to drown people out.)

"Du bist meshugeh!"

"Du bist meshugeh!"

"Du bist meshugeh und fackackt!"

"Du bist meshugeh und fackackt!"

Loose translation:

"Shut up!"

"No, *you* shut up!"

"No, *YOU* shut up!"

"No, *YOU* shut up!" Not much gets accomplished. Nobody shuts up.

I feel like an exasperated parent. *"Don't you two make me come in there!"* I try to get them to stop yelling. I might as well tell a tidal wave to turn around.

And the best part is—they tell me *I'm* the crazy one.

And the *worst*? I believe them. What the hell *am* I doing under the bed?

In *crazy,* I find a word that fits me. There's a rightness to *me* and *crazy.* Me crazy. Crazy me.

Daddy's First Name *Isn't* Y'idiot?

Twenty-five years after escaping from Poland, Daddy still screams in his sleep.

When he's awake, we all scream. I want us to talk nice, without veins bulging. But Ma and Daddy rage over brisket. It's not *really* about the brisket. It never is. Ma and Daddy are fueled by a constant inner irritation. Daddy says he doesn't start it, that he'd be happy if Ma would just shut up. Ma says if he'd stop being so stupid, she wouldn't have to complain. They both have a point . . .

One time Ma and I are watching from the porch as Daddy drives halfway down the block, stops, realizes he's gone too far and makes a seven-point turn. He often drives past our house, which isn't easy. We live at a dead end.

"Ma, is Daddy *like that* because of what you went through in the war?"

"Nah, he vas a idiot *before* da var."

"Why did you marry him if he was an idiot?"

"He dressed nice. And he had a bike."

"A bike?"

"He vas rich! And very handsome. And, *oy,* he kept bugging me. And he made me laugh, alvays making mit da jokes." Aha! Looks, money, and a sense of humor—it's what women want. But somewhere in time, Ma stopped laughing at Daddy's jokes.

As he's parking in the driveway, Ma's tongue—an insult weapon— unloads,"Y'idiot! Around da voods of Poland you knew how to get, on da vay home from *Cavendish Mall* you get lost?" Maybe he drives past on purpose.

Did being called an idiot for decades turn Daddy into one? It never made him smarter. It made him angry; and when Daddy gets angry, he gets dumber. He gives Ma more ammo. Not that she needs it; Ma *hates* Daddy. And Daddy hates Ma for hating him.

Ma tells me that Daddy's mother died when he was a young boy. His father was a harsh disciplinarian who whacked his son in the head. Ma and I look at each other in silence.

She tells me Daddy's father found a second wife. "*Oy*, he married a real beetch!"

"A bitch? What do you mean?"

Ma says, "She goes to da market on Tuesday, comes home Friday—a beetch!"

Poor Daddy, first he's beaten by his own father, then by Hitler, and then Ma comes along to finish him off. There's never a question about Daddy's behavior that can't be answered with, "Dat's because he's a idiot." There are no other explanations. Ma doesn't hear what Daddy is trying to say because she's busy preparing what she's going to say next. Not heard, Daddy yells louder. But his opinion never sways her view. There are only two sides to any disagreement and Ma's has to be right. Which makes Daddy's wrong. He doesn't like this routine.

No matter how mad Daddy is, he doesn't get as vicious and coldblooded as Ma. But what he lacks in evil, he makes up for in volume. In between the screaming, there's silence. The loud kind. If they were cartoon figures, steam would be shooting out their ears. Even when they're sitting still. They're safe here in Canada, no Nazis, no gas chambers, but. . . . Poland is a state of mind.

Again with the brisket—

Ma attacks! "*Y'idiot!* You should pay so much for a *brisket*? Vhy do you go to dat *goniff*, tell me?" (Remember, this is not *really* a question.)

Daddy's voice booms through the house. "*I'm* a idiot? You married me, dat makes you a *bigger* idiot!" Jews are a funny people. Hysterical. "You know nuting—dat's vhat you know! He's okay by me, dis guy!"

Ma's voice could trim a hedge. "And twenty years ago you said da plumber (pronounce the b, plum-*ber*) vas okay by you, he robbed you blind! You can't tell a person who's robbing you dat he's no good? You vant da butcher should tink you're a bigshot! *Dine fatter hot ingeshticken a pitskele putz, und hot gotten tsrick a groisseh!*" (Your father put a little dick in and got back a *big* one!) "You drive me crazy! I'm moving to Miami!"

Miami? When's she going? Will she take me with her? I like Miami.

The battle of the brisket continues. Daddy defends against Ma's blows with his best intellect. *"Farmach dine groisseh pisk!"* (No, *you* shut up!)

With that, Ma tromps down the hall, throws my door open, pulls me off the bed and drags me to the kitchen. "Suzie, Hanala, Poopsala, who's right, me or dis *y'idiot*?" As she's reliving the butchery, something rises in me and I blow.

"WHO THE HELL DO YOU THINK I AM—*HENRY KISSINGER*?! LEAVE ME ALONE! YOU'RE *BOTH* NUTS! WHAT YOU'RE FIGHTING ABOUT IS STUPID!"

Ma turns to Daddy in shock. "Ver did she learn to open such a big *mouth*?"

Gee, let's see . . . at the movies? But we never went to the movies.

Ma and Pa Chaos go back to brisket-bickering, and I'm in the pantry hunting for relief. I like to hide here, among the basic food groups. Ahhh . . . bagels . . . .

I fill time by filling my thighs. Ma whips *this* door open and catches me unwrapping the salami. Her disgust shifts from Daddy to me. "Hitler killed my brodders, my sisters, and all dere children, but I should live to have a daughter like you? You can't use a plate?!" She wants me neater?

Ma's upset, and it's my fault. I don't question it; I just accept this as normal. You think a fish knows it's in water?

The next morning Ma's baking pies when I walk into the kitchen. "Ma, are you gonna take me with you to Miami?" She looks at me like I've got three nostrils. "Vhat, are you crazy? I'm going to leave da Daddy?" Did I imagine that she said she was leaving? No, I know I heard her. *Didn't I?*

I wish I'd known about post-traumatic stress disorder, but it was only named a psychological condition after the Vietnam War. No one spoke of lasting emotional effects from Hitler's days. For me, PTSD stands for Punish Traumatized Suzie Daily.

Inside the *Thing* They Fed and Dressed

It's the sixties, I'm in kindergarten and clearly in over my head.

I can't relax my hands! Like homing pigeons, they hover close to my face so I can, on an as-needed basis, stick my thumb in my mouth. Things are always going in there. I have no fingernails, just long cuticles.

At home, I gnaw on furniture. I have an overbite and a nervous condition. I sit on the floor at the end of Ma's bed and soothe myself by scraping my front teeth along the top of the footboard. I make grooves, pulling wood shavings into my mouth like they're a high-fiber snack. If my body ever needs to be identified, Ma's bedroom set contains my dental records.

At school—no one's pencil is safe. *Leave It to Beaver*.

I'm the designated class paper cutter because I do it so well. At last, my unique talents are being recognized. I have great potential and could be so many things that have nothing to do with math.

Maintaining my reputation is intense. It's hard to never make a mistake with scissors. I gain a bit of pride every time teacher calls me to the cutting desk. My first kindergarten report card is spellbinding! I read down the column: "E, E, E, E," all Es for Excellent, YIPPE-E-E! But then, I see it in *RED*. My teacher has written at the bottom,"*Can't keep fingers away from face.*"

Caught! My mood plunges from elation to mortification. Who else has seen this unbecoming flaw? Does everyone at school think I'm weird? Until the tainted card, I felt like one of teacher's favorites. Will she still ask me to cut things?

"Can't keep fingers away from face" revealed the real me, the icky inside part!

Who do I talk to about this humiliation, the Holocaust survivors? I can just hear Ma: "*Dat's* a problem? A Nazi chasing you, *dat's* a problem!"

Never mind. That's when I'm allowed to mind, never.

Children of Holocaust survivors tend to develop a "Never mind, it's not important" policy. Even with flying fingers, I graduate kindergarten.

Challah and *Star Trek*—My First Addiction

I am Bewitched

Ma works as a saleslady in a bakery. She gives me a quarter to buy two egg rolls for lunch. None of my peers "do lunch." At noon, when all the other kids go home, I walk down the street with my quarter. I sit alone in a brown leather-esque booth at The House of Wong, watching the clock, dipping my egg roll into plum sauce and wishing for a regular mom. If I dip twice and nothing drips from the egg roll dish to my mouth, if I close my eyes and wish hard enough, or twitch my nose . . .

I learned how to twitch my nose *just* like Samantha Stephens, but Ma never materializes in front of me saying, "Vhat's da matter, darling?" or "How vas school today?" In my times of need, Ma's usually cleaning.

For example, the horrible day I turn on the TV to find Samantha living with a new man. His name is also Darrin. What happened? Did he lose weight and get taller? And meaner? What the fuck is going on? Is it me? I'm gonna ask Ma! I boldly reach out to her, right in the middle of Windexing. "Ma, why did they switch Darrins on *Bewitched*?"

Without breaking her rhythm, she wipes the question away like it was a speck of dirt on the counter. "Don't be stupid," she says. "Go make da bed."

❖ ❖ ❖

I sit on the powder-blue chenille chair in the TV room, eating dinner with the family. Unfortunately, it's *The Addams Family*. And the chair is covered in plastic.

TV families share stories, they get each other in trouble, they laugh. I study these creatures, these normal people, because one day I'll have to live among them. I have to act like them to avoid being spotted and turned in. Are they pod people?

As alien as TV family life looks, I long to belong. If a gang or a nice cult comes by, I'm getting a tattoo and signing up. For now, I have my nineteen-inch, black-and-white portable TV. Why it's called a portable, I don't know. At eighty pounds, where are you going with it?

It occurs to me I've been born into the wrong family. Wrong planet. Perhaps Earth is an intergalactic day care; I've been dropped off by aliens and when the *Here's How to Live* manual was handed out, I was in the kitchen looking for something to eat.

Star Trek knows how to treat an alien. Unless you personally attack the Enterprise, you're welcome on board no matter what your color, religion or celestial orientation. And if you're female, you get to kiss Captain Kirk. You don't even have to be carbon-based.

I watch TV trying to identify, but no one's from Poland.

What's *real*? The Bradys? They never get naked. Mrs. Brady wears a bra to bed. No one ever pees. They use the bathroom only to brush their teeth. Mr. Brady, the architect, designed the bathroom without a toilet—they can't pee if they *want* to; that's how six children can share one bathroom. (I'm looking to TV to show me what's normal, not realizing TV is written by high-paid maniacs living in Los Angeles.)

We don't have "dinner." At *Chez Oy Vey*, it's a table-for-one. "Da chicken is ready" is my cue to assemble the TV table. The top, a tin tray with a faded floral pattern and dinged like the doors of a big Buick parked in a mini-mall, is attached to hollow gold legs with plastic clippy things. I lift the tray, pry open the legs, click the fasteners, and there it is—my dining room table. Ma cooks, but when she's at work I have to find the food. It's under foil somewhere in the kitchen. If I'm lucky, it's still in the oven. *Nothin' says lovin'.* When Ma's not working, she serves me a plate but doesn't sit down to join me. Daddy's already eaten, or he's in another room slurping food like a Nazi is gonna grab it from him.

One night Ma's at work and Daddy tries to make me eat a bowl of lima beans. Beans are old-man food, not child chow. But Daddy says I can't leave the table until I finish the bowl. Even for an adult, it's a huge bowl. It's a Jethro Bodine bowl. (Kellogg's sponsored *The Beverly Hillbillies*, and Jethro ate corn flakes from a vat.) Daddy hands me a spoon big enough to shovel snow and leaves the kitchen. Why doesn't Ma have a garbage disposal like real moms?

I sit tall, determined to get the slimy limas down so I can get back to the TV, but halfway through, my throat closes. The beans sit in the bowl and I sit at the table staring at them. The beans have become the enemy.

Daddy checks on me. "EAT!" My forehead is sweaty, angry tears flow, but I eat every bad bean. Daddy comes back and sees the empty bowl.

"Good girl!" He's all happy with himself. I'd like to give him a mouthful. I open my mouth to speak, but instead of words, the beans come back up much faster than they'd gone down. I projectile vomit. Beany baby blows chunks clear across the room, covering Daddy in goo. From now on, I eat only what I want to eat. And I eat it in front of the TV.

❖ ❖ ❖

I decide what to watch before I sit down (two channels, no remote). I peel back the foil on the Swanson frozen turkey dinner, careful not to let the cranberry sauce in the middle compartment touch any of the *real* food. Making sure the potatoes stay away from the turkey, I finish one food group before going on to the next.

For a snack I pull the centers out of the challahs and dunk them piece by piece into milk. Ma gets upset when she goes to the breadbox and finds the empty challah shells. I put up with the yelling because I like the feel of bakery glue in my stomach.

I get excited when *Star Trek* comes on. I watch every rerun. I like reruns. NO surprises. I know how the story ends. Comfy. I've seen the "Trouble With Tribbles" episode ten times. The first time, I was nervous. How can we be *sure* Captain Kirk will save the ship, even though he does every episode? One star date, he might not! Shit happens.

As a matter of fact, it seems like shit happens whenever I go outside. So to play it safe, I stay inside. Give me another half hour of life, the way it should be.

I try not to let the outside world affect *my* world unless it's coming in through the television. I zone out to *The Twilight Zone*. I love the episodes where you disappear through the bottom of a pond and pop up in a home where you're treated nicely. Or you become part of a soap opera, and you play a much better role than you do in real life. You're the star—not an extra.

The Flying Nun, Mr. Ed, My Mother the Car . . . I'm *Lost in Space*, I'm *That Girl* flipping channels, looking for life in all the wrong places. On TV, life is funny and fair, and no matter how screw-boiled everything is, it all gets resolved in thirty minutes. I develop a half-hour attention span.

We may have a new color portable, but the picture I get is still black and white. TV land is simply defined. People are divided into *good* and *bad*. Samantha, a blonde, is a *good* witch; Serena, her black-haired cousin, is the *bad* witch. We *Get Smart* in *C.O.N.T.R.O.L.* or Nazi-lite in *K.A.O.S.* The good *Man From U.N.C.L.E.* or the evil shmucks from *T.H.R.U.S.H.* Humans versus Klingons. *Green Acres* has Oliver versus Mr. Haney. And hero Hogan combats kooky Klink.

The *good* people on TV are nice, funny, and white. The black people on TV cook for the white people. *Good* people on TV don't do *bad* things. I don't mean *Lucy-bad*: "Oops, Ricky, I cut up the rug." I mean, "Oops, I got drunk and fondled the Fuller Brush man."

Sex doesn't exist. It's never a topic. Father may *know* best, but he's not talking. The Professor and Mary Ann? Ginger maybe, but nice pie-baking Mary Ann get slippery and stinky? Nope; doesn't matter how long they're marooned on *Gilligan's Island*.

TV has strict sex rules. If two people are in bed together, one of them must keep one foot on the floor. You can't say "pregnant." If you have sex, you're bad. On *The Dick Van Dyke Show*, Rob and Laura Petrie are *good*— they have separate beds. That's why Richie's an only child. (If the show were shot today, we'd be in the delivery room. *"Oooh Rooob!"*)

On my Sylvania, men work, women clean, and only juvenile delinquents yell at their parents. Donna Reed, June Cleaver, Harriet Nelson—they're all nice, stay-at-home-moms.

Oh really? Don't we see them at work? That's why they look so good, heels clicking around the kitchen. You think Harriet wears that much makeup at home cleaning up after David, or dragging Ricky into rehab? Twenty years later, the cast of Father Knows Best *goes on* Geraldo *confessing depression, alcoholism, and sexual abuse. Who knew?*

All I know is I want to be Kitten. Or Opie on *The Andy Griffith Show*. Aunt Bee isn't hysterical and yelling at Opie in Yiddish. I want to live in Mayberry. There are no crack heads in Mayberry—maybe over in Raleigh, but not Mayberry. Otis is the only one in town with a substance-abuse problem. No one carries guns except Barney, and he keeps his bullet in his pocket. Andy doesn't beat or cheat on Helen. And Helen never has PMS. She's never moody or bloated. Howard Sprague doesn't defraud seniors with savings and loan scams. Floyd doesn't lure little boys into the back of the barbershop. Nobody asks Gomer, and Gomer doesn't tell. If only I'd been raised in Mayberry. Look how well Opie's done.

I dream of *being* Jeannie, the blonde from Baghdad. One day I ask Ma, who's dusting the plastic couch covers, "Mummy, how much do you have to pay to be on TV?"

"Don't be stupid. *Dey* pay *you*." The perfect job!

"Where does TV come from?"

"Hollyvood." Like in *The Beverly Hillbillies*? The place that never rains? As soon as I'm old enough, I'll pack up the truck and move to Beverly. Hills, that is. I know what I'm going to do when I grow up. I tell my friends at school. They laugh. In the meantime, I keep dreaming and watching the lovely, lively genie, Jeannie. I study her. Jeannie's life purpose is to please her master. She's my role model. Now they call this *codependency*. Network censors—who prohibit Jeannie from *really* pleasing him—ban her bellybutton from the show. Dirty thing! Not once will you see her navel. Meanwhile, change the channel and you can watch *Mannix* shoot someone. Why ban the bellybutton but not the breast-enhancing halter? Censors like breasts. Jeannie prances around Tony the astronaut day and night, and does he leer, grab, or beg? No. He's a gentleman! But maybe, if her navel showed . . .

I yearn for a nice astronaut to marry. Of course, I finally learn it's all a fantasy. There *are* no blondes from Baghdad.

If Ma Isn't Cold, I Don't Need a Sweater

Ed Sullivan is over, it's Ma and Me, alone.
Ma/Me . . . a difference of a vowel.

I'm in pajamas, curled in a ball on the floor, tears rolling down my face. I'm looking up at the little woman sitting in the big blue armchair. "Tell me again, Mummy, how you slept in a hole in the ground in winter." I want to know what the bad men did to my Mummy. If I can get a handle on the Holocaust and how it happened, I'd know what to do about Ma.

> *Maybe, if I could understand you, Mummy, you wouldn't be so scary. I could stop hating you, you could stop hating me, and I could stop hating me. If I'm a good girl, you'll feel better. Then maybe you'll be like the nice mommies on TV. So tell me, Mummy . . .*

Ma knows how to set up a story. With the Holocaust as a backdrop and Nazis co-starring, no embellishment is needed to grab my attention. My attention is on her all the time anyway.

"*Oy* . . . Hanala, you know da vay you love babies? Vell . . ." she sighs, needing strength to go on, "I loved my brodder's children like dey vere my own, and because I couldn't save dem, dey got chopped up mit an ax, vhat can I tell you?"

Ma gets up and starts with the dishes. Like a hit-and-run driver who doesn't realize she's flattened someone, Ma hits and cleans. She's oblivious of the impact. She leaves a heap of emotional rubble without a speck of guilt. Hey, wait! One minute her niece and nephew are being axed, the next, she's dashing off like the white knight from the Ajax commercials, brandishing a *shmatteh*. She's working the Spic 'n Span and I'm frozen. I've been Mummy-fied. Can't talk. Like the Tin Man after rain. Must figure out Nazis. Must eat cheese blintz. Reach, lift, chew . . . ahhh . . . mushy . . . sweet . . . there now, that's better. Now, go turn on the TV and make the yuck go away.

◆ ◆ ◆

Sometimes late at night after Ma comes home from the bakery, we sit at the kitchen table sharing a danish. I listen to her relive one shocker after another. A Yiddish *Twilight Zone*. Tonight's episode: "Ma's Choice."

Sometimes Ma sings songs to me at bedtime. Here's a Polish hit—

It's the story of Laybka and his wife, Raisala. The two Jews survive the war, have a baby, and are living in a poor apartment in *da Old Country*. Laybka tells Raisala he will go to America, make money, and send for her and the child. Laybka works very hard in America and becomes a big boss, and every day Raisala waits for the postman to come. Finally, a letter falls through the mail slot. She springs out of bed, tears the envelope open, but instead of her ticket to America, Laybka has sent her a divorce. She gets back in bed and, rocking her baby, cries. "We hoped and we waited, but your daddy fooled us. Sleep my child, aloo-loo-loo-loo, to America, we will not go."

By the end of the song, I need a drink. But I'm only five. Each time Ma sings the Laybka song I try not to cry.

Ma gets a tickle from it. "Hanala, you heard dis song a hundred times already, each time you cry like a baby!" It *is* silly. I know the end of the song and yet, I keep hoping Laybka sends the tickets. It doesn't occur to Ma that these tales might freak out a five-year-old. But I'm not a little girl as much as I'm a part of Ma. You don't ask your arm, "Are you okay?"

Ma says I made her tell me the horror stories. Oh. Okay.

I wonder now . . . if I had a little girl who said, "Mummy, tell me about the war," would I tell her, "My family thought they were showers, but instead of water, poisonous gas came out of the pipes"? Or would I let her find out about life's horrors later, when she could handle them better, and could afford a shrink.

In the middle of the night, I am rudely awakened—

Ma jumps into my bed. Clutching me to her, she cries, "I had a dream da Nazi vas pulling Sylvia from my arms." She wakes me up in the middle of the night and doesn't even bother to change the story so it's me—not my *sister*—they're pulling from her?

Can't worry about that now; Ma's in trouble. I stroke her hair. "It was only a dream, it's okay, Mummy." Poor Mummy! How awful. The torture continues even when her body tries to rest. Would death be the only peace Ma would ever have?

Except for My Sister, I Was an Only Child

Sylvia—

My older sister and I were named after relatives from the Nazi death camps. Always a peppy thought.

Jews and names: We have several—the Yiddish first and middle names given at birth, the English versions of those names, the surname dat you had in *da Old Country*, and the Americanized, Ellis Island less-syllabled version. Our surname was Stadtwojner. Then it became Stadowoner, which still had too many syllables for Sylvia, so she shortened it to *Stadner*.

Traditionally, Jews don't name a baby after a living relative because the angel of death might mistakenly take the child instead of the older namesake. Ma and Daddy had no shortage of names to choose from.

Sylvia was born eleven years before me in a refugee camp in Poland—*not* in Vienna like she tells people. She was named *Tsivia Ita*. In Canada, it became Sylvia Elaine.

Ma and Daddy were Mania (pronounced *Munya*) and Fishel (Fish´el) Stadtwojner (whatever). They changed their names to Molly and Felix, but everyone calls them Mania and Fishel.

Me? I'm Hana Sura. Hana isn't Hannah. Hana is pronounced like the town on Maui you take the road to. It rhymes with *Donna*. Or *wanna*. As in *wannabe*, as in I wanna be someone else. The *H* is said like you're clearing your throat. But Sylvia likes the name *Susan*. I become *Susan*. And sometimes *Suzie*. (And in Los Angeles it changes again to *Suzan*.)

Ma named me after her sister Hana who "Vas full of pep, people vould come from all around *da shtetl* to talk to *Hanala*. And she vas a beauty." But when Ma calls me Hanala, I scream at her, "Maaa! It's *Susan!*" Anything but a yucky *Yiddish* name. I need to blend in. People who stick out (are too loud, too different, too *Jewish*) are teased. Or put in ovens.

Suzie has two mommies—

I've got Ma, a loud, wrinkled, four-foot-eleven-inch refugee who embarrasses me, and Sylvia, who acts like royalty (more Marie Antoinette than Princess Di) who *I* embarrass. She's genuinely repulsed by the peasants she's been placed to live among.

> *One day in kindergarten the teacher asked me, "Suzie, do you have any brothers or sisters?" "No," accidentally dropped out of my mouth. Oops. I went through the rest of the year pretending I was an only child. If only.*

Sylvia's a slender willow with a Jackie Kennedy attitude and Grace Kelly hair. I'm Cousin It. My hair parts down the center and frizzes out, forming a pyramid, and it's so thick I disappear. In summer, it turns big. Seventies' Afro-big. Ike Turner-big. My hair supports the theory that Africa is the bed of civilization.

I'm a little girl with big body parts—big hair, big head, big eyes. I'm big inside, too. My skin barely contains my extravagant nature. Syl and I have Daddy's eyes, and all six are blue, a blue that changes with the weather, my mood, and my outfit. We have Daddy's Garbo lids and full lips. From Ma, we get round cheeks, small nostrils, and better than good posture.

I want to copy Sylvia's smooth hairdo so I sleep with cans. Sunkist, Tab, Fresca, evaporated milk. They make better rollers than the drugstore's skinny kind that make me look like Harpo Marx. I found out it works better if I empty the cans first. Dippity-Do, Alberto V-O-5, a hairnet, and I'm ready for bed. I sleep propped up like the Elephant Man, who also had problems maintaining a positive self-image.

Sylvia inherited Daddy's Prussian nose. She refuses to accept this. She sits for hours, chin in hand, pushing up the tip—as if one could train a nose. But nose push-ups will not make her a WASP. Sylvia is going for Sandra Dee—she gets compared to Sophia Loren. Awww, shucks.

Sylvia was born dead, no heartbeat. They had to run her under cold water to get her to breathe. She's been chilly ever since. She's the *American* one in the family. She underwent a Jew-ectomy. She doesn't say, "Vasn't," "dere," "den," "vhen," or "vas," as in, "I vasn't dere den vhen he vas stealing your vallet." Sylvia doesn't roll her stockings up to her knees, order shmaltz herring, or get on a bus shlepping gefilte fish in a nylon mesh bag.

But she wasn't born *American*; Ma and Daddy taught us, "Eng-a-lish, Sarana-wrap and sen-a-vich." (Years later Ma would call me on my cell-a-phone.) Sylvia stood in front of the mirror for hours practicing how to say one-syllable words in one syllable. "Wha-a-at?" has become "What?"

Me? I talk like Jackie Mason: "Sylvia? You want Ma should make you a sen-a-vich?"

I'm six, Sylvia's a cheerleader at Baron Bing High.

I worship Sylvia. I also annoy her. There's something about a self-obsessed, clingy little crybaby that irritates her. I speak, and her eyes roll. "Oh, puh-leeze! Stop being so stupid, Susan. You are *so* obnoxious. Stop *whining*." How? I'm a child raising myself. So what, I'm not supposed to whine? It's how the part's written. And how do you stop being obnoxious? I try. I can tell you, it's very hard to do. It's like trying to not be crazy.

Sylvia's not crazy, she's beautiful. And on this planet, beautiful equals credible (except for Walter Cronkite). She tells me I'm repulsive, I'm going to argue? It's obvious how smart she is. She's a cheerleader, for chrissake! I'm gum stuck to her shoe.

The more she pushes me away, the harder I claw to hold on. With one look of disgust, Sylvia can peel back my skull and rearrange my brain so that all thoughts lead to "I am retarded I am retarded I am retarded . . . ." I probably am. I secretly believe Paul McCartney and Moe Howard are the same person. (Later, I realize it's the hair.)

> *In 1964, Sylvia took me to see the Beatles. See, yes—hear, no. The screaming, mascara-flowing girls drowned out the music. I tried to shush the hysterical teens so I could hear. Why did they come here, just to yell? I could do that at home. I noticed the similarity between the rockin' mop-tops and Moe from the Three Stooges. Paul, especially. I don't like to think I'm so easily influenced by Ma's bias against long-haired or ugly people, and how she judges talent by a performer's looks. But as I watched the Beatles, I couldn't help thinking they looked like beatniks, they couldn't afford a haircut? Don't even talk to me about the genius of Bob Dylan—I can't get past the nose of Bob Dylan.*

Sylvia is husband-hunting . . .

I come home from school one day to find Ma packing boxes. "Ve're moving avay." What?! Suddenly—just like that? I'd been kept out of the loop. If I had gotten home late, would they have left without me? I don't ask.

I want to stay with Bonnie Bitteen, my buddy from next door, but Sylvia's power-dating and wants a better house to bring her kill. She's ashamed of our humble duplex in the refugee-filled neighborhood of Snowden, a part of Montreal that has more hospitals per capita than the rest of Quebec.

So we're movin' on up, to the west side—Cote Saint Luc. We go from the lower-middle-slums to the upper-middle-class. I stand on the sidewalk, looking at the antiseptic structure called "my new house." I don't belong here. Sylvia, yes. But, Sylvia's hardly ever home. When she is, she's in the bathroom.

Like the Bradys, we have only one bathroom, if you don't count the spider-filled one in the basement, and I don't. Ma wallpapered the five-by-seven room herself, and when she ran out of the blue posy paper, she finished the area over the towel rack in pink pinstripe with gold flecks. *Vaste not, vant not.*

My one chance to be near Sylvia is in the morning as she puts on makeup. It's the decade of eyeliner up to the brow. How is her hand so steady as she draws the line? I watch and learn. Will this be the day she sticks the pencil in her eye? I don't want to miss that.

What the hell *does* Sylvia do to get her hair to look so good? I remember when her hair was frizzy. And dark brown. And why can *she* get warm water out of the faucet? I get hot or cold. Like Ma—it's bipolar, unpredictable, and can cause instant pain.

One day the mystery is revealed. I walk into the bathroom and catch Sylvia pulling her frizzy hair up into a ponytail, attaching a long blonde fall with a rubber band, wrapping the fake hair around her head, and securing it with bobby pins. Hence, the silky and popular *beehive.* Does the "blonde" come from those stinky bottles in the trash?

I don't know how Sylvia showers. I've never seen her naked. For me, the shower is a wet place for pain. Our showerhead shoots out four sharp needles of water. I avoid the stinging attack by pointing the spray at my least sensitive body part—my hair. To thoroughly rinse out the Prell, I drain the tub and kneel naked with my head under the faucet. Sore knees, stinging eyes, and water up my nose, I spit out shampoo and struggle with the gnarled mass. Tame hasn't been invented yet. My Rastafarian hair is on its own.

But with Sylvia at the medicine cabinet mirror the room loses its hostility. With one wave of her mascara wand, she transforms the chamber of my horrors into a beauty parlor.

❖   ❖   ❖

One night, I'm watching Sylvia apply *evening* makeup for a date. It's different than *morning* makeup. I make a mental note. On her way out, she catches me hauling a snack to the TV room. Holding hands with her football-player date, she announces in the disgusted tone reserved for family, "Stuffing your face again, Susan?"

Yes, I am, but why point it out in front of company?

What did I do to make her *hate* me? Of course, hate is too caring a word.

I crave connection with this ice queen, but if I get too close I could get freezer burn. I can't relax around this woman who can turn my world off with her smirk. Who knows, her next remark could turn me into a toad. *Bitch*-craft.

I want to know what it was like when she was little. "Syl, did Ma and Daddy drive you nuts?"

Her icicle eyes turn to me. "Susan, I'm not like you, always trying to get them to love me. I didn't care what they did, I had my own life."

How much of a life do you have when you're a kid?

I keep trying to present myself in a way that will repulse her less. Like my cousin Jackie's bar mitzvah—I take hours to dress and re-dress. I skip into the living room, crinolines ruffling, happy because I look pretty.

Sylvia takes one disgusted look. "God, Susan! You're not wearing *that*, are you?"

Sticks and stones may break my bones, but *words* can last forever.

> *If* only I knew then what $250,000 of therapy has taught me, I'd have blown her off with, "No, I'm changing at the front door." Or, "Perhaps you'd like to examine your motive for wanting to humiliate me." Or, "Do you realize the impact that kind of statement makes on an eight-year-old, because you may feel bad when I become someone who can't leave the house without chemical support." But the only kids who talk like that are on sitcoms.

I'm cringing to death. All I can do is fantasize. "She'll be sorry after I'm dead." I want to be sisters with Judy from *Lost in Space*. She was so nice to Penny. I even look like Penny. But Sylvia isn't the kind of big sister you see on TV (unless you're watching *Dateline*).

I want to tell Ma and Daddy how mean Sylvia is, but they're out working hard to make money so that one day they can afford to send me to a therapist where I can talk about how they were never there.

There's No Place Like Home—Thank God

The better shtetl—

Our new house is done in Early-Jewish Baroque. It's a modest single-story, three-bedroom bungalow attached to another bungalow, its exact double. Except its twin isn't decorated like Versailles.

A twinkly chandelier hangs in the foyer. Because of the mirrored wall, we've got two chandeliers for the price of one. (A Martha Stewart moment for Ma.) The mirror is partially obscured by a shrine. The older the family gets, the more crowded the mantel. Picture frames, dozens—gold, silver, bronze—whatever's on sale—anoint the *froufrou*-wall table. Some frames still have the photos they were sold with. Ski-jump nosed, straight-haired strangers smile as if to say, "Hello! Vee are from the Nor-vee-gian branch of the family." The adopted-out, happy branch.

The living room, a no-sit-zone, is off to the left. The furniture, Louis XIV reproductions, is threaded with gold *fleur-de-lis*. The claw hooves on the living room set scare me. They stand on plastic cleats that dig into the white wall-to-wall carpeting. Plastic runners connect all the rooms.

Everything is covered with, encased in, or fashioned from, plastic. Ma filled the crystal bowls with plastic fruit. The bananas and grapes are smooth, the oranges have teeny bumps, and the apricots are fuzzy. I don't know how they got plastic fuzzy.

Ma covers everything in the house with plastic—the lampshades, the chairs, Daddy. Is that how he became part of the sofa?

The plastic couch covers are cold and hard. They crackle in winter; in summer if you sit down on the living room sofa, you get up minus skin. This rarely happens because no one *lives* in the living room. It's the passing-by room. Like the passing lane on the highway, you're meant to move along, not hang out.

Ma's proud of using modern technology to preserve our fancy belongings. "Because of dat plastic, in twenty years dat couch vill look like new!"

Well, she's optimistic, assuming we'll be alive in twenty years. I believe shrink-wrapping furniture is fundamentally wrong. But I have to admit, while the floor of our twelve-year-old Valiant has rotted, the seats—protected by Ma's plastic—look new. But is the larger picture getting lost? If we can't afford a new couch in twenty years, we've got bigger problems than worn cushions.

Lesson: Postpone comfort—it'll pay off in twenty years. The hitch: I grow comfortable with discomfort. Live for tomorrow, suffer today. Don't use what you've got, you may need it later. If it's money, don't spend it. If it's a good chair, don't sit on it. If it's a good towel, for God's sake, save it for the guests. But we never had guests. We had stacks of unused stuff piled in cupboards. Ma still uses the same towels I dried myself with thirty years ago. They've turned to gauze, and some are so rough you can buff your feet with them. But at least time has muted their orange and lime stripes. I've inherited Ma's stuff-preservation. Stashed in cabinets around my house are at least fifty bottles of moisturizer. When face cream gets cruddy, I downgrade it to foot cream.

"They Tried to Kill Us, We Won, Let's Eat"*

—*Somebody*

We're Jewish atheists, more -ish than Jew.

Ma used to be Orthodox in Poland. It's a secret why she doesn't keep kosher anymore. Did she give it up for Lent?

Keeping Kosher means we'd have to use two sets of dishes. One would be meat plates, the other milk plates. The milk of a cow must not touch the meat of a cow once it has left the cow. I ask Ma, why milk *plates*, not *bowls*? What of spillage? Are Jews cursed to make life more difficult than it has to be?

We don't observe the Sabbath, but I know what we're *supposed* to be doing. Sabbath begins sundown on Friday and ends sundown on Saturday, and it's a sin to work, or drive or even turn on the lights. A *good* Jew does not operate *any* equipment. (No cellphone, no channel surfing, no microwaving.) Fortunately, an average Jew does.

*The basis for all Jewish holidays.

Ma says, in *da Old Country,* the *shtetl* kept a Gentile on retainer. Friday afternoon, he'd go house to house, switching on lights and stoves. If a Jew needed to work anything mechanical, he'd call for the Gentile. (Some things don't change.) This person was known as the *Shabbes Goy.* They'd call for him—but not by phone. They'd holler out the window.

So, if I'd lived then, and had a date on Friday night, I'd have yelled for the *Shabbes Goy* to come blow-dry my hair.

◆ ◆ ◆

On Saturdays I observe reruns of *Star Trek.* Movie magazines say in real life Captain Kirk and Mr. Spock are Jewish. *That's* the kind of Jew I want to be—a Jew who's on TV!

Ma says I *vatch* too much TV. "Go outside and play, make friends."

With what?

"Ma, leave me alone." Funny thing is, she does.

She doesn't understand; it's not about *won't* go outside as much as *can't.*

I Hate School;
You Have to Go Outside to Get There

. . . and I hate outside. It's cold. It's hot. It has people.

New teacher, new building, new books . . . old me. I'm living in the new refugee-free zone, trying to pass for white.

I enter the brick box with transom windows, locker-lined hallways and hard, heel-clicky spotted floors. Floors. Floors don't give you dirty looks that destroy.

My knee socks don't match. Ma said, "Dey look like da same, nobody vill know." No they don't, and yes they will.

I've been transferred to Westminster Elementary in the middle of third grade. It's a clean school. I've been placed in Miss Sawyer's class. I'd rather be placed in one of the lockers. Or maybe I could slip into my brown flip-top desk. I almost fit, if not for the books and gum wads.

Fresh textbooks . . . ahhh . . . bright clean pages. This school gives out *new* textbooks, not scribbled-in, highlighted, dog-eared books with traces of jelly and yellow cheese. And empty notebooks hold the promise for the year to come. But I can't keep the promise. I'm a squirmer. A nail-biter. A whisperer. And a compulsive doodler. I pass around my cartoons and commentary. I spend a lot of time in detention. And in *Whatever-Whatever Land*. And in the hall outside the classroom door while stuff is being taught. And learned.

If you're a true nerd, you're good in math or science. You have confidence from knowing that even though kids laugh at you, you're better then they are at something. I'm not brainy; as a matter of fact, I can barely read. I'm not book-smart, but I can tell you when *The Munsters* airs. Too bad that's not on a midterm.

The *real* schoolwork is just trying to go to school five days a week, acting as if I'm normal. I want to act cool; it doesn't come naturally. Naturally occurring feelings are nausea and terror. If anxiety were more socially acceptable, I'd relax.

Mondays are not exactly *Room 222*. They're *Catch-22*—can't go, can't not go. Monday, the start of the prison sentence. The schoolroom is cold. Bleak. And you never know when an inmate will cut you to secure their higher standing.

Bed is comfortable. I control what happens in my bed. And I look thinner lying down.

⟡ ⟡ ⟡

While subjects are introduced in class, I'm choreographing Broadway musicals. "Step, two, three, twirl, leap, plie—again . . ." I direct plays where mommies take care of little girls, and the girls grow up to look great in Laura Petrie capri pants. Seeing as I can't keep my mind in the classroom, homework usually means covering *new* material.

Homework. Being home is work.

We get an assignment. Write a five-thousand-word essay on the French Revolution. The what? Is that in a book somewhere? What number pencil? Where do I start? Never on Friday. I'm not the kind of kid who does homework on Friday afternoon. It takes me a whole weekend to worry about it.

Homework = Helpless + Horror. Who wants to feel that on a Friday afternoon? I've just come off a rotten week. My brain can't bear more pain. If during the weekend, I think of doing my homework, I reach for another *Supergirl* comic book. I push homework into the furthest cavity of my mind. By Sunday, the cavity has turned into a root canal. Can't I just enjoy myself? Never on Sunday.

It's not like I can go to Ma or Daddy for help. Fractions are what smoked meat comes in: half a pound, quarter of a pound, and why bother. Whatever Daddy learned in Poland—stayed in Poland. Reading the Sunday paper takes him the whole week. And even though Ma speaks four languages, it takes her forever to sign her name. BLOCK LETTERS.

On weekends, I wake up feeling as though I've swallowed one hundred gum balls. How can you have a good time on Saturday when you know the next day is Sunday? Sunday is really just the long beginning of Monday. On Sunday, I'm anxious, chewing furniture, waiting for *The Wonderful World of Disney* to start, praying it isn't another story about a horse. "Please, God, make it a story about a little girl escaping." Or before *Bonanza*, "Please, God, make it a show about Little Joe." (He was Jewish, too.)

After *Disney*, denial crumbles and I crash back into the *not* so wonderful world of probable detention. The gum blob in my stomach pulsates. It sprouts tentacles.

Sunday night, I'm hunched over the kitchen table surrounded by textbooks, notebooks, and eraser particles. I have eraser in my hair. My torso has collapsed, my toes tap like I'm hammering out Morse code. S-O-S. You'd think I'm trying to pay the mortgage and feed twelve hungry kids. And, the worst—arithmetic problems!

Like I don't have enough problems already? They should call them *scenarios with numbers*: If Billy lives 1.5 miles from the 7-Eleven and his new "uncle" gives Billy a dollar to buy him a pack of Camels, and Billy walks an average of three miles per hour, and the Camels cost $1.50, how quickly will Billy be sent up the river for whacking the Hindu behind the counter?

(Or another scenario: If Hanala is in therapy three times a week at $120 per session, and the sessions last fifty minutes, how much does the therapist earn a minute? Answer: enough to make Hanala want her mother to pay.)

◆ ◆ ◆

Textbooks scare me. My mind won't stay on the page. It's planning the next defense. Who's around? What will they say, what will they see? What should I do? Pages of a book flip by while I'm thinking of noodles and if they really need butter to be tasty. I go over and over paragraphs, yet have no idea what they're about. (I'm probably thinking about something else *right now*. There's frosting in the fridge.)

I start each paragraph with an oath. "This time, I'm going to concentrate on the words." But that in itself gets me thinking about methods of concentration. How to do it, have I ever met anyone who's concentrated? Is concentration something to which I should give some thought? I know it's a TV show with Hugh Downs. I wonder what's on TV now? So I reread, or re-*not*-read. I give up after the fourth or fifth attempt. (I'm not the guy you want monitoring a nuclear power plant.)

And what would I read if I could read? Ma and Daddy don't buy books. I would go to the public library, but the public is there. So I steal a book from the school library.

> *I felt bad about this for years, it wasn't that good a book. It was a children's book—lots of white space—big letters. When I finally finished it, I started over from the beginning, like a baby being read the same story over and over. It was comforting. No one was being killed or yelled at. But I was ashamed. I wasn't a baby—I was nine.*

Reading takes forever. TV's quicker. My mind wants instant, and everything takes so long! Corn on the cob takes three days to cook.

"Maaa, is the corn ready yet?"

She says, "In an hour." What's an hour? Time. It's passing unenjoyed.

"Ma, I'm bored."

"So go bang your head on da vall."

Mattel wasn't made rich by people like Ma and Daddy. I play with Ma's china tea set. *Play* is a strong term. If I break a cup, I'll have to move out.

I try to think of things to do. I think *real* hard. Even my body gets hard. I find myself frozen in a fetal position. It takes mental force to uncoil. It's as if I've come out of a trance, dazed and stiff. An hour has passed without my knowing it (like today when I'm watching *The Sopranos*).

I remember having a violin, a beautiful, gentle violin. But I can't find it. I'm upset. "Ma, where's my violin?"

Ma laughs. "A violin you had? *Du bist meshugeh!* You vere dreaming!" Okay. But I'm not imagining my nine-inch ceramic replica of Paul McCartney. His neck has a spring in it and when you push on the giant head, it bobs up and down. I love him, yeah, yeah, yeah. There's also a bat-a-ball, the wooden paddle with a red rubber ball attached by a long elastic band. But as I said, I'm not good at sports. I hide it under the couch in case Ma tells me to play with it.

I hate doing something I'm not good at. Frustration of wanting to be really good causes anxiety, which prevents me from getting really good at the thing. Someone gave us a box of dominos. I like the feel of the tiles; I rub them between my fingers; but I don't know what the dots mean. (Still don't.)

I play with the brown wooden bureau in the TV room. It has three sliding doors. When I'm not refinishing it with my teeth, I slide one door open, then the next, then over to the right, left, middle. (If I'd had a computer, I'd have entered a chat room and met a nice man who was interested in children. But it's the sixties, a computer is the size of the kitchen and costs five million dollars.)

Ma enrolls me in year-round Hebrew camp.

There are a couple of rooms, kids get together with counselors on weekends, they do stuff. One of the stuffs is to sit in a circle, tell stories, sing, and play guitar. When I can get myself to go there, I'm too scared to be bored.

With all the angst growing inside, naturally I want a guitar to belt out the blues. It would help if I could sing. After months of pleading and bargaining, Ma and Daddy cave. I lie in bed at night looking at the fascinating instrument.

I'm scared of notes. Mostly of picking the wrong ones. Choir's mandatory in school; I mouth the words to "Onward Christian Soldiers."

I find a guitar teacher. We sit in the TV room, singing and strumming the chords of "Michael Row the Boat Ashore." You can hear the pain in my voice—from the strings cutting into my fingertips. I associate picking up the guitar with torture. I'd quit, but Ma and Daddy would kill me. After about six months, I feel confident enough to bring the guitar to camp. All the kids and counselors are in the circle. My heart pounds harder the closer it gets to my turn.

At first, Michael rows the boat without incident. Then I hit the sour note, play the wrong chord, and I row that boat right out of the room.

No matter how much Ma and Daddy yell (they paid for camp upfront), I do not return. The guitar goes the way of other discarded paraphernalia from past defeats, like ballet shoes. It's shoved in the garage, the burial site of future exercise equipment.

Internal bleeding doesn't show. I try to tell Ma about camp, but no matter what happened to me, it happened worse to her. Of course, hers was a different kind of camp.

I Go to the Badlands

"Don't be crazy. I never called you stupid!"

One Sunday afternoon Ma's cleaning the kitchen and I'm dunking saltines in milk, anticipating the week ahead. "Ma, nobody in school likes me. I'm scared that—"

"You're *scared*? Vhat, is a Nazi chasing you? Do you live in a hole in da ground? Did your family die in da gas chambers?" Yes, technically. And the ones still alive are in no state to raise children.

"But, Ma, school is so hard—"

"Hard? Vhat do you know from hard? I vork like a slave. Da Daddy's a *meshugeneh*. Listen to vhat he did now—" She tells me. And I listen.

Like Daddy's *mishugeness* affects only her?

I hate when Daddy turns into Monster Man. In the comic book, some-one ticks off Bruce Banner and he turns into the Incredible Hulk. Daddy operates along the same lines. His veins start bulging out of his neck; his eyes get bulgy, too. His nostrils flare and the sides of his mouth turn down in a sneer that says, "You make me sick." His booming threats nearly shake the gold leaf off the wallpaper. I've become repulsive to him. This seems to come out of the blue, the blue mood he's generally in.

I try to tell Ma how awful it feels. *Come in, Ma, Mayday, Mayday, child drowning, Mayday . . .* but Ma doesn't listen. "*Oy*, stop talking such nonsense."

So I start to yell. Wrong thing to do.

Ma gets more irritated. "Vhy can't you be more like Sylvia!"

I tried. I can't. I'm screwed. Why don't you like *me*, Ma?

Because I'm *bad*. Not Patty McCormick bad-seed-bad, but bad. Ma and Daddy will tell you they have nothing to do with it. Ask them, "Are you good parents?" They'll flash back, "Of course! Ve give her clothes, a roof over her head, and she alvays has enough to eat! Da problem mit her is she's spoiled! She has too much!" How could they ever hurt me? They *love* me. The sick must come from someplace inside me.

Daddy shifting into Monster Man is bad, but not as bad as when Ma morphs. Daddy uses the belt, but Ma's weapon is the fly swatter. Only, she calls it *da fly slaughter*. I don't know what's worse—the physical pain or that bugs have been squished with it.

Ma's love can be so mushy. "*Oy, Suzie, Hanala, my darling, my life! My beautiful babyala! A diamond!*" A beat later, mushy Ma disappears and a mean-looking Ma is yelling at me, "You make me crazy!" I do? Yikes!

I have no way of knowing I merely bring the crazy out in her. Irrational fury had been flowing under the surface, like molten lava, even before I was born. I provide opportunities for eruption. Pressure builds up, I'm playing nearby and—KAPLOOWEE!—chunks of molton-crazy spew all over me.

I never know what to expect. Sometimes Ma's face has such a sweetness, like Juicy Fruit gum, a burst of sweet so strong it's painful. When her love beam is locked on me, I'm not a bad girl; I am *SuperGirl*. I am invincible! But then the beam dies. And so do I.

> *Hence my bittersweet issue with Juicy Fruit gum. I put a stick in my mouth, the blast of sweetness hits my tongue, and I get depressed. I think of how soon the yummy taste will die and all I'll be left with is a lump of flavorless rubber. I can't let myself fully enjoy the yum because I know the yuck is coming.*

In a flick of a switch Ma turns from white to black. No dimmer, no indication that my light source is fading. She just snaps over to the dark side. How'd Good Ma go so fast? What'd I do? Can I get it back? She loves me, she loves me not; she loves me, she loves me not.

I want to hold Good Ma here. I tell her, "Mummy! When you die, I'm going to stuff your head and keep it with me always because I don't want to live if I can't see your face every day!" I said this before Hitchcock did *Psycho*. Stuffing a mother was *my* idea.

Flashback to me, at three . . .

I develop a theory: One woman can't be so different—there must be two of her. One smiles; she's pretty, her eyes are soft, and she looks at me like she just sewed a perfect hem. The other one's eyes are hard, she has no lips, and she looks at me like I smeared poop on the walls. Is there a Good Ma and a Mean Ma? Good Ma must beam up past the clouds to a holding place—the Mother Ship—and Mean Ma beams down, taking her place. I want to catch it happening. So, one day, Good Ma's home and I hide behind the couch. I fall asleep. When I wake up, Mean Ma's there. I missed the switch! I stay in hiding.

*   *   *

But now, I realize the Mother Ship theory is stupid. There's only *one* Ma. And *I* make her mad or happy. I try to be perfect to avoid being shut out. Out is unbearable. I need to be in. Oooh, I just hate Ma! But I *can't* hate her, she's a Holocaust survivor. I must be very bad to be mad at a *Holocaust* survivor. I bury my fury with food. But salami, saltines and social tea biscuits can't keep the anguish down. I'm getting fat. I'm so disgusted with myself, I eat more. I get fatter and madder. I regularly throw myself on the floor in a full-blown, stage-five tantrum. *That's* mad cow disease.

It's bad when Ma yells, but not as bad as when she *stops* yelling. The lips disappear and she skewers me with her eyes. And then . . . the eyes turn away.

That's when the begging begins. "Please, Mummy . . . I'm sorry. I'll never do it again!" I don't know what I did, but I swear I'll *never* do it again. I plead for connection, to be included again. Hit me, but don't not talk to me.

I follow her down the hall, around the kitchen, into the garden. "Please, Mummy, talk to me. Pleeeze!" I'm a pleeezing child.

Forget it. Don't bother asking for help, it won't come. Mummy hates me, and there's nothing I can do to change it. I'm dropping from high on the roller coaster. There's nothing to hang on to. There aren't even rails under me. I'm rocketing though space, alone, in the dark. I'm dead to Ma. Women walking into gas chambers. Is this how it feels when the oxygen runs out?

Days, maybe weeks of intensive apologizing, it looks like Ma's gearing up to speak to me again. Her words come out hard from between still-tight lips. "You're *sorry*?! Dis song and dance I heard before. I'm sick of *I'm sorry*." Not *great* words but at least she's talking!

> *Nightmare, recurring, ages four to twelve—On my way to school, I'm seized by an urgency to get back home. I turn around to find that my house has become a solid white block—cold, shiny-white, and seamless with no doors or windows. I run around the building, searching for a way to get in. Something vital is inside, but I can't find an opening. Anxiety turns to hysteria and I beat on the building. I wake up crying. Thirty years later my therapist asks if the building reminds me of anyone. I answer, "No, it's just a cold hard structure with warmth deep inside, but no crack for me to crawl in through. . . ."*

So Far, So Bad

I'm carrying a note home from school—

They want Ma and Daddy to come in for a meeting on Monday. It's a weekend of stomach flips and bad dreams.

On Monday, Ma fusses with my hair and smooths my tunic. She's mad this is making her miss work. We're in one of the offices in school. I'm getting a glimpse behind the scenes. *Oooh.* This is where teachers hatch their plots. "It's Friday, let's give 'em a book report due Monday. Heh-heh-heh!"

Ma and I sit across the desk from my teacher.

Mrs. Crankoff says, "Mrs. Stadwoner, are you aware that your daughter has a lisp?"

Ma's indignant. "Vhat do you mean a lithp?"

"Yeah," I wonder, "what lithp?"

They speak as if I'm not in the room, or like I don't even mind. Yeth, I mind.

"The lisp isn't the *worst* of it." There's a *wortht*?

"Susan speaks English with a Yiddish accent. Her speech is sing-song, and she adds extra vowels. For example, she says *sen-a-wich* instead of *sandwich*." Ma's face is blank, but I understand. I'm three feet tall and sound like Sergeant Schultz.

How'd this happen? Ma and Daddy speak to me in Yiddish. I learned English from Mr. Clean and women battling yellow waxy buildup—but with Ma's and Daddy's accents. It is confusing. Sometimes Daddy uses three languages in one sentence. "*Farmach la* door." Also, there is a refugee pig latin only Ma and Daddy speak. They speak *Polish* when they don't want me to understand. What the hell is so awful I have to be sheltered from it? Are they talking about me? Sounds like, "Yachy pachy kachy goochy."

I demand, "What! Tell me! Please! What are you saying? I can handle it. Do we have to pack? Should I get my quarters out from the flowerpot?"

I just want to be kept in the loop. "Pleeeze!"

Ma snaps, "About dis, you don't have to know!" Maybe I do.

"Shurrup! It's not your business!" Ma uses her silencer. Not a gun, the *fly slaughter.*

◆ ◆ ◆

Mrs. Crankoff's voice snaps me back to the teacher's room, "Susan needs speech therapy."

I've become Ma. I'm a refugee and a geek. I'm a *refu-geek*. I've got to run, to shrivel, to chew a bureau.

Oh, cruel nature! Not only did I skip rope at recess, sounding like Tevia from *Fiddler on the Roof*, I have a lisp! I try to avoid saying words with an S, but eventually I have to say my name. Susan Stadwoner. Thuthan Thtadwoner. How gathtly! It thuckth. I will, no doubt, be banned from any in crowd.

This pronunciation news flash puts it in concrete: I'm weird. Weird means lonely. True, often I hate and fear people, but I don't want to be alone. I have so much to share. With whom, and *how*? Sign language?

I go to thpeech clath. I conquer the lisp, if not the lisp-related self-consciousness.

Later that year, we start studying French. *Merde*. I'm still struggling with English.

What Daddy Knows About Parenting Could Fit on the Belt He Hits Me With

Still in third grade, my troubles multiply . . .

One morning, Miss Sawyer starts writing numbers on the blackboard.

Of all the things I want to do with chalk, writing numbers tops the list. Numbers are even more fun than letters. The chalk clicks at the start of each new number, and the lines are defined and end quickly. I love to work the fresh-out-of-the-box, long, smooth piece of chalk. I know how to handle long chalk without breaking it. Stubby pieces aren't as much fun, although they squeak less.

And I like erasing, too. The rectangular black felt block wipes all the old away. Little mistakes require mini, short rubs; paragraphs need windshield-wiper strokes. The board gets whiter as more is erased, and it's a dusty cloud by the end of the day. But every morning, it's shiny black again.

At my old school, Iona Elementary, I volunteered to be blackboard washer. Alone in the classroom after school, using the terry towel and water bucket, I'd clean up a day's worth of chalk—but first—I'd draw numbers and pictures of girls with big eyes. And I'd write my name over and over. My married name, "Mrs. Dr. Kildare."

But I'm not at Iona anymore.

Miss Sawyer is using chalk to draw symbols I've never seen. Odd formations. What could the strange markings mean? No one else looks confused. What do they know that I don't? See! I *knew* I didn't know!

I can't let on that I'm stupid. Not in front of the kids who all know each other. And I don't want to take up Miss Sawyer's time after class. I can figure it out myself, I'm nine years old.

The markings don't look *totally* unfamiliar, I had come across similar symbols at Iona. Sorta like plus and minus signs. Hmmm . . . this is a fancy neighborhood, maybe the dash with a dot above and a dot below is a fancy way of doing a minus sign. And the *x* is a plus sign, slanted for elegance. So, when Miss Sawyer hands out the test, I add and subtract accordingly.

I'm shocked the next morning when she hands back my test. A big red ZERO is marked at the top. What would the Beaver be thinking, "Am I going to get the strap for this?"

I stare at the zero. *None* right? I'm the most successful failure in third grade! At least I'm smart enough to make sure the test never gets home. None of them do. I bring my first report card home because it has to be signed and returned. *Excellent* and *Very Good* in art and English. *Unsatisfactory* and/or *Failure* in arithmetic, history, geography, French, and science.

Daddy takes off his belt. *Da strap* will motivate me. It does. Into a life of crime. From now on when I get a report card, I forge Ma's name at the bottom and present the card to Miss Sawyer. She signs it and gives it back. Then, I stop at the park after school and turn Us into Gs. I doctor the Fs into Bs or Es and Gs into VGs and bring it home.

Late at night.

I just got the strap for something. My thighs burn. I'm in my darkened room, my long black locks in pigtails, Mercurochrome on my knees and determination written all over my face. I stand over Adolf who's strapped to my desk chair. Adolf Hitler, the first man I obsess about.

My face is scrunched up as I jam sticks under his fingernails, one stick per question. "That doesn't feel very good, does it, Mr. Nazi? Nice families suffocated in *your* gas chambers—do you know how scared they were? Do you know how sad you made everybody? *Do you?!* Are you going to say, 'Sorry'?" The sour Kraut trembles and begs for mercy.

"Did *you* show mercy?" I push the sticks in further. He screams.

It's a good distraction from homework.

Death-camp-revenge games scratch my itch to punish bad men. I'm filled with a fury that no one, including myself, can understand. After all, *I* hadn't been in Poland. I was born here in Montreal, yet I want to reach out and torture someone. I don't have a little sister, there are no wimps at school to bully. *I'm* the wimp.

Retribution will have to wait until I grow up and get married.

> *If* only I'd had it together at nine to say, "Ma, Daddy, sit down, we need to talk. First of all, when you hit me, it doesn't *hurt you more than it hurts me.* You get over it. I, on the other hand, live with the humiliation. You say you love me, but you scare the poo-poo out of me. I may never feel safe being myself, as being myself often hurts. You say giving me da strap *is for my own good,* but history tells us that Adolf Hitler was regularly beaten by his father, and he still became a very bad boy."

The kitchen table—

One day school calls, Daddy answers the phone. They want him to come in for a meeting. Will it take time away from Walter Cronkite? Daddy turns into Monster Man. I turn to a loaf of challah.

Miss Sawyer hands Daddy a mimeographed times table sheet. (From the expression on his face, you'd think it was a draft notice.)

Every night, Daddy waves the sheet in my face, demanding answers. All I can come up with are more questions: What's wrong with me? Why can't I learn this? Why does the paper smell so good?

Daddy demands—"Nine times six!" Fear scares the answer into a part of my brain I can't access. I'm flooded by an array of double figures. (The "please wait" hourglass appears on the screen on my forehead.) Will any two numbers stand out? No. I'll have to guess.

" . . . Fifty-six?" Whack!! How close was I?

> *Thirty years later in therapy, I reluctantly divulge the secret of how retarded I'd been to think a multiplication sign was a beautified plus sign. My shrink says, "Seeing patterns is a sign of intelligence. Think how scared you must have been. And you couldn't even ask for help. You had to figure everything out by yourself. You weren't stupid, you were a naive, innocent young girl." So how bad can that be? It's what most men want.*

But for now, I'm a nine-year-old idiot, in the kitchen, getting flogged by a man determined to whip the naive out of me. "I'll give you a fifty-six! *Oy a broch!*" (Loose translation: You better marry rich because you'll never make it on your own!)

I'm not asked *why* I'm having a hard time. I should just "try harder!" Whack! Whack! Daddy knows percussion, not discussion. "You have it too good! You're spoiled!" Huh? Doesn't *spoiled* imply a kid gets whatever she wants? Ma and Daddy aren't nice to me, I'm not getting what I want.

Everyone gets wise to my report card scam.

I have to show Ma and Daddy the real thing. F in arithmetic. Failure. It suddenly occurs to me that I could *run*. The belt comes off, and I take off. Daddy's hot on my trail. The belt's off and he's chasing me down the hall. The patter of angry feet behind me suddenly stops. I look back. Daddy's pants fell down. Yelling in Yiddish, one hand waving the strap, the other pulling up his waistband, he tries to resume the chase, but trips.

My observing eye notes, "One day this'll be funny." But not yet.

Here's an equation I got: *Tragedy+Time=Comedy*. A survival skill develops. Get a sense of humor, or end up like Sylvia. Brrr.

Report Card Eve

And I'm not celebrating.

Two monumental events stand out from third grade—
1) "Robert Kennedy has been shot."
2) The release of the final report card.

There's another thing sabotaging my success as a student—something I never told anybody. I don't even want to think about it; I push it out of my mind—like if it stayed in there too long it would start to burn.

I see numbers in the wrong order. Not all numbers, and not all the time. I see seventy-nine instead of ninety-seven, and when I catch the mistake I give myself an F. FF. Fat Failure.

I flip-flop letters, too. I often start a word with the *second* letter. *A book report?* I have to read a book? Then I'm supposed to write down what I *think* about the book? What if I'm wrong?

Another secret: I can't see the blackboard. Doesn't everyone see blurry? This affects my ability to cheat. I become myopic. I think about what I *can* focus on—*me.* I have no perspective to see the larger picture—any picture. If I can't see a face from across a room, how can I care about the mind behind the face? What must the blurry people think about me? I do wish I could see the TV better.

So with all this *mishugas* working against me, I'm at risk of doing grade three over again. Tomorrow I'll find out if I passed arithmetic. Daddy, admitting defeat, hired a high school boy to tutor me, a geeky guy—no crush material there—but if it didn't work and I get another U or F, the strap will come off for sure. I'm not going to sleep tonight.

I'm in the school hallway, getting ready to go home and start my night of panic. I'm alone, the tidal wave coming, and I can't get out of the way. The incredible shrinking child. I'm a pea in a stadium-size pod. I had dilly dallied in the library, delaying home as long as possible. The hall lights go off. It's dark. I take my coat from its hook. It falls. I scream. I fall on my coat. Maybe I can sleep here tonight.

The classroom door swings open. Miss Sawyer, arms full of papers, walks out. She sees me, as if for the first time. "Susan, you passed arithmetic. You got a G."

What?! This is an elementary school high crime! Teachers *never* divulge such information! My gratitude and love for Miss Sawyer lives on. Whenever I'd think of her kindness, I'd get warm inside. Till one day, something occurred to me. Instead of returning each test with zeros, why didn't the bitch help me in the first place?

I Hate You, but Don't Move to Ohio

Nothing this big has ever happened in the family before!

Sylvia is marrying David from Brooklyn. They met in Atlantic City. He's a chemical engineer with General Tire. They'll live in Akron, Ohio—home of the tire.

I put on my pouffy pink dress with black velvet flowers and bows, and crinolines, and black patent leather shoes, and a purse big enough to hold my sparkle-lip gloss, rouge, and a Kleenex. I'm just *plutzing* with glee.

I skip into the foyer. Sylvia's standing in front of the mirror with a veil fastened to her beehive, and wearing the white, sleek, knee-length, classic sixties' dress. "Oh, Sylvia! You look beautiful! I can't wait to get to the synagogue!"

Sylvia snaps, "Why are you dressed up? *You're* not coming."

"Maaa!" I can't miss the wedding! What am I supposed to do? Stay home and hope a *Star Trek* rerun is on? "Maaa! Sylvia says I can't go to the wedding!"

"*Oy,* Suzie!" Ma says, "Of course you're coming, don't be stupid!"

With people telling me to stop being stupid, you'd think I'd stop. But how?

At the synagogue, I try not to bother Sylvia again. I hang out with my-cousin-Molly (never "Molly," always my-cousin-Molly)—who I never seem to bother.

❖ ❖ ❖

And then, Sylvia moves away. A year later she gives Ma her first grandchild. It's a boy!

I Am an Over-Feeler

I meet Margo Small—

Margo lives across the street. She becomes my best friend. Hanging out with her coolifies me. Margo's popular; I have a spot to stand in school. But there's trouble. Terri Baron lives in the bungalow attached to mine. Terri and Margo have been best friends for years. The three-way goes: Margo and me, Terri and Margo, but never Terri and me. Then suddenly—there's no me anymore. I can't understand why Margo won't talk to me; naturally, I figure it's because of some stupid thing I said or did. (No one told me about the three-girls-can't-be-friends rule.) There went *cool*, and here I go back to *refu-geek* status.

I spend months looking at Margo's house. Let her come outside, see me through my window, and tell me she wants to be friends again. Please, Margo, forgive me. I'm sick of playing Snakes & Ladders with myself. I cheat.

I need Ma to know, ya know? "Ma, I'm scared to go to school—"

"Scared you feel? *Oy!*" Ma defaults into Holocaust-ese. "Is a Nazi chasing you dat you should be scared?"

"But Ma, if Margo doesn't like me, nobody will, and I'll always be lonely."

"Lonely? Ach, I should only have da time to be lonely! Let Margo *gay in drerd!* You're better dan Margo. You should be glad dat she's not your friend!"

"But I—" Forget it, there's no *I* in *Ma*.

"You have nuting to complain about. Da problem mit you is you have too much! You're spoiled! You tink I had vhat you have in *da forest?* Ve vere starving, freezing, sleeping in a ditch! You have a roof, clothes, food." Sure, I have food. That's why I weigh 150 pounds.

Saturday, I'm staring out the window when Margo waves!

Oh my. She beckons me over to her yard. "I want to be friends again," she says. Yes! What of the troublemaker Terri? Who cares! I'm elated, ecstatic, and I run home to tell Ma.

"Ma! Ma! Margo said she'll be my friend again!"

Ma looks at me in the bad way. Oh-oh. The corners of her lips curl down in disgust. *"Don't you have any pride!* Vhat's da matter mit you?!" I don't know. There is something very wrong mit me. How could I be such an idiot! Why didn't I tell Margo, "I'll think about it"? How could I have let my guard down? I forgot to watch how I spoke, and *look* what happened!

Ma's trying to teach me to have pride. So how come I feel less proud than ever? Not knowing what to think or who to be, I turn on the TV and eat a box of Alpha-bits. In alphabetical order. But I don't feel any smarter.

Next Time I Open My Big Mouth, I'm Putting Food in It

I get hooked on codeine.

Two-twenty-twos are a Canadian over-the-counter pill with codeine. I pop them to stop the mouth pain. I can't sleep. I'm missing school. I scream at Ma, "I need to see a dentist! This isn't normal!" What is?

Some kids are told to brush their teeth—aren't they? But Ma and Daddy lost all their teeth in the war. They didn't floss in the forest. Dental hygiene, like tipping a *maitre d'*, is something that would never occur to them. Whenever I'd get a new toothbrush, every three or four years, I'd be so happy! No white crusty guck, all its bristles going the same direction. I'd take it to bed with me and massage my gums (long before it became trendy).

Ma knows a dentist who has an office in his house. He's a Russian immigrant who doesn't have a license to practice dentistry in Canada. I assume he was licensed in Russia. As a dentist.

He greets us at the door, smiling, heavy accent. "Hello, Missus. Hello, little girrrl." He sounds like Boris from *The Rocky and Bullwinkle Show*, and his gold front tooth glints in the sun.

His office is in the basement. We walk down the dark stairwell. *Is it safe?* It's bargain basement dentistry. Fillings wholesale. Extractions, two for the price of one. Cash only. It seems I should be here for an illegal abortion, not a bad tooth. There's a smell . . . disinfectant? Plaque? Cat pee?

The—I hope—dentist escorts Ma and me into a small brown room with no windows. And no diplomas on the wall. Just a chair, I think it's a *barber's* chair. I'm in *Bizzarro Mayberry*, being treated by Floyd the barber/dentist.

Ma stands behind the chair, out of my line of sight and he tilts me back. There's hardly any room between my feet and the wall. The bare bulb above bothers my eyes. The table next to me, with long shiny instruments, needs a napkin or something; it doesn't look clean.

I'm only mildly concerned about the steel probing device. I'd bitten into a tinfoil wrapper once and learned never to do it again, but I don't relate that to the pain caused by metal touching the nerve of a tooth.

Discount Dentist tells me, "Open vider. Vider!" My mouth is opened wider than it's ever been opened before.

He moves a steel probing thing toward my face and into my mouth. "Is *dis* da bad one?" He jabs the sharp metal into the crater even I could see at home in the bathroom mirror. You could see it from Sputnik!

My body ejects from the chair. My knees lock and my feet jam into the wall. My *knees!* Ow, ow. I shove Boris away before he has a chance to congratulate himself for finding the decayed tooth and run up the stairs, not taking time to scream at Ma for doing this to me.

I'm back on codeine. I don't see a dentist again for months; and when I do, it's for a root canal. He's a nice guy with a regular office and no accent. But no matter how many times he shoots me with Novocain he can't freeze the area. My arm is numb, but I can still feel the tooth. I'm crying, the dentist is crying, the nurse is trying to get patients to stop leaving the waiting room. Tears flood my ears, but I can still hear the piercing sound of the drill.

He says, "You're unusually sensitive."

"I'm sorry." I'm putting this man through a terrible ordeal.

He calls Ma and tells her I need braces to correct my overbite.

"Dat's because you sucked your tumb!"

Earlier in the year, Ma shamed the thumb out of my mouth forever by telling me it wasn't *normal.* "Now ve have to pay $800!" Is there that much money in the world?! Are we in an $800 tax bracket? Ma price-comparison shops for a hairnet.

Another note from school—

"Suzie needs glasses." I was caught squinting. How am I gonna tell Ma and Daddy? They forked over the $800 for braces because—I can't land a rich husband looking like Bugs Bunny, but glasses are not going to add to Ma's law of attraction: As long as I *look* good, does it matter if I can *see?*

❖ ❖ ❖

Asking for things means getting barked at; it doesn't mean getting the things. Me asking usually leads to me begging, which leads to me being sad and/or angry—feelings I try to avoid.

So I don't ask. When I come home with the "Suzie needs glasses" note, Daddy doesn't put up a fight. Years later it hits me. Daddy *wore* glasses, he *understood* the need.

It takes a year for me to ask Ma for a training bra. The embarrassing bumps under my blouse need to be trained. They're poking out.

Ma snickers, "You need a bra?! You have nuting!" I have bumps.

The Holocaust Follows Me
to Hebrew School

As if Monday through Friday isn't bad enough.

It's another queasy Sunday morning. I wake up wanting to barf (my gut's opportunity to express itself). Either I go to Hebrew school or Daddy takes off *da belt*. I have a choice. So how come I feel like I don't?

I shlep myself out of bed so I can get to the kitchen and crack open a fresh box of social tea biscuits. They will calm the queasy. Cramming eight at a time into a vat of milk, I wait for the perfect mushiness and spoon them out. Mmmm . . . I finish a whole row and save the second row for after Hebrew school.

(Six years of Sunday school, and I can't even recite the Hebrew alphabet. It's been wiped from the hard drive.)

I mosey along to synagogue, avoiding bees. I'm scared of anything that comes out of nowhere and hurts. Bees are heat-stinging missiles that get you just when you think everything's okay.

There it is, another brown building with another brown desk to fidget behind.

I'm at the desk, ready to start carving my initials, when the lights go off. Are they showing a *movie*? The Venetian blinds drop and the film projector fires up. I'm excited.

Wait a minute. Skinny people? Wide-striped prison garb? Armbands, piles of shoes . . . ? Auschwitz in its heyday.

Why are they showing us this? To teach us our history? To tell us "never forget"? And to make sure we never marry *goyem*?

A black-and-white gray scene comes up. It's daytime in the forest. Men with the Star of David on their arms stand shoulder to shoulder in a line.

Pow! Pow! Pow-pow-pow!!

The men . . . they don't run. They . . . fall.

THE CAMERA PANS OVER to the shooters. They're soldiers, also in a line. These men have swastikas on their arms, not stars. It was bad to be on the wrong team.

CUT TO an indoor scene. Another line. It's moving slowly. This is a line of women. They're naked. A woman carries a baby in one arm. Her other hand holds the fingers of a girl no older than the girls sitting with me in the dark.

THE CAMERA MOVES DOWN the line of women and children to the door at the end of the hall. We look inside . . .

The room has no windows; it's empty except for sawed-off pipes sticking out of the walls.

CLOSE UP OF PIPES. Now that can't be good. I've heard stories, remember? Showerheads.

NEXT SCENE. Dead people being slid into ovens, like pizza ovens. Can I slide out of this room?

CUT TO big trucks. Skinny dead bodies are being unloaded. There's what looks like a peace sign, on the grill of each truck. (I don't recognize the logo until ten years later when I see it as a hood ornament on cars in Beverly Hills.)

CUT TO the skinny dead people being thrown into a ditch. Who dug the ditch? The people lying in it? Is that a baby's body? Am I related to any of these bodies?

Barbed wire, smoke blowing from the chimney, Yiddish music playing under the narrator's voice. I'm horrified. I'm transfixed.

It's Ma's story . . . with a soundtrack.

Chochu

Ma wasn't a sole survivor.

Her cousin Freidel also made it to Montreal. I know Freidel as Chochu, which is Polish for *aunt*. She isn't really an aunt but in *da New Country*, friends became cousins and cousins became uncles. Everybody got an upgrade.

After Hebrew school, I'd walk to Chochu's and have a salami sandwich.

Chochu is *never* not home. She's stayed in her duplex for thirty years, feeding. She's as large as she's long-suffering. It takes a bar mitzvah, wedding or funeral to get her out of the house. I understand; if it weren't for school, I'd be home, eating.

The Sunday ritual at Chochu's house, like the smell, is always the same.

I let myself in. "Hi!" The door's never locked. Chochu lifts herself off the couch; this takes a couple of minutes.

"*Oy*, I have such a *copviteck*!" Chochu's had a headache since she got to Canada. She drags me to the bathroom and—using a washcloth the way you twist an orange on an old juicer—scrubs like she's trying to erase my face. After the terry cloth assault she gives me luncheon meat.

One day Chochu's headache is so bad, I have to make my own sandwich. Not knowing it's a crime, I use a *milk* dish. Resembling one of the dancing hippos from *Fantasia*—only with nylons rolled at the knees—Chochu, migraine and all, dashes across the kitchen, grabs the plate and throws it into the garbage pail. I experience simultaneous shock and guilt. The plate cost money. Chochu *hates* parting with money; although she does give me a quarter every Sunday. (I suspect she dug the plate out of the trash after I left, but I never confront her. She might scrub even harder.)

I ask Ma, "Why does Chochu hate me?"

"Ach, da Chochu . . . when you vere a baby, maybe six veeks old, I had to go get a gall bladder operation, so I gave you to da Chochu; and I don't know vhat happened. You vere such a happy baby, alvays laughing. Vhen I got you back—maybe two veeks later—you didn't smile no more."

Did Chochu scare me? She scared her kids. My-cousin-Molly never learned how to ride a bike or drive a car or travel. Molly wears black liquid eyeliner, blue shadow, lines her lips with crimson, filling the rest of the lip with light pink. Rouge sits on her cheeks. She doesn't blend.

I've never seen my-cousin-Molly happy. Even when she smiles, sadness comes through her eyes in microwaves. . . .

Fast-forward to 1967: The synagogue. Molly's wedding.

She's crying in the bridal chamber. Two hundred guests wait for the white dress to come down the aisle, while Molly clutches Sylvia's eighteen-month-old son, whom I've brought in because he can't sit still in his seat. He's looking at her curiously.

She's hunched over, black streaming down her face on to the tail of her veil. "Mark, oh, Mark! I wish I could take you and run away." Mark doesn't have the vocabulary to ask what's the matter; I don't have the guts.

My-cousin-Molly loved another boy but broke the engagement off because he wasn't Jewish. Chochu would not accept a goy in the front door let alone into the family. One might think that as a victim of extreme prejudice, Chochu would be more tolerant, but one would be wrong.

So my-cousin-Molly is marrying a man she doesn't love. But he's Jewish.

My-cousin-Molly's brother, Jackie (who I have no need to call my-cousin-Jackie), born a couple of years before me in Canada, was also affected by the H-factor. He was strange, but strange is normal for children of the Holocaust. When Jackie was in his thirties, he dropped out of rabbinical college and moved to Toronto to escape Chochu's giant suction cups.

My-cousin-Molly never lived farther than four miles from Chochu. It's as far as the cord reached.

I watch Molly slowly disappear through the years. And as she does, she gets bigger and bigger. The apple doesn't fall . . . .

Fast-forward further to 1997: Chochu's dead, my-cousin-Molly and Ma have grown close.

I'm on the phone listening as Ma tells me about a woman from *da shtetl* named Faiga Basha. As I understand it, Faiga Basha was a wide woman, and clumped as she walked. Her breasts hung down to a waist that wasn't there. Faiga Basha had perpetually red eyes—not just in her eyes—but surrounding them too. And they crossed. Ma said, "She vould look at you, and see me." She drooled from both sides of her mouth. Her nose drooled, too. And she smelled like cheese. Faiga Basha never married.

"Ma . . . why are you telling me about this poor woman?"

"Vell, Molly told me dat da Chochu used to call her Faiga Basha, and she vanted to know if I knew who dat vas. So I told her."

I want to scream, but nothing comes out.

"Hello. . . Suzie, are you still dere?"

"Yeah, Ma. I'm here."

"Vell . . . vhat's da matter?"

"Nothing."

"Vhat do you mean, nuting? . . . I said someting wrong to Molly? She asked me who Faiga Basha vas. Vhat, I'm supposed to lie?" And why not? I've heard Ma lie, she's good at it. Why tell the truth now? Ma got some satisfaction from telling Molly.

"Vell . . . ?"

"Well . . . now she knows."

"Dat's vhat I mean!"

"Exactly. Gotta go. Bye."

"Guys, It's a Sitcom About Those Darn Nazis"

Friday, 8:45 p.m.—

I'm on the floor in the TV room laughing at silly Sergeant Schultz. Hogan is using food to distract him so that Schultzy—the Nazi you hate to love—will leak top-secret information. Schultz says, "Colonel Hogan, if you escape . . ." Hogan says ". . . Yeah?" Schultz says, "Be a good fellow and take me with you."

Ma walks by with Windex. "Yeah, if only da Germans ver so stupid! My sisters vould be alive." She drops the observation, like you drop a Kleenex in the trash in passing, and continues on shpritzing and wiping. I can't breathe. Colonel Klink "heil Hitlers" in every episode. There it is—the worst salutation in history, and I never put it together with the same people who brought us genocide by gas chamber.

Hot flash! Somewhere down the road from Hogan's kooky camp . . . is *Dachau.*

I'm still looking at the TV but no longer watching it. I'm conflicted. I need the laughs from this Nazi comedy to relieve the pain of living with Nazi-traumatized parents. Do I continue to watch *Hogan's Heroes?* If so, do I watch, but only with guilt?

I have many unanswered questions. Why was a nice man like Colonel Hogan a prisoner? He doesn't seem like a criminal. And why doesn't *colonel* have an *R?* And why did the Holocaust happen?

And, come to think of it, how crazy is this world, when a comedy featuring Nazis can be aired twenty years after they murdered six million Jews? How did the pitch meeting go? "If you liked World War II, you'll love Hogan's Heroes. *You got these Nazis, real likable, and a POW camp. I know what you're thinking, 'Where are the* girls?' Don't worry, Hogan seduces a sexy Russian spy . . . ." And how many Russians did Hitler kill? And how crazy is it that John Banner (Sergeant-I-know-nuting-Schultz) was Jewish. So was Werner Klemperer (Colonel Klink). Both had fled Nazis in the thirties and served in the U.S. Army during World War II. Howard Caine (Major Hochstetter of the Gestapo) was also Jewish. Leon Askin (General Burkhalter) had been beaten by the real Gestapo and spent the war in a French internment camp. Robert Clary (Louis Lebeau) was Jewish, too. When John Banner was asked, "Given your background, how could you work on Hogan's Heroes?" he said, "I see Schultz as the representative of some kind of good in any generation." But other than getting a new Chevrolet, who thought of anything like that back then?

Ma's War Stories
Weren't Funny Like Hogan's

Okay, I guess I should tell you what happened in the war, but when Ma tells the story, she does it in Yiddish, and there's no way my translation will sound the same. I'll do my best.

Poland, 1939: Off to the ghetto we will go.

Mania and Fischel live in a *shtetl* near Warsaw. Ma's eighteen, Daddy's twenty-one. It's their wedding day. The ceremony's over, everyone's drinking schnapps, dancing the polka, eating brisket. Ma's thinking, "My modder should be here." Boom! The door is kicked open and a troupe of Nazis march in.

Now it's Germany's time to eat. And when a Nazi wants your food, you don't say no.

The party's over.

Daddy remembers it was a Thursday—

He and Ma hear shouting and fists pounding doors. The pounding comes closer. Daddy opens the door only to be pushed back in by a Nazi, "You have five minutes to pack your things and get into the street!"

Daddy and Ma, her father, sisters and brothers, and their children load what they can into the family pushcart. They are forced to walk many miles, at gunpoint, to end up at a wired-off section of Warsaw. A ghetto. Ten people, one room. No heat. No water. Ma longs for her mother, but she had died a year before because Jews weren't given medicine. If you're a Jew, and you get typhus, you die. And die she did.

Ma says, "*OY*, mine modder, dey vere putting her in da ground. Vas she a beauty! Mine sister trew herself on da box, da . . . da . . . caffeine . . . no . . ."

"Coffin, Ma. Coffin."

"Oh yeah! Tank you, Poopsala." She sighs, "Mine sister vas crying, da men had to pull her from da . . . coffing . . . coffee . . . *oy a broch* . . . how you say—"

"You say it fine, Ma. . . ."

"Hana, mine sister, such a *punim,* like a movie star! She vas crying, 'Don't go, Mama, come back!' *Oy,* like you could bring back da dead!"

The sky is gray the day Ma and Daddy's ghetto is liquidated.

Each day at dawn, Ma's younger brother, Gedala, and Daddy are taken with the rest of the boys from the ghetto to build roads for German tanks. (Roads Daddy will later help to blow up.)

They're gone when the big commotion begins again; soldiers banging on doors, barking orders. Ma's family packs up again.

Ma knows the man in charge of her quarter. Like Sergeant Schultz, he's a Nazi with a weakness for food. He'd bring Ma apples, she'd turn them into apple pies. (She makes the best apple pie in the world!) He'd bring a chicken and then stay for her chicken soup.

Ma's family is loading up the wagon when Schultz motions her aside. "Mania, don't go. You're young. You and Fishel don't have children. You can run away!"

Ma doesn't understand why her friend wants to scare her. "What are you saying?! I want to be with my family!"

"This transport isn't going to a good place, Mania." His urgency sends her mind spinning. "When my back is to you, walk away slowly, slip into the forest. When Fishel and Gedala are brought back tonight, I'll tell them where to find you." He suggests a place.

"You won't shoot me in the back?"

"Mania . . . I don't know why the world went crazy. I'm just a soldier, I do what I'm told. But I see things. Jews aren't bad. You're no different than we are."

Yeah, she is. Hitler's into blondes.

Ma goes to her father and repeats Schultz's warning. "Father, what should I do?" The old man keeps tightening ropes to the wagon. Doesn't he hear her?

"Father, if—"

"If we're going to a bad place, little daughter, you shouldn't go."

She kisses her brothers and sisters and their children. She pulls her sack off the cart and walks away, wondering if she will soon feel a bullet in her back.

Reaching the trees, she turns. One more look . . . she resists the urge to run back to her family. Will she ever see them again? Click. Her mind switches to, "What now?"

Ma wanders as night falls on the old forest. The trees block out the moon and stars. She can't find the meeting spot. How afraid is she? Who can imagine? Where are Fishel and her baby brother? Where are the Nazis? Does she feel terror? Grief? Does she feel anything but the hope to keep breathing?

She lies down, covers herself with dirt and leaves and drifts off, knowing she might never wake. But is she really awake now? How can this be real? These things don't happen.

Dawn opens her eyes. She isn't dead! But then she remembers . . . Click. She picks a direction and walks. But to where? Ma comes to a path and decides to take it.

Two Polish soldiers suddenly appear from around the bend. They're headed right toward Ma. It's too late to slip back into the trees. They've spotted her.

Ma becomes Ms. Congeniality. Striding toward them, she smiles, swinging her arms. Just as she's about to pass, one reaches for his rifle and says, "A Jew!"

Ma pulls her chin high, puffs out her chest, and demands in Polish, "Do I *look* like a Jew?!" (Ma's four-foot-eleven. Her chutzpah's six-foot-two.)

The second officer chuckles. "No Jew would have the guts to answer like that!" They both laugh, and without even asking to see her papers, wave her off and walk on.

Ma stays on the path till the soldiers are out of sight. Then, ducking back into the woods, she burrows into foliage. "Maybe it vas tall grass, like little trees. Maybe it vas corn." She'll find Daddy, but she'll wait here by the side of the narrow road till it gets dark. Hours pass. Soldiers pass. The day gets long. And cold.

In the distance, Ma makes out two children walking alone. Why on earth are they alone? As they get closer, Ma recognizes them. She hasn't seen them in a year, since her brother Gershin moved from her *shtetl*, but she knows who they are. These are *Gershin's children*! She waves her arms, trying to get the children to come to her.

"Over here! Hurry!" They don't see her. Something's wrong. They walk like zombies. There's blood . . . Ma freezes. Her niece has a bullet hole in her shoulder and another through the hand. (Ma will always point to exactly where.) The boy walks with his sister's help.

Ma runs into the road, grabs the children up, and pulls them deep into the forest. Finally, the girl tells it . . .

"Daddy took us to a barn. He said we had to hide there, with the other families. We were in the barn a whole day; then the farmer came running in, yelling. He told everybody, 'Get up, get up! The German army is coming!' He said we must rush out the back door. Everyone was pushing and the door opened and . . . then we saw the Nazis. They were in a line, with guns pointing at us. They backed us into a corner.

"Mummy and Daddy pushed us behind them. All the parents were pushing children to the back. Then there were popping sounds. And screaming. Daddy fell on top of me. Then it felt like everyone fell on top of me. I heard the soldiers get closer. They kept firing. And firing. Then the screams stopped, but the shooting didn't. I heard German shouting. Then—nothing.

"I didn't know if the Nazis were still there, maybe they were waiting. So *I* waited a long time. And I wondered, 'Maybe I'm dead.' It was hard to breathe. I had to push my way out. First I looked. No soldiers! Then I got out from under the heavy bodies.

"I saw the door and ran as fast as I could. I heard my name being called. My brother was trying to catch up to me. But something was wrong with his leg. I waited to see who else would come out of the barn. No one. Were we the only ones left?"

It's hard to imagine Ma, not much taller than these two children. Round hazel eyes, long brown hair tied back in a babushka. I know her as tough and old, but the day Ma went into the forest, she was an eighteen-year-old girl. And for all she knew, she'd never be nineteen.

Ma pulls the children close; she tells them not to worry, she'll keep them safe. But what do you do with two wounded children? Ma picks up the boy, her instincts choose the direction, and they walk.

The day is losing its light when Ma spots a man in a field. Did he see them?

Wait! She knows this man, he'd been to the house! She pleads with him and he agrees to hide the children while she goes to find Fishel and Gedala. The boy and girl beg her not to leave, they can go *with* her—they'll keep up. Ma tells them it's not possible, she promises to return soon.

Ma travels to the meeting place and hides. Late that night she hears a scuffling sound. Ambush? No, Daddy and her brother! Ma tells them about the barn, and that they must go get the children. But Daddy had been warned that Nazis have occupied the area, going to the farm now would get them all killed.

Days go by before they make it to the farm, and when they do, the children aren't there. The farmer says that when he learned the Nazis were coming, he made the children run into the forest.

Ma, Daddy, and Gedala search for days, no kids. But Daddy knows someone. A man he can trust. (Then again, you never know who'll turn you in.) Daddy's friend is the village mayor.

The three sneak up to his house and Daddy knocks quietly on the door. The man hurries them into the kitchen and pulls the curtains. He puts food on the table. They ask if he knows anything about the children. He urges them to eat.

When all the food is gone, the man sits. He tells them to stop searching for the children. He sounds sad. "Yes, the farmer told the kids to leave, but they wouldn't. They said they were waiting for Aunt Mania to come back."

Ma always cries at this part. So do I. Every time. If I only knew how much guilt you already felt, Ma, I wouldn't have tried to make you feel more.

Ma says, "Dat's vhen I found out. Da farmer took an ax, and he chopped dem up. If only I got dere earlier. If I got dere, I could have saved dem . . ."

If. Such a little word that could change such big things. What *if* I'd been in the farmer's place? What would I do to save my family?

◆ ◆ ◆

Ma's already moved on. *Move along, move along, nothing to see here, move along.*

She rips off a button from her sweater, undoes the thread, and three gold coins fall out. Pressing them into the mayor's hand, she pleads, "Take these. Go to the pub, buy the Nazis drinks. You speak German, find out where the transport took the families from my ghetto."

The mayor looks down the hall to the bedrooms, and without a word, he walks out the front door. Ma, Daddy, and Gedala wait. And wait. Hours pass.

The mayor returns and hands the money back to Ma. He's found out nothing.

Impossible! He must have heard something.

Daddy won't leave without an answer.

The tired man's shoulders fall. He speaks as if the words themselves will destroy. "The transport went to Treblinka."

Yes, they understand, they've heard the Nazis were putting Jews together to work in labor camps.

"No, not labor camps," he says, "the Nazis at the bar . . . they were laughing about the dirty Jews who thought they were getting showers but . . ." Ma remembers the hollow sound of water dropping from a faucet. The three fugitives try to comprehend the words they hear in the mayor's kitchen . . . gas chamber.

The Underground

Even though Ma has told me the forest story over and over since child-hood, so much is still fuzzy. Like *time*. What happened when? Horror blurs my hearing.

"Ma, Daddy, *how long* were you in the forest?"

Ma says, "I vas hiding in da forest for a year. Maybe two years. Two and a half."

Daddy barks, "No matter how long it vas, it vas too long."

"Right you are, Daddy! Maybe *you* can be more specific?"

"Nineteen forty-one to nineteen forty-four."

"So, what did you do while you were hiding?"

"Ve blew up bridges. And roads. I vas da *captain* of *da group*."

Ma corrects, "*Oy!* You don't do dis until ve met da Russians!"

"How about we revisit that later. So, how did you guys *live*?"

"Big holes. Da Daddy mit da men made ditches in da ground. You could put in nine, maybe ten people. Ve made a door put a bush on top so you couldn't see da door of da hole even if you stand next to it."

"Hold on. Men, what men?"

"Ve met otter people hiding in da forest. I had a friend, Rifka, ve knew Ralph and Ann, who you met. Dey also got married just before. And two more couples, dem ve never saw again."

They would forever be referred to as *da group*.

"What happened in winter, why didn't you freeze?"

"Ve slept, vhen ve *could* sleep, side by side, like sardines. And on top ve had coats, underneath ve had branches. Ve slept in da day. At night it vas more safe, ve vent to get food."

"Food from where?"

Daddy butts in, "I had connections. Der ver farmers, da store people, friends. . . . Before da ghetto, my fatter gave me money. He said, 'Take dis. If ve get separated, you vill need it.' I used dis money to buy food from good Pollacks."

The coins they tried to give the mayor went to buy guns.

"Did you think about your families?"

Ma jumps in, "Tink! Vhat vas to tink?! Dey vere dead in da gas chambers!"

Forest fugitives had to route their thoughts away from massacred families and on to—how do we get through the day without dying?

Over-talked by Ma, Daddy has given up trying to tell the tale.

As months pass, they join up with others; the sardine can gets bigger.

They encounter a group of Ma's cousins. They're the *big* branch of the family, reaching heights of five-foot-seven. One cousin is Freidel. (I know her as Chochu.) She has a husband, Berel (Uncle Berel). Daddy asks them to join *da group*, but they, as Ma says, are "*Farshtunked*" and decline. They stay on their own.

Like leprechauns, *da group* lives unseen, unheard, and short. They shiver, they starve, they hold their breaths.

One night, Ma leaves the hole in the ground to "go make da pee-pee," when she hears men speaking German.

She drops to the ground and tries not to breathe. Inches from her face, a pair of shiny boots gleam in the moonlight. She's a breath away from death.

Ma tells me, "If da Nazi heard me, or if he looked down, you vouldn't be here."

"I don't know how you did it, Ma. How could you go on, day after day, for years?"

Ma shrugs. "Vhat should ve do, sit and let dem kill us?"

She adds, in a low voice, "You know . . . it vasn't just da *Nazis* and da *Pollacks* dat vere bad. Dere ver some bad *Jews*, too."

"Huh?" I probe. She won't tell. Like the guards at Buckingham Palace, she ain't budging. I wait many years for the answer. How could I have imagined she was talking about Chochu.

Meanwhile, Back at the Forest

1941 or '42 (maybe it was '43), Ma gets pregnant.

Ma said Daddy had always been frisky, "Even in a hole in da ground mit da bombs shooting." It's not like the forest women were on the pill. Condoms? From the *shtetl's* *7-Eleven*? The men used sex to take the edge off. After all, for a couple of the couples in *da group*, this was their honeymoon. *The Newlywed Game* becomes—*Survivor*! Those *alive* at the end win.

❖ ❖ ❖

They could not survive with a baby in *da group;* the baby would cry and give them away.

There's a doctor in the village who takes care of knocked-up fugitives. Ma will go it alone. Soldiers are sweeping the country eliminating Jews as they come across them; there's less risk of capture going solo. Ma and Daddy decide on an *après*-abortion rendezvous point.

Ma creeps into town in the dark and finds the doctor's house. She doesn't need to tell them why she's come. She hands over the coins she'd taken from her buttons. A woman leads her into the basement. She's put on a table. The man comes in, says nothing, pushes her legs apart.

After, with only a rag to stop the bleeding, she's ushered out the door.

Ma finds the rendezvous point, but Daddy and Gedala aren't there. Have they been caught? Are they lost? Are they alive?

(Postpartum, with crazy-making-hormones and Nazis, and alone! *I* would have just laid down and died.)

But Ma's furious. If Daddy *was* alive—she was going to kill him!

Ma walks for hours. The trees shut out the stars and in the total darkness, she's wobbling and about to collapse when she sees a light through the trees. It's a cottage. Hope gives her strength, exhaustion gives her courage; she goes up to the front door. For all she knows, she's inviting herself into a hut of Jew haters.

An old woman opens the door and pulls Ma inside. Grabbing a blanket and pillow from a trunk, the woman makes a bed by the fire and gives Ma something to eat.

Suddenly, Ma's stomach goes into spasm. Has she been poisoned? Was the abortion botched? She runs to the outhouse. She hadn't eaten in days, and the food was too much, too quickly. Ma comes back to her bed and falls asleep.

It's still dark when Ma hears knocking. She's excited, "Fishel and Gedala! They found me!"

"No," the woman says, "you were dreaming. But you had this dream before first light, so it will come true." Poles are a superstitious people.

Ma lies back down, too tired to think. Just before dawn she hears another knock, "Am I dreaming again?"

The woman is already at the door. It's Daddy! He's found Ma. A miracle!

Ma tells me, "It vas a *true* miracle—he can't even find his vay home from da *mall!*"

I ask her, "Ma, how can you joke?"

"Hanala, vhat are you gonna do, cry all da time? Ve laughed in da forest too. Yeah!" she whispers. "My stomach vas sick from not eating, den eating too fast, but da Daddy, he *alvays* had a problem mit his stomach. *Da group* vas never sure if da noise vas gunfire, or Daddy passing gas."

1944—da group links up with "maybe 200 people from da Russian Underground."

One afternoon in the forest, the group, now over two hundred, are shooting at a group of Nazis.

Then the shooting from the other side stops. Ma hears the Russians yelling, "The Americans are coming! The Americans are coming!" The Americans have arrived, and the Nazis are running away.

"Ma? When did you realize the hell was really over?"

"Vhen . . . da Americans came. Dey gave us food, clothes. . . . Dey took us to a refugee camp."

"Did you cry? Did you finally cry then?"

"No . . . not den. Ve vent into da refugee camp. Music vas playing from da buildings. I tought to myself, 'My sisters vill not hear dis music.' For dem, da music vas over. So den I cried."

❖ ❖ ❖

The Holocaust in Europe is over, but it stays alive and is spreading like a virus through the children of survivors.

How dare I take my silly troubles seriously, knowing what Ma and Daddy went through? How could I ever be angry at them? But I am. How can I blame them for anything? Yet, I do. How could I ever raise my voice to poor, sweet Ma? Ma agrees. The problem is, their problem was so big, it left no space for mine.

Surviving Is Not the Same as Living

*1948: The Holocaust moves to Canada—
let the oy-vey-ing begin!*

Hitler's dead, Germany's embarrassed, and Jewish refugees spread around the world in search of relatives. Some roam America's gold-paved streets where Jews aren't killed for being Jewish. They're just kept out of country clubs. Others go to Israel. These will become the world's butchiest Jews.

❖ ❖ ❖

Ma and Daddy, stuck in Poland, post their names as survivors in the *International Jewish Journal*. Meanwhile, Ma gets pregnant again. She's in labor, in the hospital alone in the middle of the night. Lying in the bed, she overhears nurses talking. "You see, there's still some of them *left*!" The other says, "And she's going to have a baby. Another dirty Jew!" Ma's scared they'll kill her baby.

She's on the operating table about to deliver. The doctor cuts her open, and then after, sews her back up—all without anaesthesia. And where is Daddy?

Ma says, "Friends had to drag him out from a German voman's bed to come to da hospital to see his child." Ma still holds a grudge about this. Ma resents a bakery that sold her day-old bread ten years ago.

Daddy defends, "Dat's a lie!"

"Den vhere vere you, tell me?!"

"I, for your business, vas vorking in da black market to get supplies and food to da Jews who vere fighting."

"Yeh? Da var vas over already! You found out you vere going to live, so you vanted to live it up!" Daddy has that faraway look again. He gets up, saying something about needing to shovel the snow. He can shovel it all right.

What to believe? Daddy was a hunk who'd faced death every day for years, and survived only to be treated like an itchy sweater.

What came first? Did Daddy hurt Ma, and she became a bitch, or was she a bitch who turned him into a scoundrel?

One chilly winter night in Winnipeg, Canada—

Ma has a cousin who immigrated to Canada in 1930. His name is Herschel. Cousin Herschel's mother-in-law is warming herself by the radiator, reading the *Jewish Journal*. The eighty-year-old is catapulted out of her chair. She runs into Herschel's bedroom. "Wake up, Herschel! You have cousins alive in Europe! They're looking for you!"

Herschel's at the immigration office first thing the next morning, petitioning for what's left of his family to come to Canada. He'll sponsor them. He'll give them jobs.

Before the war, Daddy had two siblings. Ma had four. All had been married with children, except Gedala, the youngest. By 1945, Ma, Daddy, and Gedala are the only siblings alive.

As a child I met cousins (Moishe, Ruchala, and Zelig from New York) only to find out years later that they aren't relatives at all. They're friends from *da Old Country*. (They got the upgrade.)

Ma and Daddy immigrate in 1948; they come by da boat.

Always referred to as *da boat*. When I was little, I believed one really big boat brought all the Jewish refugees to North America, and the rest died in gas chambers.

Sylvia is three years old for the boat ride from Poland. Ma is throwing up the entire crossing. (Poles are not generally known as a seafaring people.) Little Sylvia is up on deck when an old man approaches her. "Your mother won't reach the new land alive. She'll get sick and die before we get there."

Sylvia doesn't stop shrieking until Canada. Was this where she started dismantling her feelings? A piece here, a piece there, she locks them away and forgets she's ever had them.

Herschel owns a mink ranch, and Daddy, Gedala, and Uncle Berel go into the fur business. Daddy is proud of his new profession. (Years later, driving on the highway in the old Valiant, we pass some furry roadkill and Daddy makes an assessment, "$7.50 for dat pelt!" Gross!)

◆ ◆ ◆

Do Ma and Daddy feel happiness or guilt when they meet their family in Winnipeg? How do they explain why they survived? Is it comforting to have family again? Do they talk about what happened?

Does Ma ever try sharing, "Vhen da soldiers came mit da transport . . . "

Do they cut her off? "Mania, dat's da past. Sit, have a nice glass of tea." Do the Canadian cousins feel guilty?

Double message: Don't talk about what happened. But as Jews, we must never forget. (Like they could forget if they tried.)

Ma says they were happy to go to Canada and leave a country that hates Jews. "In Canada, a Jew can live. You vere cold, but you lived."

Ma applies for work at a sweatshop, lying in broken Eng-a-lish. "Sure, I can operate a sewing machine. Very vell!" She's fired after a couple of days, but not before she can watch the workers and learn a little. The next job lasts long enough for her to learn a little more. By the third time she's fired, she almost knows how to sew. The next factory does not fire her.

It's 1955. Ma, Daddy, and Sylvia move from Winnipeg to Montreal.

Ten-year-old Sylvia has been coming home from school every day, begging for a brother or sister. Ma says, "She *hacked mir in chaynick*!" So I was Sylvia's idea?

Ma's still working at the factory into her ninth month carrying ME. At four-foot-eleven, her feet already had trouble reaching the floor; now with her stomach so big, she can barely reach the sewing machine. Ma's co-workers prepared a box of *shmattehs* to use as a cradle.

A born people pleaser, I arrive on Saturday, Ma's day off. The last thing I do right.

She tells me, "Vhen you vere born, I looked at you and tought, 'Oy, vhat a beautiful baby!' Such a *punim*, like a doll, an absolute doll face! I vorried maybe somebody vould steal you from me."

"How did Daddy react when the nurse brought me in? Did he want a boy?"

"Vhat do you mean?! Daddy vasn't dere."

"Vhere, uh . . . where was he?"

"He vent home."

"Who was there when you woke up? Where was Chochu?"

"Chochu should drive on *Shabbas*? Never!" (If I'd been born on Thursday, Ma wouldn't have been alone.)

"Were you mad at Daddy?"

"SURE I vas mad! But vhat could I do mit da *shturmock?* He's in da bed at home."

Nobody stole me. Ma brought me home from the hospital. That's when Sylvia realized what she really wanted was a dog.

Oh, Canada

Back to the sixties—

I don't mean to knock Canada or its people. It's a picturesque, large land with robust people and moose. And the moose are often eaten by the robust Canadian mosquito.

Other than the mosquitoes, you're unlikely to be attacked in Canada. If you travel worldwide, it's good to have a Canadian passport as terrorists tend to abduct Americans, not people from Saskatchewan.

Montreal is how I imagine Russia; everyone's in the kitchen drinking vodka and cursing the government. Surely, this is going on in Minsk—only with *babushkas*.

The sun rarely breaks through the gray blanket hovering over the island. When it does, it often brings with it either biting cold or sweltering heat. And it's a *wet* heat.

The political climate's also sticky in Quebec. You'd think with all the sexy Frenchmen they'd be a happier people. But some of them are bombing buildings. It isn't Belfast, but it's not *Hooterville*, either. There was a referendum to replace *stop/arrette* signs with *arrette/stop*. (They vote yes; tax money well spent.) Many Quebecois want to separate from Canada. So do I, but I'll do it by moving to Hollywood.

Some experience Montreal as the home of smoked meat, paper-thin crepes, and comedy festivals; to others, it's a place from which to plan an escape. Canada is boring. That's why so many comedians come from here. We're forced to make ourselves laugh, because if we don't, who will?

Monday through Friday has too many people. Weekends, not enough. Weekends are spent starved for stimulation. I'm a tongue in search of spicy. I want pepperoni; I get Melba toast. I'm dying from bland. Since going outside is too scary—what with mosquitoes, bees, and mean girls from school—my life depends on finding *something* to watch on TV. The emergency broadcast signal blares in my head. *See me, hear me, get me cable.* But it's the sixties; the only cable I get holds my braces to my teeth.

Weekend TV is mostly nature shows, political programs and sports. The political programs have topics such as the preservation of beavers. And sports? I don't get the fascination with balls. I've never been tossed to. When someone throws something at my undefended body, I flinch and knock it away. I don't know how to describe my terror of pucks. Hockey, a game in which a hard black thing flies into your face at 60 mph, must be the invention of a sad Canadian man. I want no part of the violence.

We have two English-speaking TV stations. If you want to watch NBC, you play with the bunny ears till you find Buffalo, New York. But is the snowy picture worth it? For *The Dick Van Dyke Show,* yes.

Canadian TV is like the Yukon—there's not much to see, unless you like shows produced by the Audubon Society, which produces shows about the Yukon. Turn one of them on, chances are you're looking at flying ducks. Switch channels, turn back ten minutes later, and the ducks are still flying. It's like watching wallpaper. Or tune into *The Irish Rovers*, filmed in a pub. People swing beer mugs, tell bad jokes, and sing. Kind of like an alcoholic *Laugh-In.* They get drunk and *I* want to puke.

Ma and Daddy's favorite? *The Lawrence Welk Show.* They clap along with "Beer Barrel Polka." Quick, hand me a gun, I've got a clear shot to my ear.

❖   ❖   ❖

So one day I'm in the TV room, twisting tin foil around the antenna, trying to add enough juice to watch *The Newlywed Game* coming from Plattsburg, when Ma shouts from the kitchen, "Get dressed, ve're going to a movie! To see a cartoon."

What? A cartoon??? Oh boy! The only movies I ever see are the ones in Hebrew school with the gas chambers. What's gotten into Ma and Daddy, suddenly we're moviegoers? And they're taking me to a *kids'* movie? I figure this is the transformation I've been waiting for. We're finally switching into The Nelsons. I put on my fancy white dress with the black velvet ribbons and climb into the back seat of the Valiant. Salt from twelve years of winters has now rusted through the bottom so I can see the road under my feet. It's like the Flintstones' car.

Yabba-dabba-doo, we're in the theater! I'm wiggly with anticipation, waiting for the cartoon to start. The credits come up, and that's when I realize . . . the movie is called *Khartoum*. It's not a cartoon. It's an Arabian war flick where someone's finger is chopped off and put in a jar. The surprise is on me—it *is* like Auschwitz!

I don't say anything. It's dark, no one can catch me crying. Jeepers, I got it *so* wrong!

My First Drunk

Ma and Daddy's twenty-fifth wedding anniversary . . .

Our basement has never looked so festive. The brown paneled room isn't as dark crammed full of people drinking, eating and laughing. Jewish music plays on a turntable in the built-in-the-wall cabinet. This is an actual celebration, like real North Americans have! No Nazis to barge in.

Yesterday, I took my quarters out of the flowerpot, and took two buses to buy Ma a jewelry box. When you open it, music plays, and a ballerina in a pink tutu rotates; beveled mirrors reflect her image a hundred times. Ma will place this black Oriental treasure chest on her French provincial dresser. It'll replace the old shoebox in the underwear drawer: we'll save the burglar a couple of minutes.

We're *finally* at the opening-gifts stage. The crowd watches as Ma, in a high-backed chair, receives her spoils. My heart pounds as she unwraps my present. Ma opens the painted box. I'd wound the key to make sure the music plays. The ballerina turns.

Her face is in a lemon-sucking scrunch. "*OY! Dis is a present for a baby!* Ver did you get it? How much did you pay? Ve can take it back!" Everybody heard.

"D-d-downtown, in . . . in a store . . ." But my answer isn't important. Ma continues opening gifts. I shrink back into the crowd.

How could I think she'd like such an immature jewelry box!

(This is saved to the hard drive: *Never get that excited again, it only leads to humiliation.* If I don't want to cringe through life, I have to contain my gushy emotions.)

Ma's right, I'm not normal. But, I need to be normal, not weird. Normal people have lots of friends. Weird people have lots of cats.

And that's when I discover penicillin. While Ma is *kvelling* over the crystal bowls her friends brought, I—making sure no eyes are upon me—find abandoned, half-empty shot glasses. I bang back my first whiskey. Blech. This is no vanilla ice cream! Why do people drink the stuff like it's so good? It's so gross! But it's also so *warming.*

Suddenly the jewelry box doesn't matter anymore. My braces don't matter anymore. Nothing matters but *the moment.* I'm free to express myself as a creative talent! I begin speaking Yiddish, which I hadn't done effortlessly since I was five. I cha-cha. I sing. Wow! I can't understand why anyone would have a party without drinking. (Eventually, I can't understand why anyone would have *breakfast* without drinking.)

It occurs to me that it's my *parents'* anniversary, and I bought only Ma a present. Drunk, and feeling divine, my gift to my father becomes—my song.

With an audience of Holocaust survivors (and the token Gentile couple Ma calls *da Italianos*), I begin a soulful rendition of "My Heart Belongs to Daddy." I'm singing seductively in some mysterious key when Daddy cuts me off in the middle. "Enough of dis, Suzie!" I melt into my patent leathers.

> *I* have always remembered this night as yet another time when I screwed up and caused chaos. Decades later my shrink says, "The jewelry box sounded like a lovely gift! It wasn't a present for a baby, but a present from a baby. A sweet baby who loved her mom!"
>
> "But I wasn't a baby! I should have known better. Wasn't I asked to intervene in Ma and Daddy's fights and judge who was wrong? And wasn't I tried as an adult?"
>
> The shrink says, "No, you were a child. And it's normal for children to give gifts they'd like to have. If an adult humiliates a child for their choice, the child could grow up with a giving complex."
>
> Ah! That explains my anxiety at the mere thought of Christmas.

Is it an alcoholic gene telling me at nine years old, that alcohol holds healing properties? Perhaps it's not genetic, but learned. On *Bewitched,* when Darrin gets mad at Samantha, he goes to the bar behind the stairs and fixes himself a martini. Or he and boss Larry Tate meet at a bar, with the recurring featured drunk. Darrin feels much better after his martini. You can tell because he smiles more.

The second Darrin doesn't drink as much as the first. Maybe if he did he'd be nicer to Samantha. I hate Darrin number two! The first Darrin was sweet, he had a temper, but underneath his anger you could see how much he loved Sam. Underneath Darrin number two's anger is more anger. (In the nineties, Darrin number two reveals he's gay. That's why he was so snotty— he'd wanted to be with Larry. Sam, the wife, didn't do as much for him as Sam the butcher from *The Brady Bunch*. That would have been a whole different show.)

Fireman! Save My Child!

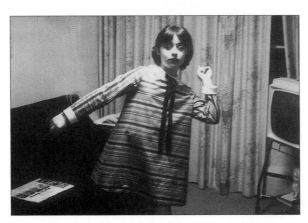

Daddy's found the solution to our family problems.

He's going to kill the television. He believes the evil box is sucking out our brains. (And sometimes, Daddy's *not* a *y'idiot.*)

It's seven o'clock. He wants to watch the news, Ma and I want to watch *anything* but. We're at the TV, fighting over the dial, and Daddy stomps off. Satisfied, Ma and I settle back to watch a contestant in curlers and a mumu jump all over Bob Barker on the evening version of *The Price Is Right.* (Curlers? Where's she going *after?*)

Daddy barges back in the room waving a hammer. He's going to smash the Sylvania. Ma and I descend on him like lionesses defending a cub.

This isn't just his belt on my butt; he's attacking the one component on the planet that can comfort me! I *need* television—I haven't discovered Quaaludes yet.

Ma and I jump on Daddy. He shoves Ma off of him—part of me enjoys this—then he turns, pushes me, and I fall back on the couch. He walks toward me, hammer raised, eyes beady with hate.

Daddy hovers above me, I protect my face with my arms, lift my legs and thrust both feet into his stomach. Daddy falls. Ma and I look at him. He lies motionless, in the fetal position, still clutching the hammer.

"Should I call an ambulance, Ma?"

"Nah, he'll get up soon." Does she think he's faking?

We sit and turn our attention back to *The Price Is Right,* where life is right. Eventually, Daddy gets up and returns the hammer to the kitchen drawer. That was the last time Daddy tried killing the TV.

To Sleep, Perchance to Scream

Some people fall asleep to escape their problems. I fall asleep preparing for le nightmare du nuit.

> *The dream: circa 1970–1999—There's a high building, maybe eight stories . . . a man is balancing on the edge of the roof. At his side, a little girl holds his hand. Swinging her arm, he forces them to jump. Nobody sees the crash, but everyone assumes they're dead. They're not. They've just fallen into the basement where they lay crumbled and out of sight. People down on the road wonder how a father could do this!*

To me—he's *Daddy*, but other than that, who is this man? Sometimes he's mean and scares me, but sometimes he's nice.

I yearn for more insight into this man called *Y'idiot*. Perhaps, if I can learn to see him as a person, rather than as "my Daddy," he won't have the same power over me.

"Ma, tell me more about how Daddy was when you first met him."

"Vhy you asking?"

"Maybe one day I'll write a book."

"Oh.

"Vell . . . I vas seventeen. Da Daddy vas handsome."

Ma doesn't admit it, but Daddy's looks played a big part in mate selection. He'd been Ricky Ricardo handsome. And tall, if you consider the average height of the village people was five-foot-four. I saw a picture of him when they were in the Displaced Persons camp. It was taken before the heavy in his head drove his eyebrows down to cover his Garbo lids, before the years turned his eyes vacant and sad, before jowls formed next to his sculpted lips, which had thinned as his black hair turned white.

Looks mean everything to Ma. She's critical of physical imperfections and in awe of beauty. She was the Blackwell of the Warsaw Ghetto. *"Oy, gib a kik! A groisseh tuches!"* (Oh, look, a fat ass!) She's all about "be pretty or *plutz*." This woman puts on a girdle before going to the butcher. Belted, boned and barely able to breathe, she comes home, unleashes the repressed flesh, satisfied that she's made a good appearance. So, nabbing someone handsome would have meant more to her than hooking up with a guy she could *talk* to.

"One day, da Daddy said, 'Let's go for a ride.' On his bike. On da handlebars. It gave me a bruise. He tried to kiss me. I vouldn't let him!

"Den, I moved to Warsaw to live with my sister. Da Daddy wrote me a letter, 'Darling, I had a dream dat I slept mit you. If you tell me da dream vill come true, I'll come visit you.' I tore da letter up. Vhat kind of a *y'idiot* writes dat to a girl?!"

Ma's married sister, Hana, the one I was named after, thought Daddy was a good catch and didn't want Ma to lose him. So, like Cyrano, Hana wrote back. And Daddy wrote back, for two years. Ma knew Hana was doing this but didn't care. Then Ma went back home to Paprotnia.

Daddy started hanging around the house, buying her jewelry. Whenever Ma saw something in a store, she went in and told the shopkeeper she wanted it. Then Daddy would come around later to pay. Ma fell, not in love, but into the prospect of having money.

"Da Daddy vas very nervous. If you said *blue*, he said *gray*. He vasn't agreeable. Ach, he's da same vay now. You can't finish a conversation. Da whole vorld is stupid, and he knows better den anybody.

"You know, my modder didn't vant I should marry da Daddy."

"No, I didn't know."

"*Oy!* Dere vas a man, he lived in da *shtetl,* a idiot. Everybody vould laugh how stupid he vas. His name vas Magoolski. So my family, dey called da Daddy '*Meshugeneh-Magoolski,*' vhat can I tell you?"

"Ma, there's only supposed to be *one* idiot per village."

Ma says, "Dis vas Poland. You could have two."

"So . . . Ma . . . uh, what was the wedding like?"

"It vas 1939. It vas a miserable wedding."

"What do you mean, *miserable*?"

"Terrible."

"How many people were there?"

"Plenty!"

"How many?"

"Not so many." Aha!

"Were you wondering if you were making a mistake?"

"No. I vasn't vondering."

Daddy comes in from the TV room, Cronkite's over. He must've heard us. "I had *many* girls, dey vere crazy for me!"

"Yeah, Daddy? How come?"

"Vell, first of all I'll tell you. I had lots of money. I vas alvays nice dressed. I vas in a society . . . vhen everybody jokes, I vas not behind. Vhen people discussing about business, serious anyvays, I tried to listen. So people liked me."

"Daddy, do you remember your wedding day?"

"No. Vhat happened?"

"I wasn't there, you tell me."

"It vas a long time ago."

"You remember blowing up a bridge don't you?"

"Sure!"

"*That* was a long time ago."

"Yeah, it vas."

"Uh, okay, well . . . were you and Mummy ever standing in front of a rabbi?"

"Rabbi? Dere vere no rabbis. Ve got married in da Mummy's sister's house, da whole house vas big like dis kitchen. Small."

"Do you remember . . . like . . . wedding vows?"

"Ve said da Jewish prayers, dat's all."

"Were you scared about getting married?"

"Dis vas not a scary business."

"When did you know when you were in love with Ma?"

"Who knew from love? She vas okay, a good girl. Talented! She used to make pants. In da forest mit a needle and tread, no machine, she made pants."

"What else did you love about her?"

"Love. Dis is silly."

"Daddy, tell me what Ma was like."

"She vas from a poor family, I vas rich. I vorked in my daddy's store fixing da machines. I vas da top fixer!"

Ma can't stand it. "*Oy*, Fishel, Hanala vants to know *vhy* you loved me."

"Dere ver tventy-six Jewish families, dat's all. Six families in one room. I moved in mit her and her family."

"But why *Ma?* Why not *another* woman."

"Da Germans came in and . . . "

"But Daddy, you *must* have liked her."

"Dere ver no more girls vhen da Germans came and . . . "

"So you're telling me—and Ma—that you married her because there was no one else?"

Ma's had enough. "Ach, he's a *Y'IDIOT*!" she says. "He came to my house, all da time, day and night! He vas mit me because he loved me! I couldn't get avay from him!" Separate realities.

"Daddy, what did Ma look like? There are no pictures."

Ma says, "I never had a picture of my modder vhen she vas alive, so, vhen she vas dead and in da box, I asked if I could take a picture. I took one. It vas da only picture I had of her. I gave my pictures to Mrs. Nierupca. I never saw dem again."

"Me and da Mummy vere friends. I used to read comics, fifty, sixty ev-a-ry veek! I vanted da Mummy to read, too, but in dis and in politics, she vasn't interested."

Ma's plutzing. *"Meshugeh!* Sixty comic books he read? He read sixty comic books like I'm da qveen of Egypt!"

"Daddy, Ma said when she was having Sylvia that you were with another woman. A German woman."

"I'm telling you *dis* is impossible. I never slept mit dat voman. I vas a smart man, not stupid, a man mit power in da army!"

(So was Bill Clinton.)

"Daddy, Ma told me your sister committed suicide. Her boyfriend left her and she jumped off a bridge."

"Dis never happened."

Ma rolls her eyes.

"How did your sister die, Daddy?"

"I don't know." How could Daddy not know how his sister died?

"Did she die before the war?"

"Yeah."

"So, how did she die?"

"I told it you a'ready, I don't know."

"But how could you not know? It was before the war."

"But ve didn't live in da same place!" Nobody lives in the same place as Daddy. Trying to talk to him is like trying to pick up a puddle. Where do you lift from?

Daddy's fed up. He leaves the room. I grill Ma for more.

Turns out, after living in Canada for a year, Daddy got sick. He was hospitalized. I've heard three versions: (1) hepatitis, (2) malnutrition, (3) mental meltdown. You never get a straight story from these people.

Daddy doesn't *look* sick. He doesn't limp, he doesn't get a special parking space, his condition doesn't show up in bloodwork. If his malady were *physical*, we'd have more tolerance. But it's hard to feel empathy for someone who's towering over you and yelling. It's easy to feel sympathy for cancer patients (with the possible exception of smokers).

Daddy chooses to exist, for the most part, in a dimension of his own. Failing to ever make a connection with him, I've almost given up. Almost.

Daddy likes his whiskey. I like Daddy after his whiskey.

* * *

He looks especially nice when he gets spruced up for night school. Daddy's learning to speak French. He takes so long in the bathroom Ma and I figure he has a crush on his French teacher. He positions his hair and puts on his best suit.

He takes pride in the fact that he's worn the same size belt since he was twenty. Daddy is an exercise bulimic. He walks off everything he eats. (If you add up the miles he's walked in the past thirty years and put them in a straight line pointing out into space, he's walked halfway to the moon.) Was he looking for his mind?

One night while primping for French class, Daddy runs into the TV room. *"MANIA! Vos host du geteen?!"* (What have you done?!)

Undaunted by his bluster, Ma keeps cleaning. "Vha-at?"

Daddy, arms spread out to his sides like Jesus, "Vhat kind of *dreckisha* deodorant are you buying now?" Daddy's armpit hair is stiff.

Ma looks up at the can in his hand. *"Y'idiot!* Dat's my hairspray!" He's confused the Arrid Extra Dry with the AquaNet.

Daddy drops his arms. Crunch. He slides his glasses down his nose and screws up his eyes to study the evil can.

Closer observation doesn't assuage his anger. *"Finstera nevileh!* You buy all da cans to look da same! You have too many cans mit all da makeup dat you vear!"

Ma says, "I vear makeup?! *Azameh zach!* Okay, so I'm no good. You hear dis, Hanala? Ver do I have da time or da money to vear makeup, tell me!"

The way she looks, it can't take more than two minutes. Ma uses AquaNet to form the football on her head (she wants to look taller). She shmears on Maybelline blue eyeshadow, black eyebrow pencil, red lipstick, pink rouge. Strangely, no mascara, the main staple of my arsenal.

The entire beauty kit fits on top of the toilet tank.

Linda Is No Ethel Mertz—
More Like Linda Tripp

I'm eleven, it's mid-September—

Ma hadn't read the letter saying I needed to register at the newly built school two blocks from my house, so I started sixth grade at the wrong school. Oops.

I'm at the *right* school now trying to find the principal's office. I tiptoe down the hall, registration papers in hand, afraid to disturb the classes already in session.

That's when I see her. She's standing outside the classroom door. In punishment. I *hate* when that happens. She doesn't seem to mind.

She's a curly-haired blonde with a big nose, lips collagen that patients ask for, and bright blue eyes that check me out as I pass. If Shirley Temple and Danny Kaye had a daughter, she'd be Linda. Her expression is irony, mixed with amusement. And sadness. I know this breed of human. We would end up in detention together many times.

Linda Resnick becomes my best friend. Not so much best as *only*. She's odd. Actually, she's nuts and I feel comfortable with that.

Linda never poo-poos my opinion; as a matter-of-fact, she's *interested* in what my opinions are. She sees things the way I do. When we're together, I feel real.

The following February . . .

Bouncing on the ducks-on-coils in the barren playground, Linda and I make a pact. If one of us ever attempts suicide, the other will not attempt a rescue. (Who knew she'd be so touchy about a broken pact? More on that later.)

Linda wears makeup to bed. During a sleepover, she's getting out of the shower and I catch her without makeup. She screams. And goes running for the mascara. I watch her coat her lashes in wads of black. They end up looking like spider's legs. "You've got spider legs!" I think it's funny . . . but I see a hurt look flower on her face.

Our sleepovers are usually at Linda's house, a creaky Victorian mansion nestled in tall maples next to the train tracks. *Twilight Zone.* Her sheets smell like the backyard, and she has gigantic feather pillows. They're cozier than the starched balloons I sleep on at home.

Linda and I are allies against the world, but like Italy and Germany in the forties, the relationship is conditional. Linda's condition? "I'm on your side until it stops working for me. Then I'm with them." Sometimes she sides with Ma during our fights. She calls it "good diplomacy." I call it Benedict Arnold.

I go loco when Ma compares us. "Vhy can't you be more like Linda? Linda doesn't yell at her modder!" Linda is a lying slut who introduced me to shoplifting. But to adults she's Emily Post.

Mrs. Bulford is our teacher. She's divided into two sizes. From the waist up, average weight, but her lower half, the *Titanic.* With the rafts. She's my worst nightmare.

She sounds like Julia Childs, if Julia was from Newfoundland. Newf'ies have the most severe of all Canadian accents. They shorten A, E, I, O, U, and sometimes Y. They rely on consonants. *Rs* are said, har-r-rd. Put Scottish, Irish, and French together, now remove lips. Now teeth. Now add "'Ey!" on the end of every sentence. Add "by jeeze" and "alr-r-righty then."

Linda does a killer impression of Mme. Bulford. On our way home from school, she starts swaying, "Our pr-r-rincipal would like to know who r-r-ripped the pages out of the library book, 'ey? We're missing pictures of naked people from New Guinea. 'Ey. Should anyone know the whereabouts of the naked natives of New Guinea, they're to r-r-report it, r-r-right away, 'ey. Alr-r-righty then!" I fall back into a snowbank, laughing, and I can't get up.

In awe, I watch Linda in action, studying how to be funny.

There *is* a library textbook with pages missing, and Bulford's been asking the class who did it. Turns out it was Linda. Some of the pictures appeared in a geography project she turned in.

Bulford tells me I'm wanted in the principal's office. She escorts me. The principal asks, "Susan, did you cut pages out of the destroyed book?" The clean, cheese-free, un-dog-eared book? Never! But will they believe me?

I'm deer-in-headlighting, a feeling I'm accustomed to. "Me?"

"Linda Resnick says that you did, and that you gave her the pictures."

"No, she didn't!" This must be a trick. Are they trying to elicit a confession? Why trust the people who cause insomnia by keeping grades top secret till they hand out report cards?

Bulford and the principal look at me for a long time. Linda had set me up. They send me home without punishment, so I figure they didn't buy her story.

I go home and tell Ma what she did.

Ma's mad. "Vhy did you let her do dat?" Yeah, vhy?

Because it's hard to do something when you don't know *what to do*. You could do something that ends up making things worse.

I call Linda wanting to yell at her, but I'm afraid that will make her angry. Instead she laughs as I tell her what happened in the principal's office. "They are so stupid, they'll believe anything." But they *hadn't* believed her. Confused, I hang up, find food, switch on *Green Acres*, and file the incident away with the other unsolved mysteries.

I hate Linda, but I'm desperate for a friend. High school is coming!

Forgiving Linda is easier, knowing the family she's from.

Her mother's Jimmy Hoffa in an apron. She's butch and today would march for gay rights in her ESSO shirt. Her hair is salt and pepper and cropped. Her Playtex Cross Your Heart Bra crosses at her stomach. The weight of her hefty breasts pulls her shoulders forward and the bra straps make troughs in surrounding fatty tissue. Mrs. Resnick and Mrs. Bulford would make a dainty couple.

While Mrs. Resnick looks like a bulldyke, Mr. Resnick rages like a bull. Weighing in at 300 pounds, he stomps and snorts through the house. His voice, like Daddy's, booms. I relate to this un-Brady bunch.

One night, Linda and I are in her bed, lying back on pillows. We've been yakking all day and haven't run out of things to say. Linda has stretched her arm up and behind her so her head is resting on her elbow.

I say, "God, Linda, your hand doesn't look like it's attached to your body."

Linda's face goes blank. "What hand?" And the fingers crawl up her cheek, creep inside her mouth, and *yank* her head back. I scream! Then I have my first ever belly laugh.

Mr. Resnick charges down the hall. He's spitting and steaming and wagging the finger, "One more squeak . . ." He makes the usual parental threats and leaves. Linda jumps up and does an imitation of him. I bury my face in the pillow to silence my laughter.

And then, she gets quiet . . . .

Paul is one of Linda's two brothers. Paul's room is next door.

Linda's demeanor turns downright lascivious. "Paul likes to get in bed with me. He . . . does things." Of course, this comes from Linda, and Linda lies. Does he do *things*, or is she just crying wolf? What things? I don't want to ask.

Paul looks a little like Davy Jones from the Monkees. And I'm starting to get the hots for him. All that separates us is a wall. Maybe a wall with peepholes? Is he listening or watching now? I breathe a bit heavier. But other than that, I do nothing.

Ever Wonder Why It's Called a *Crush*?

Onomatopoeia: A word that imitates or sounds like what it is.
Say *Crush.* Once more with feeling—
make it into two syllables: *Cu–rush.* See?

I'm twelve—

Steven Cape is the cutest boy in seventh grade. I can barely fantasize about him without feelings of inadequacy. Why can't I get a crush on some *shlemiel* nobody wants?

He looks hot in uniform. Quebec is a Catholic province, kids are required to wear school uniforms. For the girls—a navy blue tunic: v-neck and fitted, or square-neck, pleated and belted at the waist. It's the micro-miniskirt era, and we wear our tunics just long enough to cover our snug gym bloomers. To complete the Catholic-schoolgirl look: a starched white blouse, knee socks, and navy blue penny loafers. The pennies must be heads up and parallel. Such details rule me. The boys' uniform: white shirt, dark pants, and an optional book held at crotch level. A giggling girl bending over the water fountain presents the boys with easy fantasy material.

It's a chilly afternoon . . .

Leaves reddening, people counting down to the shortest day of the year, goodbye peacoats, hello 50 degrees below. I walk home from school, loving the way the chromatic leaves have started to fall. Up ahead, Steven Cape and some popular Cote Saint Luc girls are laughing and dawdling. Eventually, I'll have to pass them. I can move through the pack, maybe saying, "Hi," or walk up on somebody's lawn, or step off the curb and crunch through the leaves. So I do what any girl with I'm-not-entitled issues would do—I cross the road. Why did the chicken cross the road? To avoid the snobby chicks.

Steven Cape and the girls are laughing when he turns toward me and says, "Susan has one."

One? I smile as I move back onto the road. He's looking at my lips. Just this week I noticed a rather cute dimple developing when I smile. Has Steven Cape noticed it, too?

"One *what*?" I ask, playfully.

The group doesn't answer. I skip along the road, looking up at Steven Cape. "I have a what?"

Steven Cape says, "Oh . . . it's nothing."

"C'mon, tell me, what?!"

The girls chant, "Tell her, tell her, tell her . . . "

"Really, it's nothing."

Determined to worm that compliment out of Steven Cape, I insist, "Tell me—a *what*? What *is* it I have?"

"A mustache. You have a mustache."

Cu-rush.

A Cote Saint Luc girl may have peach fuzz. *Refu-geeks* are Eddie Munster.

Everything I do, I do with one basic goal: to fit in. I'm physically challenged. I have Jerry Lewis, Nutty-Professor buck teeth riveted in re-bar. Luckily, my nose is so big it prevents the sun from bouncing off my braces and blinding schoolmates. My face is Elmer's-glue white, except for the rosy color that comes from my acne. Cover Girl does what it can. I'm a twelve-year-old Norma Desmond. I've got bulky legs, blubbery arms and now, apparently, a mustache. I look for commercial images to relate to. But they don't make *Eastern Block Barbie.*

Ever Wait for a Surprise Party
That Doesn't Happen?

April 14—

On previous April 14ths, John Wilkes Booth shot Abraham Lincoln and the Titanic *hit an iceberg.*

Normally, I wake with a death grip on the mattress, clinging to unconsciousness; getting me out of bed involves a crane. But this day I spring to my feet. Ma's vacuuming. She doesn't usually vacuum at 7:00 a.m. Then the thought strikes, "She's waking me on purpose so we can begin celebrating!" I'm thirteen today.

I open my door, anticipating Ma's over-the-top "Happy Birthday!" and my toes get sucked into the Hoover.

"Move," she says. Strange. Okay, I'll wait. Daddy comes home and now both of them are saying nothing. And I wait. There has been no talk of a bat mitzvah, but they *can't* ignore this birthday entirely.

I wonder, "Maybe I should drop a hint?" Then I figure, being a periodic optimist, they must've planned a surprise party. The surprise comes when Ma goes off to work at four o'clock and Daddy's in bed by seven. At ten p.m., I finally give it up. There is no party.

Do people *really* forget their daughter's thirteenth birthday? People *do*.

I take the phone to my talking place, the spot in the living room farthest from where parents roam and the phone cord reaches. It's time to reach out and touch someone. Even though Linda is neither a true friend nor family, I'll call her.

I keep the lights off and look out the picture window to Norma Milks' house. Ma calls Norma "Crazy Norma Milks." The kettle calling the *chaynick* black? I'm glad Crazy Norma Milks lives on the block. I get to feel superior over someone.

It's rained. Big shock. The pavement is wet and steamy. The streetlight illuminates the plastic covers and throws long shadows on the floor and walls.

I can see why an animal will chew off its own foot to get out of a trap. It will detach from a limb to gain freedom; *humor* detaches me from feelings that would entrap and eventually kill me.

I tell Linda about the day and she laughs. She imitates Ma. I start laughing and after a while, it's as if this ugly day happened to someone else.

Da Beatings Vill Continue Until
Morale Improves!

It's a scream-filled Sunday, I get on my bike and escape to Linda's.

Ma hunts me down by phone. She isn't done yelling. I whip out the communication tools I inherited from her and scream out something I'll feel guilty about for thirty years. "I wish Hitler *had* killed you! Then *I* wouldn't have been born!"

Mr. Resnick overhears and all 300 pounds of him move into the basement like a storm. He's appalled by the disrespect and banishes me *for life.*

I'd rather die than go home. I'm thirteen. It's not like I can say, "Ma, this living together just isn't working for me."

There's no way out. It'll be years before blow-jobs-for-cash comes to mind.

I pedal to the drugstore, walk up to the counter, and tell the pharmacist my mother has sent me for sleeping pills. He disappears into a backroom for a long time, maybe two minutes. What's he doing? He returns empty-handed. Did he tell Ma? I don't wait around.

Now what? Is there an easier way to commit suicide? Doing a wheelie off a bridge into the St. Lawrence is something a *shiksa* would do. I'm cold, hungry and I need to watch TV real bad. I pedal home slowly, zigzagging up and down blocks, my teeth chattering. The closer I get, the harder they chatter. I ride up on our lawn and Ma bolts out of the house, *fly slaughter* in hand. She yanks me off the bike as she screams and whacks me. *"You vant sleeping pills to kill yourself?! How could you embarrass me like dis? Oy! Vhat da pharmacist must tink?! You von't have to commit a suicide, because I'm going to kill you!"*

I imagine Ma at the funeral. "I gave her everyting! How could she do dis to me?" I feel a wrongness about Ma's reaction. Mostly, I'm embarrassed for thinking the pharmacy scam would work.

> *Thirty years later the therapist asks, "Didn't your mother talk to you about why you wanted to kill yourself?"*
>
> *"Talk? Well, of course! Over brunch at the club, then we went shopping at Saks. No, we never talked about **why** I did anything. And we never bought retail."*

Now I'm banned from my sanctuary, doomed to spend nights in my blue bedroom with a book I can't read, listening to Super-Fishel and Maniac's screams from down the hall.

But I have a good fantasy system. I'm no longer sticking sticks under the nails of Nazis. Now I fall asleep as a celebrity guest on *Password*. Or I'm dating in Hollywood. My boyfriends are Robert Wagner, Richard Chamberlain, and the Beatles (Paul, then John, and sometimes George; he seems so *alone* at the mike). I swoon over Adam West, "Holy Bulge, Batman! Is that a banana in your utility belt, or are you just happy to see me?" I have a periodic crush on Tony Curtis (real name: Bernie Schwartz, a Jew, too!) I buy movie magazines with his picture and take a picture of me, trim around the face, and paste it over the head of whatever woman he's with.

I pretend my pillow is one of my Hollywood boyfriends, and I kiss it. It's not a good kisser. Better for cuddling. Sometimes it's tough picking *which* celeb will be the pillow. Dr. Kildare or Captain Kirk? A three-way?

I've become every alien Kirk ever kissed. My men switch in the middle of a pretend kiss. I start kissing Tony Curtis and end with Mr. Levine, the biology teacher.

May, still in seventh grade . . .

Mrs. Bulford announces in front of the whole class that Linda is wanted in the principal's office. I wait in the park after school. Linda shows up with a note:

> *Dear Mr. and Mrs. Resnick, Due to Linda's poor grades, she will be required to repeat seventh grade.*

No. This cannot be. I can't do high school without her. I sit on the spring-coil-duck, rocking and crying. I rock far back, deep in despair, and fall off the duck. It's what I do, I fall. Over and over. (Like Chevy Chase in the future *Saturday Night Live*.)

Linda is laughing. What strange pattern of thought does the girl have? Does she not know the inconvenience of flunking?

The next day Mr. Resnick storms into school passing Linda and me in the hallway as if he doesn't see us. He's headed in the direction of the principal's office. Through the classroom window, I see him leaving about half an hour later. He's got the look of a man who begged rather than demanded. Whatever he did, worked. They didn't flunk her.

◆ ◆ ◆

Then, one of those strange things happens. Mr. Resnick has a heart attack.

I come home after a tough day of acting normal, the phone rings, it's Linda. We had just said goodbye, and I'm laughing. "Yeah, okay, so what?"

"My father died."

And I say, "You're kidding!"

"No." I didn't think she was, it was just too weird to be true.

"He was on the couch. I walked in and saw him on the couch, he's blue."

Bad news, her father's *dead*. Good news, I'm allowed back in the house.

Geeks to the Right,
Prom Queens to the Left

Linda and I enter Wagar High like new Auschwitz residents—

We're soul-inmates.

Between summer and Christmas break, I got my braces off and Linda sprouted breasts. There's something devious about this girl. What will she do next? She's curiously mature. Linda started her period before me, but she never says when. She was probably five.

I *became a woman* at thirteen (if the defining characteristic is that you start leaking from a new place). My first ever period hits, and I'm standing at the bathroom mirror thinking, "If I have to go through this once a month, I'll kill myself."

> *I remember the day in sixth grade when they separated the girls from the boys for that special "Isn't It Great to Be a Girl!" class. I suppose the boys were in the "Isn't It Great to Have a Penis!" class. The teacher told us all about sanitary protection, but no one mentioned antidepressants. Perhaps she addressed moods and hormones in the sex ed class, but when the boys were escorted out of the classroom, I split, too. Or, in shrink-speak: I split off. My body stayed in the room, but my head went soaring through the galaxy, scanning for anything else to think about.*

Was I the only thirteen-year-old girl to find herself roaming the feminine hygiene aisle of the pharmacy, bingeing on doughnuts and wishing I were dead? Suicide fantasies soothe me. I think, "There's always a way out." This mood thing is no fair! I felt irritable and hopeless *before* PMS.

Linda's cycle and my cycle start the same time each month—it's something about the moon and the pull on bodily fluids. Exercising our right to choose, we choose *not* to strap on the traditional sanitary napkin. They don't seem very sanitary. And the Sealy-Posturepedic pads are neither visibly undetectable nor odor-resistant. And it's hard enough for me to walk normally without the *Hindenberg* between my legs.

With much cringing, we buy Tampax on the way to school. We split the contents in the girl's bathroom, shove the spares in school bags and enter our respective stalls. They look like miniature space capsules. Houston, I have a little problem. As a virgin tampon user, I don't know how to proceed with the installation. *Why didn't I listen in class!* Like they covered *that* in class.

I try to read the directions on the thin page with tiny type. You need a microscope. They would be hard to follow for someone who *could* pay attention. Had the typeface been big and bold like that of books in first grade, it would have been helpful:

> See Jane run. See Jane run to the bathroom and shove a tampon up her vagina.
>
> See Dick watching with envy and fear.
>
> See Spot. See Spot in Jane's panties because she didn't get to the bathroom in time.
>
> See Dick trying to avoid Jane who has become a raving bitch.

I position the tampon like a pad horizontally. I don't know it's a device intended as a plug that you put inside. I don't know there *is* an inside.

Linda and I exit the girl's room, tampons at half-mast. I go to take the final geometry exam, she goes . . . who knows for sure? I sit on the hard wooden chair trying to figure out the right angles both on paper and in the chair. If I sit on only one cheek, the tampon, lodged like a hot dog in a bun, won't hurt as much. As if finals aren't tough enough!

After the test, I run to the bathroom. Pain motivates me to read the directions, and, boy, am I shocked. First, I learn, you have to remove the cardboard.

Oh. And then I discover I had the geography wrong. Location, location, location. I move the thing to where it's supposed to be.

I leave the bathroom feeling like an idiot, but a more comfortable idiot. When I bump into Linda, I tell her about my discovery. She doesn't look surprised. Another reason not to trust her.

We're at Linda's, in her bed . . .

She says, "Have you ever kissed a boy?"

"Yes, it was awful, I was five. Warren Lebowitz kissed me in the alley behind my old house. I ran into the house and told my father. I'm like, 'Daddy, Warren kissed me behind the garage!' Well! My father grabbed me and jerked my arm almost out of its socket, and then he goes, 'You should be *ashamed* of yourself! Do you know dis is verrry bad?!' I'm confused. Was that a trick question? Man! Do you believe how dumb I was to tell my father? What the hell did I expect, '*Mazel tov*?' I try not to get too excited around him anymore."

Linda says, "Listen, you know what I think? I think we should practice kissing."

"Who?"

"Us."

"*Us*?" See, I told you the girl's no Ethel Mertz.

I'm caught in a snow flurry. Everything's gone white. Then I get an idea of what she means, and I think *yuuuck!* But remembering how hurt she was when I called her eyelashes spider legs, I keep the yuck to myself.

"Okay," she says like she's just discovered garlic bread, "let's take off our clothes and get in bed. I'll leave the room, you get in first, then I'll come back in." She leaves. What would Daddy say about *this*?

Not wanting to appear small-minded or to offend my sensitive friend, I get in bed and take my clothes off under the covers, keeping an eye on the door. I pull the blanket up to my neck. She knocks.

"Yes, I'm ready, come in." (Like I'm in a spa and she's my massage therapist.)

She enters—and undresses. I've got my eyes closed. Maybe this will all go away. We're covered up, staring at the ceiling. *Laverne and Shirley* gone gay.

She turns to me, "Has anyone touched you . . . there?" She points to my boobs.

I throw her the universal *are-you-crazy* expression.

She says, "It feels good." How does she know? I don't ask.

After a few minutes of silence, she reaches over and places her hand on my bare shoulder. Then she slides it over my collar bone and brings it down to my chest. I'm trying to relax, but my eyes follow her hand. It's a deadly spider.

The phone rings. It's in the kitchen, which means echoing and amplification. Can't examine budding, young sexuality with church bells pealing. (Well, maybe some priests can.)

I grab one of the blankets, wrap myself up, and run to the kitchen.

If not saved by the bell, would my fear of angering Linda have made me do something I found disgusting? Not that lesbianism is; I mean trying to avoid Linda's anger rather than being true to myself is disgusting. Luckily, I'm in the kitchen so I can deal with this mystery with a cheese danish.

Just When You Think Things Can't Get Worse, They Introduce Communal Showers

Can school actually kill?

High school means harder homework and bigger mean kids. Jealousy, hate and fear rule. (If only I had access to assault weapons like kids nowadays.) Ma and Pa Holocaust know one thing: High school is a building where I spend time. "Vhat do you mean, you hate school? Vhat's to hate?"

How can I explain the absurdity of studying things like who sailed through whatever strait, in what year—rather than what to do about the zit that just popped up on my chin.

High school means my first real gym class. Real gym means sweat trickling, hair frizzing, and tinted Clearasil sliding off my zits. Real gym means standing, thighs exposed, trying to look like I like myself while two girls—with the thighs I want—choose everyone but me for their teams. What, was I Lizzie Borden in a past life to deserve such karma?

Real gym means running around Wagar High. Me, run? Just pulling on gym tights gets me winded. (I've been putting on weight.) I plod around the school as fast as my wide load allows. My heart bumps around my chest, protesting the violence. Eighty-year-olds from Maimonides Retirement Village pass me.

I fantasize about a convulsion, maybe collapsing, a nice seizure. They'll rush me to the hospital and I can finally lie down. Then they'll be sorry.

I get back from the "run" before dark. The gym teacher, Miss Groisenbacher, is waiting for me with a kind, empathetic look on her face. *Not.* That's my fantasy. In real life, she scowls and points at the ropes. At 140 pounds—of mostly thigh—I ask her to excuse me from the exercise. "Ergonomically, my body type, those ropes, bad combo."

She grabs the back of my collar and directs me to the mat where a 200 foot rope dangles from the ceiling. "Climb!" she commands.

Yeah, fine for Cathy Rigby. I inch up. Nineteen . . . twenty-eight . . . thirty-five . . . and . . . there I hang, like a salami, unable to go any further up, too scared of Groisenbacher to come down. Suspended above the mat, I cling to the rope, my hands burning, praying for a fire drill.

The rope gets slippery, I start to slide, and just before my palms burst into flame, I land back on my feet. I don't think anyone noticed. In Siberia.

After two hours of torture, gym is over. But the worst is yet to come.

We're safe in the locker room, so I think, when Groisenbacher tells us to strip, line up and twelve at a time, move into a square, tiled room with shower spigots jutting out of the walls. (Did you see *Schindler's List?*)

Strip? I have trouble being naked in a locked bathroom at home. Does she mean underwear, too? I can shower in a bra and panties.

Groisenbacher stomps over and snaps my bra. "Off! *Everything off!*"

She picks up a towel and slaps it into in my hand. It's so small. Guys are lucky. They can have small towels. But husky girls like me don't know what to cover. Boobies or cellulite, one or the other's gonna show. I wrap, cover, and keep my eyes focused on the floor, hoping the other girls are doing the same.

I don't know how much of my aversion to organized showering comes from my family dying in gas chambers and how much is my fear of being naked, but I know there has to be a way out.

New get-out-of-gym strategies race through my mind. "Chafed thighs? High ragweed count? Killer bees?" I use what I can.

"Please excuse Suzie from gym class today because her Aunt Hana died." I don't mention it was fifty years ago in Poland. I sign Ma's name. I'm the Corporal Klinger of P.E. (I remember Miss Groisenbacher, the rope, and that tiny towel years later when I'm on stage, half-naked, teaching an aerobics class at the most famous gym in the U.S.)

Life Begins at Leonard

Thirteen-and-a-half . . .

I'm having a thin month when our eyes meet in the hallway, between math and French. Leonard Goldfarb, also in the eighth grade, plays lead guitar in a band. He sings "The House of the Rising Sun" and "Louie, Louie." *Oooo.* Leonard is never Lenny or Len—always *Leonard.*

I hear from a girl, who heard it from a girl, who knows a boy, who's friends with someone Leonard knows—that he likes me. That's why he ignores me so much! His ignoring feels more like attention than when Ma is talking to me. He ignores me all week, until one afternoon when he approaches my locker. "So, wanna meet at Westminster Park?" It's the hang-out for Wagar kids.

" . . . . ." The sound of me, nodding my head.

I'm afraid of going alone, so I bring Linda. She stays off by the bushes.

Leonard and I talk of life and death. And hair. His is red and reaches past his shoulders. We share our struggle with frizz. Dippity-Do doesn't *do* it for Leonard's hair. The humidity of the Saint Lawrence River has a disastrous effect on the unfortunate Jewish population of Montreal.

He admits, "My mother irons my hair with Vaseline."

"Me too!" I'm impressed with his openness and am inspired. "I straighten *my* hair with appliances! And tubs of gook! But in five minutes, if it's August, I have a complete Afro!" Unfortunately, it takes *six* minutes to walk to Westminster Park. Fortunately, it's late September.

I want to iron Leonard's hair till the end of time. Or until it falls out. I don't care, I love him. So, you'd think I'd be dying to kiss him.

And now, for the kiss of death.

Linda signals from the bushes. She's cold and wants to leave. Leonard and I stand under the streetlight next to the man-made lake now drained for the coming winter. I can see my breath. He's moving his head close to mine and just as our lips are about to meet, I yank back. I ask him to try again, that I won't retreat. He tries. I retreat. Like Lucy, Charlie Brown, and the football, I promise I won't do it again. But I do. You'd think he had cooties.

It's as if the Enterprise's force shield is up around me. I don't know what I think will happen if we kiss—matter meeting anti-matter, global annihilation?

"Please, Leonard, I know this is weird, but I really *do* want to kiss you." He tries again, I push him away again.

He says, "Just kiss me once."

"Uh . . ."

"Just one."

Suddenly, a frozen Linda shouts from the shrubbery, "Just fucking kiss him! I can't feel my fingers anymore!"

I take a deep breath and pucker up. It's a warm, soft kiss. Nothing blows up. I don't fall down. It's nice. I just wish it had occurred to me that I could exhale through my nose.

Within a week, we're necking for five hours at a time.

Leonard's bedroom: Black light, Beatles posters, purple walls.

Leonard has been trying to get me to smoke hashish with him. Nope to dope; this offering and refusing has gone on for weeks.

Tonight he gives me the ultimatum. "You're a bummer. You bring me and the whole band down. Either you get high or we break up." He passes me the pipe. I hold it to my lips, but I don't inhale. I swear, I didn't. Really. You know I'd tell you.

Okay, I'm cool. Leonard asks me to go steady and life finally begins. I feel loved. It's a foreign feeling, and I like it.

We're at an outdoor Chicago concert the first time I do inhale. We're on a bench, Leonard hands me the splif and I suck in slowly, as per his guidance. I hold the smoke in and cough out lung tissue. So I do it again. I spew more lung tissue on the lawn. I must lie down on bench. Leonard is playing air guitar along with Chicago's "25 or 6 to 4." Forget "Does Anybody Really Know What Time It Is," the question is, "What the hell is 25 or 6 to 4?"

I notice an army of ants crossing the cement path. I hear them marching. I try to get Leonard to hear the clomping of their feet. "Listen! You can hear them."

Leonard says, "Next time, don't hold the smoke in as long."

The concert's over, I'm famished. But Leonard spent his allowance on hash, and I don't get an allowance. He says, "If you want to get something to eat, we gotta panhandle." *We* meaning *you*. Normally, I would say no, but I'm hungrier than the week I lived on Melba toast. So I come up with a story. "Excuse me, but my boyfriend just dumped me, I'm afraid of calling my parents, and I need bus fare home." I make ten bucks. I buy four hot dogs. And a Tab. I give one hot dog to Leonard.

❖   ❖   ❖

Ma refuses to speak Leonard's name. She calls him *da roita kopp* and she says it like she's spitting a foul thing out of her mouth.

She follows me around, demanding, "Vhen are you going to break up mit *da roita kopp* a'ready?" I run away screaming. She follows. "You're ruining your life going steady mit da *shlemiel*. He's ug-a-ly!" I run into the bathroom. Finally, a door with a lock!

I ask her, "What's wrong with someone who gives me love and attention?! Why don't you want me to have that? Leonard loves me. We talk! He's *Jewish*!"

"He *loves* you?! He's *using* you!"

"Ma, he's important to me!"

"*Oy*! Listen to dis! He's *important*! Dat *dreck*!"

Was she sad that she was losing her little girl? Or did she just hate red hair? She's telling me I shouldn't like what I like? Well, what should I like?

Ma needles me. I get the point.

I'm recovering from an operation on my big toe. They don't teach the important stuff in school. "E=MC^2, and aggressive trimming may lead to ingrown, infected toenails."

So on the night of the surgery I'm hopping down the hallway on my good foot when a jolt of pain propels me in the air and I land on the post-op foot. *OY!* Such an *oy,* I jump back on what was the good foot. Again—*OY!* And I'm back on the operated foot. I figure I should take a dive. On the ground, feet suspended in midair I'm wondering what could hurt a foot so much? And that's when I see it. The tip of a sewing needle is sticking out of the bottom of my foot.

Damn it, Ma! She's Hansel and fucking Gretel, leaving sewing paraphernalia instead of breadcrumbs. The carpet's more like a launch pad with miniature ground to air missiles. Oh, Ma doesn't do it on purpose. It's never on purpose.

The needle is in deep, and I, a practicing nail-biter, I can't pull it out.

"MAAA!!!" She comes running, takes one look, grabs her chest and swoons.

She's Gloria Svanson. *"Oy a broch! Ich Halesh! Es vert mir nisht git!"* (Oh my! I'm fainting! I'm feeling sick!) "VERE DID DAT COME FROM?"

She's mad at the needle?

Ma's up against the wall, holding her stomach. I'm down on the floor with Excalibur. I can almost bring my foot to my mouth. Can I bite the tip and pull out the needle with my teeth? Almost. "Tweezers! Ma, get tweezers!"

"Tveezers?"

"What you use to pluck your eyebrows!"

"*Oy!* Dat's a good idea." She sprints down the hall. A minute—and twenty of Ma's *"Oy gevalts!"*—later, with the skill of Hawkeye Pierce, I remove the needle. In between *gevalts* she marvels at my bad luck.

She's stumped. "In da whole house you had to jump on da place dat had a needle?!" Luck? Is she afraid if she takes responsibility I'll hate her? Not apologizing is making me hate her.

I try explaining how it wasn't my fault. "I couldn't see it . . . the hall was dark and . . . and . . ." And then I break. "GOD, MA! You're always sticking me with pins! I told you a million times to be more careful!"

She's composed herself. "Okay, fine. I vill never sew nuting for you ever again!"

"Fine!" Then I start to feel bad that I yelled and that this incident made her *nisht git*.

Of course, Ma would go on to sew many things for me through the years. And I would get stuck. Sometimes I'd flinch, maybe yelp. She'd be annoyed, "Suzie! Stop being so narish!*" I hate the process—but I want the clothes.*

Mr. Hole

4:00 p.m.—my French teacher holds me after class.

Mr. Hole (his real name) and I are alone in his classroom and he's about to flunk me for not doing my book report on *Le Chien Jaune*, a book about a yellow dog. (*Old Yeller* with a bad attitude.)

Robert Hole is the hippest male teacher at Wagar. Most of the girls, and probably some of the boys, have a crush on him. He's got a sexy, make-me-suffer look. His chin is square with a cleft you could lose a tooth in. Mr. Hole wears dark glasses in November. We know behind those Foster Grants are bedroom eyes reddened by hashish use.

My heart thumps beneath my tunic. I lean over his desk all-a-gush with adolescent whoremones, suppressing an urge to pull Mr. Hole onto his desk and squiggle all over him. My fantasy comes to an abrupt stop as I realize this man can send me to summer school. "Mr. Hole," I say, "I hope you're not holding the comic book incident against me, are you?"

I had created a comic book based on the life of Monsieur Hole capturing his family in cartoon form. I'd drawn the whole Hole clan to look like Robert—avec le short, curly hair, and le square chin au cleft. I gave them names like Selma. Selma Hole. Ophelia Hole. Lisa and Frieda Hole. I drew Mr. Hole looking stoned, muddling through a lesson on conjugating the verb "fart." "Je fart, tu farte, nous fartons, vous fartez . . ." The new "f" word. I have trouble saying the word fart, *but I love to write it. Mr. Hole confiscated the comic book one day as it was being passed around the room. Giggling woke him from his morning-after stupor. I could see the confusion on his face. He was appalled by the* Hustler *version of his family tree, but he's an educator who can honor talent and originality in the face of degradation. A trait I admire.*

I plead with the man I've ridiculed. "Monsieur Hole, you just have to pass me! I don't really need to know French anyway. I'll be moving to Los Angeles to be a TV star. If anything, I'll need Spanish."

I say this in French (*my* version of French, which has occasional Yiddish mixed in). Whether he decides this valiant effort deserves to be rewarded, or he just wants the pitiful groveling to end, he passes me.

I'd like to say I win all such battles. I declare my higher purpose to Mr. Druker, my algebra teacher. I explain I won't need to divide fractions on the set of my sitcom, but he tells me that unless I pass the final exam he's sending me to summer school, which wouldn't be so bad; I'd get to see more of Leonard and Linda, who spend most summers there.

Does Rejection Have an Impact?

The drama department is putting on "South Pacific" —

My big acting break! Preparation for my sitcom—but the show is a *musical* comedy. Comedy, I got, but *musical*? The memory of Michael rowing *da boat* ashore is still paddling down my subconscious. If I try singing on stage again I could capsize and drown in the South Pacific.

I don't know any songs from *South Pacific,* so I'll sing "Big Spender" from *Sweet Charity.* Maybe if I present an extra-sensual gusto, they won't notice I can't sing. Sex sells. Would they buy?

The acting part of the audition comes first. I have Linda sitting, back to the audience, holding a newspaper open. I prance around in a robe trying to get "Harold's" attention. Everybody laughs. At all the right places. I'm thrilled. And now, the song—

The guy at the piano asks if I have music.

"No, I'll sing it *acapulco.*" Nobody laughs. I strike a pose, take a breath—the only one I'll take till I get home—open my mouth and unleash the first note. Although this note *is* in the song, it isn't the *first* note of the song. I adjust, and by the fourth note I'm caught up. But then, lyric by lyric, my voice climbs up and up, higher and higher until it lifts up where it doesn't belong.

"Thank you! We've seen enough." A voice shouts out of the audience stopping me just before my ears blow off my head. It's Risa Bramon, who's directing the show. (She's now a casting director in L.A.)

I'm at the bus stop in tears. *Idiot! Idiot! Idiot!* I decide I'm never going back to school.

I'm home. In bed. And that's where I stay, in the fetal coil, replaying the moment of humiliation. "The minute you walked in the joint (boom, boom) I could tell you were a man of distinction, a real big spender . . ."

"Thank you!"

If this were a TV show, Ma would come into my room, sit on the bed, and put her hand on my forehead. She'd stroke my hair. She'd listen with interest to my self-disgusting experience and say, "You're talented, you'll get bedder parts in bedder plays, poopsie." Yes, yes, that would have been helpful.

But I don't tell Ma and Daddy about *South Pacific*. If they said, "You're *meshugeh* to feel bad, it vas a play, not a Nazi." I'd have to kill them. Besides, I don't think I have the energy to speak even if they wanted to listen.

A week later, Ma swings my door open. "Vhat's da matter mit you!" She doesn't stop for an answer. "Dey called from da school! Dey said you didn't go today!"

The next day I show up at school to find I've been assigned to paint the sets for *South Pacific*. I work after class every day, slapping paint on backdrops while listening to the rehearsals. I paint palm trees, the tropical sea, Bali Hai. I hear the chosen ones do lines I could do better. I think of van Gogh. I want to cut off *both* ears. I mix colors longing to be back in bed, but at night when I am in bed, all I hear are the songs over and over. "I'm gonna wash that man right out of my hair, I'm gonna wash that man right out of my hair, I'm gonna wash that man right out of my hair." Waaa, Ricky, I wanna be in the show. I can't wash the damn show out of my hair. I could probably still play every part, even the boys'. *If* I could sing.

Finally, summer.
No more teachers
No more books
No more bitches' snotty looks.

Houston, I Have Another Problem

I'm in bed, cuddling with my pillow Rock-Bixby-Wagner.

Ma's on the porch hanging the laundry out to stiffen when the phone rings. Who would call at 7:00 a.m.? Is it the warning to pack and run? Is someone dead? I throw Davy-Shatner-Moore aside and run to the phone before it stops ringing. It's David saying Sylvia's had the baby.

"Sylvia had the baby? Is it a boy or a girl?" (Ultrasound's not around yet.)

In David's normal blase way, he says, "She had twins."

"Funny David. C'mon, is it a boy or a girl?"

"Twins." David's a sadist.

"*David,* stop kidding! Is it—"

"PUT YOUR MOTHER ON THE PHONE!"

"Maaa, it's David. Sylvia had her baby and he won't tell me if it's a boy or a girl!"

Turns out it's true, twin girls. Ma says we'll spend the summer in Akron. Two and a half whole months! I shudder at the thought of parting from Leonard, but I have *nieces*! They need me. I need to be needed. Besides, Leonard and I will have a lifetime of summers ahead. We'll be together forever—like the Beatles.

Ma and I pack up the Valiant. Daddy drives. We've been driving around Ontario for way too long. And I mean *around* Ontario. That's what happens when he doesn't listen to my directions.

I learned to read maps. I was tired of getting lost. On a previous trip, to Toronto, we'd gotten stuck in the Bermuda Triangle of Montreal known as the Decarie Circle. Highways converge, the signs come fast and move-over time is short.

Ma and Daddy were fighting in the front seat, I was attempting to enter the trunk from the backseat. Ma screamed at Daddy as he passed our exit for the third time. "Y'idiot! Ve're never going to get home!" But I have to get home! All I wanted was a box of Sugar Pops and The Dick Van Dyke Show. *I took Ma literally. "Ve're never going to get home." I went into full-body clench. I had to get out. I rolled down the window. Ma screamed, "Vhat are you doing?!" I screamed back, "I'm going home. "Vhat are you crazy?" "It's only a few miles. I know the way." "Ve're driving on da highvay!" "I want to get home." "Dat's vere ve're going!" "But you just told Daddy we're never going home." "Don't be stupid, of course ve're going home." Seven hours later we did. That's when I decided to learn to read maps.*

I find Ohio. Then I find the twins. They are the cutest babies ever born. I play mommy. They are mine. End of story.

They're less cute at 2:00 a.m. Sylvia has me sleeping on a cot next to the crib. Every night I wake up to their crying. One starts, then the other joins in. I press the pillow against my ears but can still hear Sylvia's chilled bray from the next room, "*Susan . . . SUSAN! Get up!*"

Why is this my job? I hadn't even had sex. So I'm in the kitchen warming bottles, thinking, "This is what happens when you have kids? I can't have kids. I'm not going to have a little sister to come and help me. Maybe I should get fixed." Then again, the girls are the greatest source of pleasure I've ever known. Nothing, not even *Leonard-love*, comes close to the love I feel for these babies.

❖ ❖ ❖

Ohio is a humid abyss. I have no friends and a sister and brother-in-law who call me a selfish brat who messes up when I should be cleaning up. I find comfort at the local ice cream parlor; it feeds my needs. But I'm getting squeezed out of my jeans.

Sylvia's neighbor has kids and one day we go to the community pool. Hoping to please my new friends I shout, "Hey! Let's dive for my ring!" I slide it off my finger and toss it across the pool. We swim like fast fish. I don't know if a filter sucked it away or if one of my new friends stuck it in their trunks, but that's the last of the gold band with the emerald stone.

Wrinkled toes and fingers, shivering and whimpering, I give up my search only when the lifeguard makes me get out of the pool so he can lock up for the night. For twenty years Ma refers to this incident as proof that Suzie cannot be trusted with good things.

July 20, 1969—

Ohio usually means soap operas and summer reruns, but right now I'm about to watch a man step on the moon for the first time.

I'm babysitting. My nephew Mark is two-and-a-half. He keeps disrupting my TV viewing. I've been trying to get him to stay in bed for over an hour. I'm losing the battle, and my mind. He wants water, he has to pee . . .

"Aunt Susan, I just have to ask you something . . . " I'm not falling for this again. I don't answer. In his jammies, Mark inches his way back into the living room as I ignore him. He gets closer. And closer. One small step for Mark, one giant headache for me. If I miss seeing the first human set foot on the moon, I'll kill the boy! I come up with a creative way of getting him to stay in bed.

"Mark," I speak in a ghost-story voice, "There is a man in the neighborhood who walks at night with a big shotgun and he shoots little boys who aren't asleep by ten o'clock."

Despite my holding him and swearing that I was making it up, that there was no man and no gun, Mark screams. And screams. The closer it gets to ten o'clock, the louder he screams. He finally stops screaming at 10:10. I guess he fell asleep.

At 10:56 p.m., Neil Armstrong steps on the moon, and I'm feeling too guilty to enjoy the event. I'm a stupid meanie. Mark's still asleep when Sylvia and David come home. None the wiser. Except me.

Mark learned nothing from the lone gunman episode. He continues to disrupt my TV viewing. Erica Kane is seducing somebody's husband and he wants macaroni and cheese. I can't take it. I start yelling at him. What was I going to do next? Take off my belt? Through my angry haze I see two humongous brown eyes with foot-long lashes peering up at me. Mark's tiny mouth is trembling.

Did *I* cause that? I drop to my knees and remorsefully kiss and soothe the little boy.

It occurs to me that Mark is not why I'm mad. It's the pain from years of desperate pleading with Ma and Daddy. I stop taking it out on him the moment I realize all Mark wants is what I wanted—attention. He's the ignored brother of newborn twins.

Lesson: You should hold off on having kids until your own issues are in check. But would I still be able to have kids at sixty?

It's the beginning of September, we leave Ohio.

I'm not going to see the girls again for six months. After ten hours of driving around northern Ohio, we stop at a motel for the night. I fall on the bed, bawling. I'm sick of Daddy's driving, but much worse—the babies are gone.

Ma thinks my behavior is cute. "*Oy gevalt, da girls aren't dying; da vay you cry! Stop a'ready!*" But the girls I love *will be no more*. The babies I held all summer would no longer exist. I would never bathe them in the plastic wash basin with the diaper put at the bottom for softness, and dry them, powder their tushies, and put their tiny wriggling feet inside the one-piece sleeping things. No, when I see them again at Christmas break, they'll be crawling little humans. They won't even know me. At least I know that when my nieces first experienced the world, they were taken care of by someone whose sole function was to treasure them. That has to count for something.

From Akron with Love

Home from Ohio, school starts again.

Before I could say, "Like, ya know," a clique of snobby girls picks me to pick on. The leader of the picking is the evil Reesa Rabinowitz. She and the also evil Lana Liebman are best friends, and one is meaner than the other. They torture me with whispers heard through the school. I don't know why they have it in for me, I figure it's because they know that I'm a *shlemiel.* Thank God I have Linda.

Linda and I decide to paint a mural on the kitchen wall. Ma loves it. I'm painting a little bird. Linda's painting the sky. She's pissy. I'm staring down at the gold-speckled Formica counter with the plastic fruit, trying to figure out what I've done to get her mad.

Out of the blue she says, "You think you're so great." I *do?*

She cops a royal-family attitude. "You know, I could have Leonard anytime I want!"

I'm overcome by flabbergastment. "Uhh . . . no you can't!"

"Wh-ell" she says all loftily, "I already *did.*" Major *HUH?* Where's a reverse-the-time-machine when you need one? I feel dizzy. The gold speckles on the counter are moving. I don't believe her.

"I went to Leonard's to iron his hair because you were gone. Let's just say I straightened more than his hair." Linda goes on to tell me she gave my future husband a *hand job.*

I'm *mortified.* All I can think is, "*I* never gave him a hand job!" I don't know what a hand job is, but my immediate instinct is to go find him and give him a better one.

Leonard and I had gone only to second base—under the blouse but over the bra—and *that* left me feeling filthy.

I journey to the telephone. "Leonard, meet me at the park, *now.*"

He's there first, standing next to the swings, watching me come up the street.

First thing out of his mouth, "From far away, you looked like Mindy."

Fat Mindy Mendel from school? Is Leonard mental? He's not in *enough* trouble? I want to kill him. The anger lasts a second, then turns into—I want to kill myself. He's right. I gained ten pounds in Ohio. We sit on a bench.

"Well, Leonard? Is it true? Did you and Linda . . ." I can't bring myself to say it. Mostly because I'm not sure what *it* is.

Head bowed and hair hanging over his face, he says, "Yeah."

The bench has no back. I tip over into the shrubbery. Can't move. Can't breathe. Maybe if I don't breathe, it won't be true. How could it be true? I trusted Leonard. He's my savior, my ride out of Hotel Holocaust. After a couple of minutes, I start to worry about spiders.

I call out from the bush, "Please tell me you and Linda are making this up. It's a joke. Right? . . . Leonard?"

Leonard climbs in the bush with me. His eyes are illuminated by the light from the lamppost. He's crying. Such a sweet look on the little boy face. I want to comfort him. He promises to be faithful if I forgive him. I do. And I dump Linda.

I make new girlfriends. One-hundred-and-sixty-pound Mindy Mendel (standing next to her makes me look thinner) and Gail Beener who's three feet tall in both directions (next to her I look taller). The three-girls-can't-be-friends rule works for me now. I'm top girl. But mostly we get along great. We cut gym class together. We sneak over to the bakery where Ma works. We're inseparable. The Three Musketeers. Not the swashbucklers, the candy bars. One for all, and all for chocolate.

Sex Is Dirty and Should Be Saved for the One You Love

I'm thirteen and three-quarters—

Leonard has a projector and a film he found under his father's *Playboy* magazines in a box marked "legal papers." We start to watch, but when I see the actor's fingers going toward naked crotches, I scream and cover my eyes.

I don't know how people appear in pornos, when I can't even *watch* them. I'd like to look, but I feel it's rude.

To Leonard's disappointment, I make him turn off the projector and turn on the TV. We watch *Rowen and Martin's Laugh-In* instead. During the commercial, Leonard tells me he wants a blow job. "I'd *really* like one."

"I'll have to look it up in my *Funk and Wagnall's*." Ha-ha. Leonard gives me the definition of blow job. Sock it to me!

"You want me to . . . Y-U-C-K! People *do* this? And *live*?" I don't want a rerun of the Linda/hand-job episode, so I do what I have to do. But first I make him shower.

Not too bad. I just pretend I'm watching *The Saint*. I'd do anything for Roger Moore.

Later that year—

With blow jobs a done deal, I figure, "Let's go all the way." I'm damned for sure. Might as well go to hell for a blast of fireworks as for a runty firecracker.

"Leonard, buy a condom. This Friday afternoon we're going to cut class and go have sex." Sex is portrayed in books and movies as a fun act. I want to know what all the commotion is about. Also, I think if I *please* Leonard, he'll be more likely to hang around.

Friday, we cut class . . .

Leonard's mother works days. We go downstairs to what was once the maid's room.

Leonard asks, "You *sure*?" I pull the curtain on the transom window that looks up to the lawn. The room is black except for the fuzzy line of light that marks the window.

I start unbuttoning, working steadily toward the goal. I take off the last of my clothes and in the name of research, assume the horizontal position.

There's a problem with insertion. It's like trying to re-cork a wine bottle after the cork has expanded. Only the wine bottle isn't screaming in pain. Leonard's tenacious. If he put this much effort into homework, he wouldn't need summer school.

He pushes, I scream, "Wait!" I have an idea. "We need moisture!" I wrap a blanket around me and go hunting in the bathroom. I come back, Vaseline in hand. But the pain is still too great. Leonard pulls off the condom (it had torn anyway) and circumstances improve. This is pre-AIDS, we're not risking death. The worst that could happen is, I'd end up becoming the mother of a teenager like me.

I'm under Leonard, thinking, "What the hell are people talking about?" This is more painful than the tampon, and messier. This is not how it works in the romance novels where the man sweeps the woman into bed, she pants, squeals, and glows. This is more of a Nancy Drew novel—a total mystery! I'm supposed to be having sex, but I'm picturing Nancy Drew having sex for the first time. Were they Hardy boys?

Leonard stops. "Wanna smoke some hash?" In all our frenzy, we had forgotten to get high! I don't know how much of the relief comes from the drug, and how much is from taking a deep breath, probably for the first time all afternoon, but my body relaxes into a warm tingly state.

We're on the floor, leaning back on what used to be the maid's bed, and Leonard says, "Louise, she cleaned our house for a few years, invited me in one night when my parents weren't home. I was twelve. She was old, like— *thirty!* But she still looked good." *That's* how he learned what a hand job was. First hand. Leonard's father also had a hand in some *mishugas* with Louise. Leonard's mother is now cleaning her own house.

Leonard describes his seduction and my body starts to show interest. I close my eyes and I am Louise. "Leonard, dear, take your hand, and put it here."

We're actually having sex, and I'm semi-lost in the moment when, oh darn, I find myself returning to reality. I'm coming down off the hash. Bored with the ceiling, I decide sex has gone on long enough. How do I ease out of this? This is the first time I fake an orgasm. That done, Leonard has license to get on with his. This investigation into sex has been anticlimactic to say the least.

But we continue having sex weekly. I never like it any better, but it burns calories. And it keeps my mouth too busy to eat. Miracle—I don't get pregnant.

The most exciting thing that ever happened in bed, is one night, this new song comes on the radio, and in the middle of middle-play, Leonard becomes wild. He's jumping on the bed, shouting, "It's *the Beatles*! They reunited!" Turns out, the boys singing are from England, but they are called the Bee Gees. Darn that Yoko.

With each sex session, I grow more and more confident about our relationship. Why do I do that?

Desperate Meanies

I'm fourteen—

It's been a cold winter. But it's a *dry* cold. Leonard is walking me home from school. The snowplows have cleared the streets, leaving lumpy, white and gray mounds along the sidewalks and on everybody's lawn.

We're walking down Eldridge Avenue when Leonard says, "I have something to tell you." I'm hoping it's something nice. This was before I learned that, "I have something to tell you" means: "Life as you know it is about to change, and you are powerless to stop the horror."

Leonard says, "So, like uh, I want to tell you . . . I'm in love."

I'm about to say, "Me too!" when he says, "With Reesa Rabinowitz."

Ha-ha, very funny, the girl who tortures me. I'll kid too. "Does Reesa know?"

"I told her last night." Leonard describes the time they spent together and how he struggled with his feelings. *Reesa Rabinowitz! My archenemy.* Was he trying to get me to kill myself?

I tip over, like in the park, only this time in snow. *"Reesa?"* I'm too frozen with shock to be cold. This time there's no hurry to get up, spiders aren't out in February.

Again he's crying. "I'm sorry." Yeah, me too.

Reesa has the biggest nose in school, but I find no solace in that. I spend a week in my room. I can't make it to the kitchen, let alone to school. For the first time in my life, I'm too depressed to eat. I stay curled up in bed, staring at my poster of Tony Curtis.

One morning Ma yells something like "Go to school!" She noticed I wasn't going? I could have been building bombs in my room for all Ma and Daddy knew. As long as I wasn't having sex. School had called. Why don't they leave me alone!

A few weeks later Reesa, perhaps satisfied with her victory, dumps Leonard and he calls begging me to take him back.

"I'll have to think about it. Meet me in the park." (I'm not a quick study; it took me thirty years to stop putting earrings on over the bathroom sink.)

Da roita kopp meets me at the park. I need him more than hate him.

"Leonard, I've decided I will take you back, but you'll have to marry me." I want to make *sure* he doesn't leave again.

We plot and make plans, which include Niagara Falls (not too far a drive). We end up performing a mock wedding in Leonard's basement surrounded by friends from ninth grade. I wear a crinoline on my head. It's what he lifts to kiss me.

We never talk about Leonard's sabbaticals. I put the betrayals in a separate compartment I don't look in. That chunk of life doesn't exist. He did not have sexual relations with that woman . . . Reesa Rabinowitz.

Never Remember!

At the ice cream parlor . . .

Leonard and I are parked in front of a giant statue of Elsie the Cow, Borden's trademark and the prototype for what you're going to look like if you eat there too often.

I'm enjoying the chocolate cone Leonard bought me. He's sitting still, and some of the ice cream is running down his cone into his hand. I ask him why he isn't eating.

"I . . . I . . . I want to play the field." Such an expression! An image pops into my mind of a herd of cows alone with Leonard, the frisky farmer.

He's breaking up *again*. And the week before my sweet-sixteen party?

Don't we just *hate* him?!

That was my last chocolate cone. Switched to vanilla, forever. I'd even scoop the chocolate out of the box of Neapolitan Ma bought at Steinbergs and toss it. Me throwing away ice cream!

❖ ❖ ❖

I don't cancel my party. My friends and I are in the basement celebrating when Ma calls me to come upstairs. Leonard is standing at the front door with Lana-the Bitch Liebman!

"Leonard, what are you doing here?"

He smiles. "We should be cool, man." If I *were* a man, I'd . . .

"You aren't invited," is all I can say, and like at the OK Corral, we stand waiting for someone to make a move. My teeth are gritted as I stare him down.

The visibly whipped Leonard says, "Well, can I get my Beatles albums back?"

"Now? Okay, wait here." I go downstairs, pull *Abbey Road* off the record player, and smash it against the cabinet. And it feels *good*. I grab *Rubber Soul*. Holding it by the rim, I press the *Apple* record label against the edge of the counter and the album cracks in half. I mutilate *The White Album*. I kill *Sergeant Pepper*, which I don't see as a big loss.

I'm on my knees on the floor, picking up the pieces and shoving them back into their jackets when I realize that everyone in the room must think I'd lost my mind. Nope. Found it.

I explain. "Leonard's at the front door with *Lana Liebman*." Guests gasp, mouths drop open, hands fly up to hearts. "And he wants his Beatle albums back. He didn't say he wanted them back *in one piece*."

Everyone helps me gather Leonard's prized possessions, and they follow me to the front door where I hand Leonard the vinyl rubbish. "How do you like them *apples*." Leonard looks different, like a carrot, a big shocked carrot.

I close the door on Mr. Goldfarb for the last time, but a big part of me believes the problem in our relationship was *me*. If I could have been cooler, slimmer, better at hand jobs . . .

Being *sans*, Leonard leaves too much time on my hands, which translates into too much fat on my thighs, my weight rises to an all-time high. I'm a size fourteen.

Linda approaches me in art class. She heard about what happened at my party. We end up laughing together. Leonard's out, Linda's back in.

> *I wish I could say that I quit blaming myself for everything, but remember, I'm not a quick study—I'm over forty, and just now figured out what to do with my hair. I believe when any of my relationships sour, it's because of something I did or didn't do, or because of some- one I was—or wasn't.*

The Pool Boy

Ma and Daddy decide we're going "for da veek" to the Catskills, the New York Riviera. A *vacation*? What's with that? I drive, not Daddy. I don't want to end up in Nova Scotia.

The scenery is fantastic. Busboys, waiters, and pool boys—all students from New York colleges. I'm out by the pool, holding my stomach in, talking to a skinny girl in the chaise next to me. Her veins protrude. And she has no eyelashes. She catches me staring.

"I was in the hospital and my lashes fell out," she explains. Even her voice is thin—a thin Brooklyn. "I had something called anorexia nervosa. I stopped eating and got sick. So my parents put me in treatment for a month." She looks this bony *after* a month of care?

I want to give her hope. "Well, don't worry, with the food they pile on plates here, you'll put weight on soon."

"Are you kidding!" she's appalled, "I'm fat! I just push the food around on the dishes, sort of compact it, but I don't *eat* it!"

"It should only happen to me." Be careful what you wish for.

The pool boy who gives out towels, a sophomore at NYU, offers to shmear baby oil on my back. Then he asks me to meet him after dinner. I do. We neck on the dock.

On the teary day I leave for home, Pool Boy swears to keep in touch. There are some calls and five months later we make a date to meet in Manhattan for New Year's Eve. I sell dresses at the Cavendish Mall to make money for the trip. Ma tells me I should stay with our "cousins," an old married couple in Brooklyn.

December 30th . . .

I fly into La Guardia. Pool Boy is working, so I take a cab to Brooklyn. The eighty-somethings live in a heavily doilied apartment, staying in touch with global issues by way of their twelve-inch black-and-white portable. They move, speak, and smell identical.

The wife asks me, "You like cottage cheese for breakfast?"

"No, I don't, but I'll go out for breakfast, don't trouble yourselves, please."

She's stunned. "You don't like cottage cheese?"

"No, I hate it." She's depressed.

I walk into the kitchen the next morning, she's dishing out white, lumpy mush into a bowl. "Look!" she's excited, "I bought cottage cheese special for you today. I went to the market—so fresh! I bought two kinds!" I eat the two varieties of mush, and call Pool Boy. He's working and will pick me up at seven. We'll do dinner, then Times Square to watch the ball drop. It's only ten hours away, it takes me that long to dress.

Before I start getting ready, I want to see a bit of New York. "I'm going for a walk."

"*No!*" They corner me. "It's not safe!"

She's gonna bribe me. "Stay here, I'll make a nice cottage cheese sandwich." Her head is filled with cottage cheese. I sneak out, but instead of a walk around New York, I walk around the block, get scared (of nothing in particular), and go back to the apartment.

Seven o'clock comes, then eight, nine, ten. Finally I take off my coat (the eighty-somethings keep the thermostat at eighty-something). In a black velvet midi-skirt, a black chiffon blouse, and a coat-on-lap, I'm positioned between the door and the phone.

At 11:00 p.m. Pool Boy calls. "My car broke down." (Isn't that supposed to happen *on* the date?) I can hardly hear him for all the whoopie in the background.

I shout, "Are you coming?"

"Take a cab. You can probably make it to Times Square by midnight if you leave now." Yeah, NYU boy, look for me, I'm in black. I hang up furious with myself. I should've known this would happen. I put on the shoes that the old woman placed on the mat in the hall and say, "Bye." Ma and Pa Kettleberg, using bionic speed, throw themselves in between me and the front door.

"You can't go out by yourself! It's dangerous!" They start crying. I'm not going to Auschwitz, people! Why do their faces have to go all puppy-dog?

"Okay, okay, I'll stay, we'll celebrate together." Get the Manischewitz. By midnight, they're asleep and I sit in my velvet and chiffon, with ginger ale and two cottage cheeses, watching the ball drop in Times Square on the twelve-inch black-and-white TV.

I get back to Montreal. "Ma, it was terrible! He stood me up!"

Ma said, "Vell, it could be vorse, he didn't shoot you."

It got vorse.

I agree to go out with Sheldon, Ma's friend's cousin's son. He's a Ph.D. from MIT. But brings me chocolates and while waiting for me to finish smoothing my hair, proceeds to eat the chocolates himself.

After dinner he says we should go to his place to listen to music. I sit on a bean chair, he sits on me.

"No!" I yell. I try to push him off. Getting out of a bean chair is hard enough without having a body pinning you down. I'm struggling with him, but also with myself. On the one hand, he's repulsive—no one I would want to have sex with. On the other hand, I think I owe him for dinner. I check out—and give in. (A pattern I perfect later in life.)

Here Comes the Bribe

Linda has come up with a great idea.

We should sign up for beauty school! We're optimistic. We've had experience with hair, remember? And everybody has a head. Forget college. I close the book on studying. Ma and Daddy scream and threaten, I turn up the TV.

Daddy gets my attention by saying the most inspiring thing. "If you stay in school, I vill buy you a car."

Linda flunks out, Leonard is expelled, but thanks to the multiple-choice question, I graduate high school.

But until Daddy buys me the new car, I'm still using his . . .

I'm driving to the grad dance at the Holiday Inn on Decarie Boulevard, when the car in front of me stops suddenly and I rear-end it. Daddy's gonna take off the belt for sure! He loves this car. He'd kiss it good night and put Ma in the garage. I consider just driving on to Toronto.

I'm crying as I get to the dance. Luckily, someone spiked the punch, and I get drunk, *so* drunk that Dr. DeGroot, the principal, says, "I'll drive you home." He escorts me in the house and talks to Daddy. We all go look at the car and Daddy says, "Dis happens. Ve can fix it."

I'd heard Dr. DeGroot helped to smuggle Jews out of Holland during the war. But what he did for me . . . priceless.

So, Now It's a Cat?

One of the top twenty worst nights of my life, so far—

As a graduation present, Carole Irgo, my art teacher since eighth grade, gives me a white kitten, a runt rejected by her mom-cat. I don't name her. If she doesn't live, a *Jingles* would be harder to bury than *the Cat*. I'm also terrified that the same fate will befall this kitten as did Goldie, Pookie, and Ted. Daddy had found Ted in his shoe. Before I could save the little guy, Daddy took revenge. Ted the turtle met a watery grave. The last I saw of little Teddy, he was spinning on his back in the toilet bowl. I stood by helplessly, wishing I could throw Daddy in the toilet instead.

Goldie the fish. Fish are fish. They die.

I was twelve when Pookie, the beagle/spaniel named after Liza's character in *A Sterile Cuckoo*, was hit by a car.

I was in my room, drawing a girl kissing a boy in my algebra notebook, when I heard Ma scream, "*Oy!* Da dog is dead on da road!" What was da dog doing outside? I ran to see what happened and froze at the front door. A man, I suppose the driver, was lifting my Pookie from the road and carrying her to our lawn. Her body was limp as he put her down on the grass. Someone carried me, it seemed, over to her. Pooks wasn't moving. She was white, brown, and tan with a bit of black, now with a bit of red, too. Her chest rose and fell as if by hard effort. Her big brown eyes were gazing into my soul.

She blinked slowly, signaling that she needed my help. "Aren't you going to do something, Mommy?" Blood was pooling next to her nose, the nose that lived to smell crotches, other dogs' bums, and sidewalk smears. The nose was dying. She kept her gaze. "Mommy?"

At that moment I knew complete powerlessness. Tidal wave. I dropped to my knees. Sorry, Pookie, I fucked up. I should have been more clear with Ma and Daddy regarding front-door rules. I should have been more vigilant. I will watch that in the future! Never relax. Suzie can't be trusted with good things.

I touched Pookie. No, this wasn't a dream. Silky hair. Her Snoopy eyes spoke. "Don't feel bad, I was lonely anyway. You didn't play with me that much." She took in another breath, and exhaled, and there was a pause. No next breath? No.

Ma, in her oblivion, had opened the front door and love left our house.

Turns out, the driver of the car was the mayor of Cote Saint Luc. He seemed to be having a nervous breakdown. He offered to buy me a new dog, but I screamed at him, "Go through this again? Are you nuts?" He never tried to talk to me again.

> *Daddy never warmed to Pookie. He called her* da hint *(the dog).*
> *He was glad to be rid of the dirty animal. Ma was so impressed that*
> *it was the mayor who ran over Pookie! For her, the celebrity aspect*
> *became the salient element of the event. If I were Opie, Pa and I'd go*
> *fishin' and he'd try to console me.*

Based on all that, do I dare introduce another furry victim to Neurotics Central?

The kitty is three days old. She's tiny. I bring her home in a box with a blanket. I beg Daddy to let me keep her.

Disgusted, he booms, "No!" End of discussion.

"Pleeeze, Daddy. Ple-e-eze, I'll take care of her, I promise! She'll never bother you."

Daddy spins into fury, "Suzie! You don't know vhat you're talking!" His voice hushes to a low yell. "Vhen you sleep, cats come and dey put der mouths over yours, and den dey suck out da air from you. You can't breathe no more!"

Why hadn't I been warned about this? Cats are common, you'd think they'd have mentioned cats-that-kill on *60 Minutes*. I look at the piece of fluff in the box. How could such a tiny thing secure a vapor lock on any-one's mouth? She's as threatening as a pompom.

Daddy tells me to put her on the porch. It's so cold.

Walter Cronkite's over, Daddy falls asleep, and I sneak the kitty, a bowl of milk, and an eyedropper into my room. Miss Irgo said the kitty was too young to lap from a bowl, that I'd have to nurse her from a milk-filled eyedropper.

Here's when the life and death struggle begins. My kitten will not eat. Am I going to bury yet another pet? I wrap my ticking alarm clock in a blanket to simulate a soft mother so the kitten won't feel alone. She makes barely audible baby meows. My heart pulls apart like pieces of velcro.

At 4:00 a.m., after refusing the dropper one more time, I realize the kitty will starve. Another innocent who depends on me for her survival, and now she will die!

> *Was I seeing myself in kitty? Was she a target for my love, a vehicle for my need to fix and help rescue? Was I trying to save the starving cat because I know what it's like to starve from lack of attention?*

I spend the night next to the kitty's bed, dropper in hand, trying not to fall asleep. The room is getting lighter. Once more I fill the dropper and put the tip in Kitty's mouth.

Oh, the miracle! Kitty begins to suck the milk. She doesn't stop until she's had five droppers worth. I fall into bed crying.

Each afternoon I come home from school to see Kitty curled up on Daddy's lap. He's a furrier, he smells like animal pelts, maybe she thinks Daddy is a relative. The mother who abandoned her?

◆ ◆ ◆

A few years later, when she crawled under autumn leaves in the street and was run over by a car, Ma and I were sad, but it was Daddy who grieved the most.

Acting 101

My first year of college. . .

I major in commercial art. After months of re-creating the straight line, I switch to theatre. I know how to *act*. And besides, there are more drugs in the drama department.

I land the part of Natalia in Chekhov's *The Marriage Proposal*. Comedy. This I can do.

Ma and I are in a fight. She decides to boycott the play.

Once more I'm groveling. "I'm sorry, Mummy. Please come to the play. Okay, so you'll come?" Ma's lips are glued to her front teeth.

I leave the house, pleading, "You *are* going to come, aren't you? I have a big part! Are you going to come?" The play is running only one night. I can't believe she won't come. And yet, how could she? Does she even know where the school is? Why didn't I tell her? Maybe I want it to be *so* important that she'd make the effort and get there somehow.

I want to see her *kvell-face*. When she's proud of me, she beams; and the ray of light fills me with love. But it's dark as I peek through the stage curtains before my entrance. I scan the audience. No Ma. I steal glances during the performance. I look after the curtain goes down. She didn't come. There ought to be a law.

> *Relationship Lesson: Withdrawal of affection occurs when you make people mad, so don't speak your mind if doing so makes others stop speaking to you.*

I come home and tell Ma how the audience laughed and applauded and, "I was hurt that you didn't show up."

"*You* should be hurt?" She's offended, "*Oy!* I only hope one day you should have a daughter like you!" She's the victim, I'm the perp.

"I never talked to my modder da vey you talk to me—"

"Well, Ma, maybe your mother didn't talk to you the way *you* talk to *me!*"

"She vorked every day like a horse, cooking and cleaning, who had time to talk!"

The wheels on the bus go round and round . . .

End of second year, the final theatre production consists of three one-act plays.

Shocker! I'm cast as the female lead in *all* three. Each of the directors wants *me* for their productions! I have to choose one. I turn down the two better roles and take the play in which I get to kiss Richard Billingsley. I love Richard. I've loved him since he played Hamlet, in tights. This play might be the only opportunity I have to kiss Richard. Perhaps not the best career move. I realize my mistake. And I hit the pub before every rehearsal.

Opening night, I arrive at the theatre too drunk to pass for not-drunk. I stagger into the communal dressing room. People are buzzing around me, applying my makeup, and helping me get into costume. They look concerned. That's nice.

My first entrance onto the stage involves descending the highest staircase ever built for a production in the Dome Theatre. I make my entrance and stand on the landing, looking down at Richard, who is sweating. I see the audience and realize it's my turn to talk. I start down the stairs saying my lines. The cast and crew utter a group sigh as I reach the bottom step. I've had years of rehearsal, my body acts normal, independent of what my brain is doing. I can talk through anything my brain has to say.

I don't miss a cue. I get good laughs, and most importantly, my lips hold onto Richard's a little *longer* than they did in rehearsal.

After the performance, Richard kisses me backstage. I see entire solar systems, bombs are bursting in air, my knees are *flubber.*

Richard pulls back and in a startled manner asks, "What's wrong?"

"Huh? Nothing. Why?" He had opened his eyes before I did, and saw my face.

"You scrunched up your eyes and forehead like you were in horrible pain."

"I did?" *Oh God!* He'd seen my pain!

The kiss must have triggered my longing to be loved and—the horror of the inevitable abandonment to follow.

In Case of Emergency, Break Bread

Except for school, I'm alone a lot, watching TV.

I'm going to my bedroom with my evening snack—a loaf of challah and a tumbler of low fat milk. I spend a lot of time dunking. The bulk of my 160 pounds is stationed between my hips and knees. On my journey down the hall, my thighs brushing the walls, I get the feeling that someone's looking at me. I turn around. Daddy, still in his kitchen chair, is leaning out of the kitchen doorway. Staring. At my butt.

He talks like he's spitting out sour milk. "Suzie! You—getting fat like a *PIG*!" Does he think I hadn't noticed? Is this meant to be constructive?

It isn't. After Daddy goes to bed, I go back to the kitchen. I'm a pig. Peanut butter will help me deal with it.

The next day Daddy puts a padlock on the pantry door. Unlike Ma's bedroom set, I can't chew through it.

You Have to Be Crazy
to Go to a Psychiatrist

Christmas break, the Ohioans are visiting—

Sylvia's family has taken over our sleeping quarters and I have to bunk with Ma. We share the hide-a-bed in the TV room. I'm asleep, having a delightful dream in which I haul off and slap Ma across the face. It feels so real and *so* good. You know the dreams that feel so real they wake you up? I open my eyes. Ma's sitting straight up next to me with her hand on her cheek and her eyes wide, staring at me.

"Ma?"

Ma says nothing, she just keeps staring.

"Ma, d-did I-I just slap you?"

"YEAH!" she spurts out.

"Oh. Sorry." Delicious. I plead the "sleep defense."

◆ ◆ ◆

Sylvia and the kids go back to Ohio. I pack, too. I can't be alone with the Holocaustals anymore. Linda and I move into an apartment downtown.

Ma calls. "It's stupid to vaste money on rent. You leave a good house for an apartment. And don't buy new towels, I have towels for you." The ones from Winnipeg. The see-through ones.

Whatever the subject is, Ma and I are screaming within ten seconds of hello. She throws her hands in the air. "Vhat's da matter mit you?" Another not-question. We know the answer: I'm lazy, selfish, and crazy. I wish Ma and Daddy *would* wonder what's the matter with me. I wonder what's the matter with them, and with me. Something's the matter. Let's eat.

"It's absolute crazy da vay you scream. You should get your head examined!"

"Okay, I will. I'll go see a psychiatrist."

"A psychiatrist? Ach, you have to be crazy to go to a psychiatrist."

"I *am* crazy Ma. You said so!"

"Don't be stupid, I never called you crazy."

"AAAAAAAA!"

Ma says, "Tell him I give you everyting and you scream at me like a crazy person—ask him if dat's normal."

"I can probably see one at the Jewish General Hospital." It's Canada. Socialized medicine. Maybe a psychiatrist can help me get more social.

I call and take their first appointment. I fill out forms. In the box that asks for your mother's name, by accident, instead of writing "Mania" I write "Maniac." How *Freudian*. I'm assigned to a male psychiatrist, around thirty, not grotesque, but he looks kinda like Gomez Addams. He's got a small office on the ground floor of the hospital. I sit on the lime green leather chaise, too self-conscious to lie down like some mental patient. For fifty minutes I try explaining the dysfunction of our family.

Before I leave, he scrawls something on a pad. "Take one of these a half-hour before you see your mother." A prescription for tranquilizers!

He asks, "Would you like to come back to see me again?"

"Yes. I would like that." I am so grateful to have someone listen to me, I don't care how much it costs Canada.

The end of our twelfth meeting—

Dr. Gomez says, "Do you like me?"

"Uh . . . yeah." I want to be polite.

"Do you think your attraction to me is interfering with our process?" Attraction? I was more attracted to the idea of feeling better, for God's sake! A guy, for once in my life, is *not* an issue.

He says, "In therapy there's a thing called *transference*, where you start to have feelings for your doctor. It's normal. It can be exciting."

He moves closer, "Would you like to kiss me?"

I've been motor mouthing for forty-nine minutes, but now cannot organize words.

"... No."

"Are you sure? I get the impression you've been trying to seduce me."

"No, I haven't."

"You come dressed in sexy clothes." It's August, I should wear a coat?

"Well, we can talk about it next time."

There is no next time. I don't report him or tell anyone about this session. What if I *had* been seductive without knowing it?

I had never filled the prescription he'd given me. Drugs were scary. But today, I go to the pharmacy, pick up the pills, and proceed to tranquilize the entire affair. Better life through chemistry.

The Subject Was Roses

Linda doesn't go to college. Actually, she doesn't go anywhere.

Our rent is seventy-five dollars a month. I see a job in the want ads: "Girls! Make *BIG BUCKS* working only a few hours a night!" I become a flower child, forcing roses on diners at restaurants in downtown Montreal. I'm a pedal pusher.

Every night I pick up my basket of roses from the dispatch center and walk from table to table, disturbing people. I'm timid, but when I get the nerve to ask someone if they want to buy a flower, they often do. It's not too bad until the night another flower girl threatens to break my legs. She's big and mean enough to do it. Unbeknownst to me, I had muscled in on her turf. The flower business is too high stress. I quit and get Ma to pay my half of the rent for a couple of months. I don't know where Linda's half is coming from. She never leaves the apartment.

It's summer. Tan, drink, paint—

Linda and I walk up to the roof with Bain du Soleil and reflectors to work on aging our necks. We also take a canvas and brushes to work on an oil painting together. Our styles are almost identical, and although I don't admit it, Linda is the better artist.

We have paint fights. I paint a leaf, lift my brush from the canvas to pick up color from the palette, and she moves her brush to the leaf and alters it. I rework a nose she's just finished, she adds white to the eye I'm on.

One of our paintings is special. It radiates. It's a portrait of an African woman in a headdress done from a photo that Linda had ripped out of a *National Geographic* at a newsstand. There's an undertone of pain. What had this woman seen, what had she experienced? We call her Matumba and keep her on the easel in the alcove.

School is back in session. I've been at class . . .

I come back to the apartment after a long day of trying to pretend I'm normal. The easel is empty.

"Linda, where's Matumba?"

Linda mumbles something. She's wasted. I pour a large glass of wine to catch up. Before I can get an answer, I'm too drunk to remember there was a question. But the memory of the empty easel wakes me the next morning.

"Linda, exactly what happened to the painting?"

"I sold it."

"You . . . WHAT?!" I don't know where to file this one. Rhoda wouldn't do this to Mary.

I check the closet. All the artwork we'd done together is gone. The only pieces remaining are the paintings I did in my Sylvia Plath period. They look like they were all done on PMS. Lonely women and children painted in monochromatic browns. They were probably too depressing to sell.

I forgive Linda. She needed to come up with the rent, but I stop painting.

So *That's* How She Makes Rent Money

Morning class has been canceled. I come home early—

Linda is anxious. "You have to leave the apartment for an hour." She explains, but her story doesn't make sense, she's in her *spin* cycle again.

After I sift out the lies, she confesses. "The baker's coming by."

I hesitate to ask. "Baker?"

"The baker. I show him my buns."

"You show a baker your buns?"

"For fifty bucks." Are we doing stand-up?

She says, "I take off my underpants and he plays with himself while looking at my butt and then he . . . you know."

"*Oy!*" I don't want to know. Yuk! Ick! Blech! I grab my purse and the Quebec equivalent of Ripple, walk up five flights to the roof where I sit chain-smoking, trying to figure out what life is about. An hour goes by, I assume it is safe to return home. I walk in the apartment to find a fat forty-five-year-old heading toward the door.

"Hello, hone. I didn't know you girls work as a team. How's about I get a friend to come over and we can have a time of it—'ey?"

"I'd rather be lying in a gutter choking on my own vomit, but thank you for asking." (That's what I want to say, but I'm not that assertive.) I graciously decline and try to move out of his way.

He insists. "C'mon sweetie, I'll give you a hundred bucks—'ey?" That was all Linda needed to hear! She was already jealous of me, now I'm being offered double her pay. I look to her for help. She avoids my eyes.

The baker's intensity scares me. "Thanks, sir, really, but I've gotta go, I'll come back—'ey." And I run out the door.

Does This Coma Mean You were Serious About Killing Yourself?

I stay away for two hours to be sure the baker's gone.

The apartment is dim and unusually quiet. Is the TV broken?

Linda is propped up in bed, la Ripple in her lap, drawing deeply on a Winston.

"Remember," she's got that twisted Danny Kaye look on, "we have a pact. Don't call the hospital."

"What are you talking about?" Then I see the almost-empty bottle of anti-Ma pills. Linda must have taken twenty.

I plop down next to her. "Thank God you didn't take them all! I need a few." I toss two pills into my mouth and chug them down with the wine.

I start to feel the warming chemical glow that makes things right. "Linda, do you really want to kill yourself *now?*"

She slurs, "I hate the world. I wanna die."

I urge her to maintain perspective. "If everybody who hated the world killed themselves, there'd be nine people left alive. And, if you had cancer, you'd be fighting to live!"

She looks at me. "I have to tell you something." *Oy,* that phrase is never good. Six words that live in infamy. She pops another pill. I take one too. I need to relax. And the more pills I take, the less she takes. I don't want my best friend to die, and yet, after hand-jobbing Leonard, ripping textbooks, and saying I did it, siding with Ma, etc., part of me would be relieved to see her go. I'm evil. I take another pill.

"Susan—I love you."

"I love you too!" I say (*way* too peppy).

"No, I don't love you the way you love me, I love you the way you loved Leonard. When I was with Hilly, Ronnie . . . Louie . . . I wanted to be with you."

I'm way too sober for this. I take another pill. And a swig from the bottle. I've never seen Linda cry, not even when her father died.

"Linda, it's okay. You sleep. It'll be different in the morning." She's quiet. I crawl into bed next to her, stroke her head, "It's okay, it'll all be okay."

Like okay is possible.

◆ ◆ ◆

The next thing I know, it's morning. She's still breathing. Good, she'll sleep it off while I'm at school.

I come home after a day of practicing denial. "She'll be fine, the pills aren't that strong . . ." Linda's still lying in bed, in the same position. Her breathing is raspy.

I can't stand the suspense. Linda, do something, help me, die already! What am I *crazy*? A selfish pig! I want her to die because of what she did to me in *seventh grade*?

I shake her. "Linda, Linda, wake up!" She doesn't open her eyes. And I notice, she's wet the bed. Her words reverberate in my head. "We have a pact, no rescue . . ." But as Ma would say, "Pact, shmact, call da hospital."

But who's to say she's not better off dead. It's her life, if she wants to die, who am I to stop her? I walk to the easel. I draw. Chalk pastel on black velvet. No, not Elvis. It's a naked woman, lying over the edge of the bed, hair hanging, an empty pill bottle next to her. One pill left on the sheet. The look on her face—relief. Hours later, I put down the pastel. Linda's eyes are still closed.

I go to the phone. "Operator," (before 9-1-1) "I have an emergency. My friend is dying." The ambulance takes an unconscious Linda away as I watch. I figure, I'll go pick her up from the hospital after they've pumped her stomach and take her back to the apartment.

When I get to the hospital, Linda's mother and brothers block me from entering her room. Paul looks at me the way I'd look at Hitler. "Linda's in a coma. They don't know if she's going to live!" A coma? Like on *Medical Center*?

Her mother points to me, "Murderer!" Hey, when you're right you're right. If Linda dies I could be in big trouble. Why didn't I call for help sooner? The boys pull me down the hall and shove me into an elevator. I can take a hint.

I call the nurses every day. Two weeks later, one of them tells me Linda opened her eyes. I drive to the hospital and run into brother Paul in the hall.

He's mean. "Go ahead, go on in, take a look at her! Linda can't feel the left side of her body. She's paralyzed." It can't be true. I go in.

Linda is staring at the ceiling, her lips tight, her eyes dark. Black like Ma.

"Linda?" She doesn't answer. "Linda, please, say something." *Pleeeze, Mummy.*

She makes eye contact. "Get out. I don't want you here. I don't *ever* want to see you again." The elevator drops ten floors, but I'm not in an elevator.

"You can't *mean* that. Let me explain, when you—"

"If you don't leave, I'll tell Paul they were *your* pills and you told me to take them." That would be worse than blaming me for the vandalized textbook. I could be expelled from life. I'd finish my degree in prison. It'd probably be the only way I *could* finish it.

And yeah, she *meant* it. I didn't see Linda again for twenty years, and when I did, it was creepy.

P.S. Post Suicide—

Ma and Daddy say they'll buy me a new nineteen-inch color portable if I move back home. They know my price.

I've been back a week, and am feeling black and mostly blue. Ma and Daddy are fighting and I'm the one feeling beat up. Every scream is another punch.

I announce, "Until further notice, I'll be living in the basement."

We move my bed, desk, and new TV from my room upstairs to the black hole downstairs. The only reason we ever went into that cold, dim room was to get winter clothes out of the cedar closet.

So I'm living in spider base camp. I can always count on at least one hairy-legged tarantula trapped in the tub or the sink. Spiders can swing from a maple tree to a birch a block away, but they can't escape from a porcelain basin? I get used to checking the floor for spiders before getting out of bed. I don't drink water after 7:00 p.m., so I don't have to go to the bathroom in the middle of the night.

I'd never gotten over—when I was nine—waking up to find a thick black spider on the pillow looking at me. I screamed. Ma was laughing. "Vhat are you scared? You're bigger den dat spider!"

Living with spiders is better than listening to the fighting upstairs.

I paint a mural on the wall next to the bed. A cute snail is climbing a long road up to a cliff. What we see, that the snail doesn't, is that there's nothing at the end of her hard journey but a sudden drop into oblivion. We want to say, "Don't bother, sweet snail," but we know she has to do what a snail has to do. After her effort, she'll find nothing. Because wherever she goes, she takes her shell.

College Daze

I'm majoring in Drama—

Major Drama. An ambulance is rushing me to Montreal General, but I pass out and miss all the fun. I wake up in the ER wondering, how'd I get here? . . . I'd been cast as the bride in *Blood Wedding* . . . shouldn't I be at the theatre? I try to think back to the last time I could think straight.

Yesterday. Lunch. I'm at Hingston Hall Hell. Rebel students have converted Hingston's cellar into an underground tequila bar.

The sexy senior behind the bar fills a small glass with tequila. He puts a wedge of lime on a napkin, salts the web between my thumb and index finger, and says, "Lick the salt, swallow the shot, and bite the lime!" I do exactly what he says. I don't want to fail Boozing 101.

The first drink doesn't do anything so I have another. Then another.

The next thing I know, it's night, and two guys are holding me up as I stumble to the campus theatre for my dress rehearsal. Lucky for them, I've lost twenty pounds due to Melba toast. Then, everything goes fuzzy again.

Until . . . I'm lying on the couch in the dressing room calling for the director, my married drama professor, who I secretly have the hots for. "Carl . . . Carl, I need you—where *art* thou? Come to me, Carl." Then another quick nap . . . .

I awaken, like Snow White, to find my prince Carl standing over me. I confess my love and hurl into the metal trash can.

And now . . . is it . . . morning? I'm in a *hospital bed?* My eyes try to focus. Is that Ma and Daddy standing at the foot of the bed? *Please*, God, let it be two short doctors.

The taller short one is shaking a finger and growling through teeth, "Suzie . . . da whole trouble mit you is . . ." (what comes next can't be good if it starts off like that) "I didn't hit you *enough!*"

"No, Daddy, " I want to say, "you hit me plenty." But who can argue with logic like that?

✦ ✦ ✦

The next night I'm back at rehearsal. Carl and I are alone in the dressing room. He says, "Don't let me down." *Now* he has doubts?

On stage all I'm thinking is, "Everyone's looking at me!" It's what I want, but only if they're thinking, "She's brilliant!" And I know that's not the case. I want to be back home, *dreaming* of one day becoming an actress.

The actor I play opposite spits when he speaks. My motivation becomes, "Try not to get hit in the face by saliva." He eats garlic. I hate him.

But I love Carl. I'm willing to die for him. I just don't want to die *on stage*.

What the hell made me think I could act? I can't even remember my lines.

By opening night, I have the flu. I wait behind the backdrop listening for my first cue and wondering what would happen if I ran. I have no right to be here. I have monologues and everything! Carl has made a mistake. Poor Carl. I'm going to ruin his whole play.

I hear my cue. The stage manager motions to me. I'm frozen. Then, as if pushed—I step onto the stage. My feet are moving, my mouth is speaking, but as far as I know, I'm home watching Carol Burnett.

All in all, I consider my performance a success, because at no time did I fall off the stage.

Tell Her What She's Won

CFCF, Channel 12, is searching for contestants for a game show . . .

I show up. I get on. I lose. My consolation prize—one year's supply of orange soda. We end up stacking 365 cans in a line in the garage, forming the great wall of soda. My *real* consolation prize is Meyer Birnbaum, the other contestant. His name is an onomatopoeia. If anyone ever *looked* like a Meyer Birnbaum, it's Meyer. Ma calls him *da shlub*.

I lose the game to Meyer. The announcer's voice-over catches my interest.

"Meyer, you've won an all-expense-paid, eight-day, five-star vacation for two, to sunny Mexico!" Meanwhile, winter's battering Montreal with ice and wind.

The host of the show is thanking me for coming on today, and I say, on camera, into the mic, "*Thanks* is nice, but I think Meyer should take me to Mexico for letting him win." They all laugh. But Meyer takes me to Mexico.

(I had given him my number, he called and asked, "Were you serious about coming with me to Mexico?" I suggested we go out in Canada first. We do. I tell him I'll go on the trip, but it doesn't mean we'll fool around. We'll have to see how it goes.) Oooo, I'm so smart.

Mexico—

The first night, in the five-star hotel room, I'm trying to figure out how to get out of having sex. I'm conflicted. He didn't just take me to dinner, he took me to Mexico! But he's *Meyer Birnbaum*. The answer comes as I projectile vomit. No, I hadn't drunk the water, but I did have ice in the margaritas at a no-star bar near the hotel.

And I keep vomiting. I miss the trip to the pyramids, the river, the mountains. My temp is 104°. We call for a doctor. He gives me a shot in the butt, and Meyer's watching. Is that a camera?

"No," I try saying to the doctor, "no butt shot . . . . Meyer, no butt shot." I'm too weak to fight.

I go back home still a virgin—I'd previously converted back—and ten pounds thinner.

Meyer and I get together one night to look at the pictures: him standing next to a pyramid, next to a river, next to a blonde. He's brought over wine. Two bottles. The rest of the evening happens without me.

This is the old days, before men put pills in alcohol to knock women out so they can have sex. The date-rape drug is alcohol.

I awake with cottonmouth and my body hurts in places that shouldn't hurt. What's that about? My white princess phone rings. It's Meyer. "Hey, baby. You okay?"

"Whadaya mean?" I search my memory banks. What's he talking about? It's not like we had sex or anything. No way in my right mind could I let that bloated, hairy drooler, with the huge Hebrew honker and lips that slung like flour in a sack, touch my body.

But I hadn't been in my right mind. What exactly did my mind let my body do? I'm wringing my brain trying to squeeze at least one memory from last night.

"Wow!" he says, like we're sharing a secret. "You were amazing! You're even hotter than you look! I didn't think you'd let me . . . y'know . . . " His voice is smirking.

I look at the phone in my hand, it's turned into a disgusting spider that won't shut up. Stop it before it says more! I hurl the thing across the room so hard, it cracks the wall mirror. I pull my knees to my chest and stare at the phone like it might sprout eight legs and crawl back.

I sift through the evening looking for scraps. An image comes, so vile, worse than when I jumped on Ma's sewing needle. I vow to go back to being a virgin again, again. Me and Doris Day.

Three weeks later. Midnight, I call my favorite radio station from the spider basement.

The D.J. picks up. "Request line! Tell me yours!"

"'I Honestly Love You' by Olivia Newton John, please." I hang up and get ready to cry.

Next commercial break, I call the radio station again, this time for something peppier. "I'd like to hear 'Lonely Days, Lonely Nights' by the Bee Gees, please."

"Didn't you just call in for a tear-jerker?"

"Yes, I'm into jerks. Ones that bring on tears. You one?"

"What's your name?"

"Lilly. Lilly Pad . . . dle . . . man." Snappy patter ensues. Commercial ends, D.J. asks me to hold on. *He plays our conversation on the air*! Then plays the Bee Gees and gets back on the phone. This part of the conversation he doesn't record, "Look, I never do this, but I have an appearance at a trade show on Saturday, wanna meet me there?"

> *Lesson: If you want to capture the interest of a man, don't give a shit about him.*

I go to the trade show and find D.J. on a stage being clever and in command, holding a microphone, standing next to a rotating muscle car. He's cute, kinda looks like Kent McCord from *Adam-12*. I get tingles in dark places.

I smile, "Hi."

"Lilly Pad . . . dle . . . berg?" Four hours later, we're in my basement drunk and naked. The *tramp* made me do it.

I hear footsteps coming down the stairs. A flurry of zipping, tucking, and smoothing begins. Halfway through our attempt at looking like we're doing something wholesome, Daddy barges into the room. This is worse than when I told Daddy that Hymie Lebowitz kissed me in the alley.

D.J. leaves, and Daddy won't look at me. He hasn't been this disgusted since he sprayed AquaNet in his armpits. Weeks go by. When he passes me, he spits on the floor. Usually, it's *Ma* who gives me the silent treatment; no matter how angry Daddy gets, he's over it in an hour. This time's different.

High Crimes and Meaner Misters

Game Show #2 . . .

"CFCF is now holding auditions for a new game show." Sylvia, visiting from Ohio, reads this in the *Montreal Star*. She says, "Let's go, it'll be fun."

Being a game show contestant isn't about fun. It's about not sleeping and obsessively reliving best- and worst-case scenarios. Best: You'll be driving home in *"your BRAND NEW CAR!"* Worst: You'll be enjoying "a year's worth of home-delivered sausage."

Sylvia and I sit in a room with two hundred strangers. The woman conducting the interview tells us about the show's host. "He's originally from Canada, but he lives in Hollywood now. He's a TV producer. And he's gorgeous."

My plan: I get this gig, meet the Hollywood hunk, bewitch him, he brings me to L.A., I move in with him, get a sitcom, and tan in February.

Suddenly, I have no doubt it will happen. It's a given. Oh, c'mon, that's nuts! I say to myself. And another self inside says, Yeah? Just watch.

I see it as a preview, as clear as a TV show:

Rod Serling steps into the frame. "We call this episode, 'Susan and the Power of Visualization.' Not even having auditioned, Susan knows her fate.

From the spider basement of her home in the frozen tundra-suburb, she has the vision."

CUT TO Rodeo Drive, Susan, behind the wheel of her yellow convertible.

CUT TO the studio, she's in front of three cameras.

CUT TO outdoor café. She's doing lunch.

Screech—put the brakes on Kreskin—get the job first. Not a problem.

I am the quintessential game show contestant—perky, lots of teeth, and a head full of otherwise-useless information. I put on my least *Jewish* persona, I shorten vowels, beef up consonants, and remove all sing-songiness. Sylvia passes the quiz but fails the personality test. She's given a smoked meat sandwich on her way out. I'm torn. Do I stay and risk rejection or do I leave and eat.

L.A. calls. "Come . . . bring the Bain du Soleil.

Two hours later the results are in. I'm one of the chosen people.

My ticket to L.A.

I show up at the studio in a halter top and miniskirt. Trampesque. It's 400 degrees out. The host of the show stands on stage, he's being powdered down. He's got a David Niven attitude—amused by it all. He should be wearing a smoking jacket. How is he staying so cool and crisp, so unaffected by the August heat and stage lights?

I can make him sweat. Hee-hee.

"Bad girl!" The nun in my head is freaking.

Oh, shut up you vigilant prude. Think of what's at stake!

So I don't let on that I'm *plutzing*! I *plutz* quietly to myself.

❖ ❖ ❖

The show's going well. I manage to say clever things and smile a lot, fulfilling my contestant duties. I'm losing, but I don't care—the prize I'm after isn't behind the curtain.

Then it happens. During the commercial break, the hunky host walks over from his host-post and says, "You're funny." I could die now, and it'd be okay.

He's so good-looking. Big inner-*plutz*. Will I collapse to my knees in a heap of trembling flesh? Not now, later.

My turn to talk, but I've left the building. Fortunately, the tramp's stayed around. She talks for all of us. It's a sober blackout. Whatever she says must be good because during the next break Host moseys over again.

All bedroom-eyes, he whispers, "What are you doing after the show?" I'm as good as on the beach in Malibu.

The taping is over, we're at the food services table. I'm too wound up to eat.

Host says, "Would you hold my chicken?" The tone sounds more like, "Would you hold my genitals?"

I say, "Yes, I will hold your chicken." Carrying a plate of BBQ, I follow Host backstage. This is the first professional dressing room I've ever been in, and he's undressing in it! Man—they do things differently in L.A.!

"Meet me for dinner tomorrow," he says. My heart skips with glee. Pulling me close, he brings us face to face. I don't know which eye to look in. Then he leans in and presses his sorta mushy but not moist, gentle lips to mine. The tramp's celebrating, the nun's tsking.

Pack the sunglasses.

He says, "Give me a tour of Olympic Village." He thinks I know where it is? I'm not going to admit that while I live in Montreal, I rarely go out *into* it. Yes, I went to the closing ceremonies and saw the streakers run through the schoolchildren (Sylvia and I fought over the binoculars), but I didn't drive, so I didn't pay attention.

We go to dinner instead.

This is to be our first and last dinner. Unless you count room service.

I drink wine. Host doesn't seem to need any. We smoke some hash.

He's doing everything right, but I'm having a terrible time. The nun and tramp are still duking it out. But I'm nineteen and totally in love. Or in something.

Host flies back to L.A. between tapings.

One-night Host calls from Buffalo . . .

The airport is snowed in and he can't make the connecting flight. He'll come up to Montreal by limo. I sneak out of the house and take the bus downtown to his hotel. Three busses. The front desk knows I'm coming and the bellhop escorts me up in the elevator. I want to say something full of wit to the bellhop as we travel the long corridor. I'm imagining what he's imagining. I'm so embarrassed.

I wait in the hotel room until 4:00 a.m. It's fancy.

◆ ◆ ◆

He shows up and we jump in bed. He mumbles in my ear, "There's someone I want you to meet; she works on the show. I invited her up."

"Huh?" I tend to verbally dissociate when I'm with Host. My language center closes. He could be naked in black socks and still intimidate me. I'm either speechless or words rush out of my mouth at the same time, getting stuck behind my lips, "Blubs, mudth, d-d-duh."

Knock, knock. He's naked but gets up to open the door. He's *so* L.A.

I throw his shirt on. In floats a doe-eyed waif. She looks twelve and timid. It's like she's walking into the principal's office. Host instructs her to lie in bed next to him and tells me to get on his other side.

An aspect of my self makes a sudden appearance. "I don't *think* so!"

I put on my pants. Host takes the hand of the doe, who looks even more perplexed than when she arrived, if that's possible, and escorts the poor thing to the door. Yay! I won. What'd I win? The who's-the-biggest-booby prize?

He leans against the wall, still naked, and crosses his arms over his chest, "I just don't understand you, you're a complete enigma to me."

I smile—my best Mona Lisa smile—as if to say, "Yes . . . I know." Then I go home and look up *enigma*.

What's not to understand about me? *He's* the mystery.

His next trip . . .

We're in bed (where else?) when the phone rings. He answers and motions for me to put my ear to the receiver.

A woman is crying, "B-b-but you . . . you said you'd be here. I need you. Please tell me you're coming to Toronto—*please!*"

He covers the mouthpiece with his hand, "Guess who this is!" Her voice sounds familiar. He mouths her name. Yeah, I know her—as a *singer,* not a sobber. What is this rich, talented, Ivory-soap-singing mom doing with the likes of Satan? Me, sure. But this is a woman of importance and good reputation?

◆ ◆ ◆

Oh, Host, you are evil. Why can't you have bad breath? Or gas? Or black hair on your back? Why don't you say shlubby things? Why can't you smell weird or have flabby flanks? Or bony shoulders? I have no problem seeing other men as morons, why can't I see it in you?

Because I need you. I will *never* forget when you said, "Baby, if they gave an Oscar for blow jobs, you'd win." All the thumb sucking paid off. I can make my man moan. I'd given Host my personal best and had gotten an enthusiastic thumbs up.

The trip where it finally happens.

Host is as excited as Host gets. "Norman Lear called for a meeting. He wants *me* to produce a spoof of a talk show. Come up with something, create a character, you can be on the show."

By the next trip, I have the character ready.

I sit in the half-lotus, and use my best Galleria accent. "Hi, I'm, like, from the *Valley.*" I do the tilting-head *Val* thing . . . a floating brain looking for a spot to land. "Y'know, herbs and yoga and chanting-with-crystals, is like really important y'know. I'm a Capricorn with Pluto rising. My moon is in Mars. And my head's in Uranus."

He's smiling "Perfect! You'll play her just like that. You should come to L.A., stay at my place."

Ah, finally the actual invitation to fame and good weather. There are some problems. I still have a year to go for my degree, I'm terrified of change and, as it turns out, Host is married. It's always something.

A month later, Daddy's still spitting on the floor as I pass. I call Host at his new office and leave a message. "Tell him it's Susan from Montreal, and I'm coming to L.A.." I ask my friend Annie from the drama department if she wants to visit Hollywood for the summer. She says, "If we can take my sister." They sign on.

I pack up the car and head south. I make a right at Ohio.

PART TWO

Unrelaxability

A Debilitating Condition

Cured by Dedicated Drunkenness

And Into the Fire

It's midnight in Missouri—

I've been driving since Montreal, with only a one-night stop in Akron to kiss my nieces and nephew, grab a meal, and take a nap. Annie says she'll take over. So my eyes are closed, I'm falling asleep in the backseat when I hear the engine making a sound I've never heard before. It's crying. It's given its all, and more is expected of it; I could be projecting.

Annie has decided to pit our Pontiac Astre against a 900-cylinder Corvette. She's trying to pass, but the Corvette isn't letting her. I see the headlights of an oncoming truck. The three of us are screaming. I try telling Annie to slow down, drop back, and get in the lane *behind* the Corvette but, like when I was little, I can't be heard above the front-seat hysteria. I know what to do to avoid a crash, but I'm in no position to put on the brakes. I'm being driven crazy.

At the last second, the Vette speeds up, we drop back into the right lane, and the truck shwooshes by. I take over.

The girls are sleeping as I pull into a darkened Texas gas station. The radio says a tornado is headed toward Amarillo. That's where we are, Amarillo. It's the middle of the night, no one is in the gas station but us. The wind kicks up. I light a joint and watch devil winds whirl cigarette butts around on the ground. Between the hashish and sleep deprivation, I'm hallucinating. My Pontiac is flying in circles through the air like Dorothy's house. Auntie Em! Auntie Em! I want to wake the girls, but why terrify them as well. Plus, I'd have to share the joint. What would *really* be scary is getting caught by the Texas police. You can legally carry an AK-47 assault rifle in Texas, but holding a joint could get you sent *to* the joint. I stay parked, and awake, high on tornado watch for hours. No tornado. Finally, bored and unable to keep my eyes open, I fall asleep.

At sunrise, the girls wake me up, and after a tinkle and Twinkie run, we're on our way. By the time we reach L.A., we hate each other.

I call Host from a phone booth under the Hollywood sign. "I'm here."

"Where?"

"Here, in L.A. And I brought a couple of friends." Silence.

"How did you get here?"

"I made a right at Ohio." It's a good line, I like to use it often.

"Good!" he says. "I'm at the studio, we've started production on the show. I'll meet you at the house tonight." He gives me directions and says someone will be there to let us in.

Then he asks, matter-of-factishly, "By the way, how do you want me to introduce you to the wife, as my friend or my *lover*?"

It's the seventies. I suppose they have one of those "open marriages."

"Friend—I pick *friend*!"

The girls and I find Mulholland Drive. The housekeeper shows us to the backyard overlooking the San Fernando Valley.

Host's wife is sitting on a chaise by the pool nursing a baby. Her baby. Her big baby. Yikes! Host is a new father. Perhaps I'll just jump off the cliff into the big valley. Host had told me she was a singer/songwriter/actress.

She's also a mother. She's tanning, nursing, and writing on music sheets. Multi-tasking.

"It's *nice* to meet you, Susan. Host has said such *nice* things." Nice? Twice?

Toting the infant, the wife, with no seeming resentment of my presence, shows us to the guesthouse. They are the greenest rooms I've ever seen. Green-flowered wallpaper, green carpet, drapes, furniture, I think money. They're probably thinking "green room," where the guests wait to see the stars.

The sisters and I unpack the Pontiac and within five minutes are out by the pool, lathering ourselves with baby oil, looking down at Van Nuys and marveling at the smog. I, ever the game show contestant, inform the sisters, "Smog, a combination of smoke and fog." Thanks for sharing.

That night, we're on the green couch smoking a joint and watching *Family Feud* when the phone rings. It's Host. He tells me to come to the main house, "The door's open. Hang a right, go down the hall to the back."

I move down the long hallway, I hear a roaring sound. I'm in a sleazy B-movie. I'm either going to be hacked to death, or I'm going to be having sex. I walk into, what I guess is the master bedroom. It's dark red with velvet. These are a bold people.

Host is sitting in a sunken hot tub, arms spread, his elbows resting on the edges like Nero. The sound? The Jacuzzi motor blowing bubbles up his ass. Where's the martini and cigar?

The huge red bed is propped up on a platform. You have to climb five stairs to lie down. It's not so much a bed as it is a *stage*. And it's got a king-size mirror on the ceiling over it. Aren't they concerned about "the big one"? I mean earthquakes, not his wee-wee. It isn't that big "a one."

Host sounds sinister. "The wife's out of town for a few days. With the kid and the nanny. Hand me that towel." He turns off the motor, rises like Venus from the wet, and steps out of the bathtub toward me, now holding terry cloth. He wraps himself in the fluffy bath sheet, the kind Harlow has in old movies. We stare at each other. The towel drops to the floor. I stare at the floor. I'm not pickin' that up. I'm in a Bel-Air bedroom with a damp, naked producer. My hands are shaking, but my head's singing, "If they could see me now, that little gang of mine . . ." Host pulls my chin up and kisses me. *I'm mel-l-l-ting.*

I like having sex in this bed. I look thinner lying down.

Afterwards, Host says, "I have an early call," and suggests I return to the green room.

"When am I going to do the show? You know, play the character . . . ?"

He reaches into the nightstand and pulls out a bag of pot. "Here, take it. The Jackson Five left it last week." Was that an answer? If so, I missed it. But I don't say anything. It'll be okay. Besides, I have the pop star's pot to placate me.

Two weeks go by . . .

I still haven't been to the studio. I'm afraid Host isn't serious about having me on the show. And if that's the case, I don't want to know.

The sisters and I are hanging out by the pool one morning when Mrs. Host, baby at breast comes over. "You know, Susan, most people come to L.A. to see the sights. They don't usually lie around in the backyard every day."

More *shame on me!* She's right, but she doesn't understand, I'm not a tourist; I'm waiting to be invited on Host's new show. Besides, we tried to get to Disneyland and got lost, so we ended up back at the pool.

The girls and I drive down Sepulveda. We find a pub in Westwood. A suave, dark-haired Englishman named Lewis buys me a drink. I tell him about Host and the show.

He hands me a dime. "Call him, luv'." I get Host on the line. "Host, hi, it's Susan. I was just wondering, are you going to ask me to come to the studio soon?"

"Come down now, I'll arrange a pass."

The sisters have found a group of UCLA students. I'm happy to leave them; they've been teaming up against me. Annie's accused me of eating all the food. "I thought you were trying to *lose* weight, but I don't see the pounds falling off!"

On the set in the studio, Host introduces me to an actress. Her wardrobe's flowy, she's wearing gypsy earrings, and crystals hang around her neck. There's only one role she could be playing—the one I created.

Host says, "I named the character after you. Meet *Susan* Cloud."

Host and I are alone by the cameras between takes. I gather up courage to confront him. "Host . . . so . . . *Susan* Cloud?"

He nods, "Yes?"

And I say, "So . . . "

He says, "So?" So I leave. I'm scared to show him how angry I am. He may still give me work.

There's a Denny's across the street with a neon sign in the window that says, "Bar." I cross Sunset Boulevard, sit at the bar and order a White Russian, then a Black, then a Screwdriver.

By the time I make it back to the studio, the taping's over. I start shmoozing with the actors. Host ushers me out into the hallway where we bump into Norman Lear, the creator of *All in the Family*! A hero!

Mr. Lear agrees to pose for a picture with me. I dig in my purse for the camera, and when I try to hand it over to a wardrobe guy, it drops. I get sweaty. We can't get the camera to work. I make conversation, trying to keep Mr. Lear engaged so he doesn't leave, he even offers to help, but it's broken. Host looks like I've just thrown up on his boss.

But Mr. Lear stays sweet and patient, treating me like a person. I'd marry him if he asked, even if he *weren't* a big producer. And when he leaves, he says goodbye graciously.

I'm alone in the hall with Host. Me and the oil slick across my face, in a slutty halter top, with Black Russian raunchy breath emanating from my excessively apologetic mouth. He doesn't have to say anything. I gather up my belongings strewn on the floor and flee the studio.

Exodus

Later that night, Host calls from the main house.

He sounds stern. "I want to have a *talk* with the sisters. I'd like to know if you've always been like this." Like *this*? Pathetic? Yes, I have always been pathetic, but I'm usually better at concealing it. He wants to interview them about me? (Surely, the Menendez sisters would validate all of Host's criticisms.)

He says, "I'm coming down."

"NO! Uh, I mean, the girls are late . . . for a date, at a restaurant, with people. I'll come to you."

I hang up and shoo the girls off. "Take the car, drive into oncoming traffic, I don't care, just get out *now*!" They don't like it, but they leave.

I undress for the meeting. In my skimpiest nightie, I walk to the big house slowly, preparing for slaughter.

Host sits in the hot tub; this time the engine's off and it's quiet in the room. Too quiet.

"Do you have any idea what an idiot you were today? You acted like a *tourist*. You'll never work in this town."

"UH . . . if that's how you feel, why did you want to keep seeing me?"

"Frankly, my dear, I have no idea. Go back to Canada. You don't belong here." Canada! No! Can he deport me?

"I want you packed and out by tomorrow night."

I shlep back to the guesthouse. There's nothing holding me together. I'm a glass of water without the glass.

I'm going to plunge into the San Fernando Valley. After I've thrown myself off Host's cliff, he'll regret his cruelty, he'll reform, and future young targets will be spared the ride I've had.

I think about my contribution to the relationship. If I weren't such a wimpy idiot, Host would have treated me with respect. Then again, Host wouldn't have been with me had I been respectable.

I'm alone. (Not as alone as I think. Years later, I discover, that if all of Host's victims were used as San Fernando Valley landfill, we wouldn't be looking *down* on Van Nuys anymore.)

The girls get back and phone home. They'll be on a plane in the morning.

I stay up, smoking, and just after sunrise, call Lewis, the British actor from the pub. I can always kill myself later.

The New Land

I'm twenty-one—

Lewis is a twenty-two-year-old actor. So he delivers pipes for the Hirsch Plumbing Company. Lewis—never Lew—looks like Potsie from *Happy Days*. His British accent makes "three-quarter-inch-galvanized-steel" sound like Hamlet. I move in.

It's a studio apartment in the Valley that doubles as a sauna. My first night, the bed, which doubles as the couch, suddenly starts vibrating. Earthquake?! No, Harley-Davidsons. The building is on Sepulveda, under the 405 off-ramp.

To relieve the heat and drown out the noise, I beg Lewis to keep the air conditioner on while we're sleeping. He says no. He's broke. And I'm in no position to contribute to the electric bill. I have no self-esteem and no green card, who can work? Exchanging sex for air conditioning doesn't occur to me, and Lewis doesn't seem to enjoy sex enough to spend money for it anyway.

The call to Ma and Daddy is sickening.

I shake and stammer and finally blurt out, "Ma, I'm not coming home. I'm living with an actor, and he's not Jewish."

The screaming on the other end streams like ticker tape. "But you have a job as da drama counselor at summer camp, you have a year more to get your degree, for dis I bought you a car, vhat do you mean you're living mit a *goy!*"

Ma tries crying. "Suzie, you said dat you vould never do to me vhat Sylvia did. You said you vould live in Montreal forever!" Yeah, I said that when Ma was crying after Sylvia moved to Akron. But, I can't go back to Daddy's disgust and Ma's needling.

"I'm sorry, I'm not coming home. I'm sorry."

They beg, I cry, they threaten, I cry, they demand, I hang up. Lewis goes next door to the liquor store. We get very drunk.

◆ ◆ ◆

Lewis and I audition and join The Laughing Stock Company. We perform skits at The Comedy Store and The Improv. I love/hate it; love getting the laughs, hate the pre-laugh terror.

◆ ◆ ◆

I apply for a job at The *International* House of Pancakes. After all, I'm Canadian. I use Lewis' Social Security number but don't want to use my real name. I come up with an alias. Something dramatic. I change the "s" to a "z." Suzan. They'll never catch me now.

I'm hired as hostess.

Platform shoes are *in*, if not ergonomically designed. I wear Herman Munster shoes. They cause clomping. The IHOP manager tells me to wear more sensible shoes. I pull a Herman and jump up and down with fists clenched, "I won't, I won't, I won't!" The manager doesn't understand. I *must* wear platforms. My ass is too close to the ground.

> *A tip: My background in art taught me—that the higher one's butt is from the floor, the thinner one appears.*

So I continue to stomp around the restaurant, ushering patrons to their tables, but that's not what gets me fired. Part of the job is working the cash register. I still use my fingers to add.

One night a customer stands at the counter, staring at me. He's given me a fifty and now he wants some of it back. *Six times nine! Nine times seven!* I start to cry. The pressure to hurry slows me to a stop. I stand in front of the open drawer of money, sweating and crying. This is before cash registers told you how much change to give back—they simply *register*.

A scene from *Sea Hunt* pops up on the two-inch-portable in my head; I recall it perfectly.

Lloyd Bridges is trapped underwater by kelp, his air is running out and his voice-over (which lets him have dialogue while diving) says, "The more I struggled, the more entangled I became!" Lloyd relaxes, and works his way free.

I need to do what Lloyd did, calm down, but my oxygen's run out. Just before my head blows up (like in *Scanners*), I give up and guess. I give the customer a ballpark amount of change. He looks at his hand, smiles and leaves.

"Suzan, I need to see you in private." Oh God, the principal's office. The manager had seen the *ex-change* and fires me. Just as well, I'd gotten in the habit of consoling myself after each shift by having the cook whip up a little dessert, a crepe really: a scoop of vanilla ice cream with chocolate sauce melted between two buttermilk pancakes, smothered with syrup. Which I'd have after my tuna melt.

So now I'm chubby and out of work. Lewis' grump grows.

At least I have more time to tan.

Another tip: The darker your thighs, the smaller they look.

She's Not the Queen of England?

I'm twenty-one—

One morning Lewis is out delivering pipes and I'm watching *The Philadelphia Story* on Channel 11. I call this comedy research. Actually since getting fired I can't seem to get myself to leave the couch.

The phone rings.

I clear my throat. "Hello" I say, trying to sound normal, like a responsible person and not a malingering bimbo.

"Hello, is Lewis home?" It's a *woman.*

"No, he's at work and I'm here so I can answer the phone. Can I take a message?"

"Yes," the woman says in an all-American accent, "please tell him his mother called."

"Oh—hi! I'm Suzan. I didn't know you were from the States. Is Lewis' *father* from England?"

"Excuse me?" She's confused.

"I mean, Lewis talks like he's still living in London."

"I'm sure I don't know what you mean. Lewis was born and raised in San Diego."

Which explains why, when I wake him up in the middle of the night, he sounds more like John Ritter than James Mason.

Macbeth comes home from work. I'm cooking stroganoff, his favorite of the Hamburger Helpers family of fine nourishment, and I've turned the air conditioner on *high.*

"'Ello, luv!" he says, coming through the door, surprised to feel the cool air.

"How was work?" I ask.

"Not too bad," he responds, still not knowing what to make of the air conditioning. "The traffic was a bit 'eavy all day."

"Yes," I say, trying to sound empathetic, "and it must be even harder for you, having to drive on the right side of the road." He shifts books on a shelf.

Stirring meat into the mix, I add, "Your mum called today."

"My . . . my . . . m-mother?"

"Yup." I talk. He fidgets.

"She rang you up all the way from *da Old Country*—La Jolla. I didn't know San Diego County was still part of the Commonwealth, *luv*!"

His shoulders drop along with the phony accent. "I've been meaning to tell you . . ." Maintaining the screwball sitcom plot couldn't have been easy.

So he's not British—

Actually he's an extreme right-wing Republican. He presents me with rules by which I have to live. Drinking is okay after 5:00 p.m., but *no* marijuana. I hate the taste of alcohol, so I force myself to drink at 5:00 p.m. Every day.

I don't go gently into that good night. I present my case. "Lewis, smoking a joint would make the Hamburger Helper taste better."

"Suzan, it's an illegal drug. I will not tolerate—"

"Lewis, are you aware most of the women who are murdered in the U.S. are shot by *loved ones*, and in the majority of those cases, the guy has been *drinking*. If he'd smoked pot, he'd have killed a *burger*."

"If the wife's a *JAP* that doesn't shut up, maybe she deserves what she gets." He's an idiot. I will straighten him out.

"Oh, *that's* an intellectual comeback. Did it take *all* your brain, or only the 6 percent you usually use?" And he punches me in the arm. I tip back and fall on the floor. Wow, I haven't been hit by a man since Daddy.

I'm down, but not out of the fight. "Lewis, I'm calling the cops."

"Maybe you should go back to Canada."

So I don't call anybody. But I have proven my point. If he'd been smoking pot, I'd be making popcorn and we'd be watching *The Waltons*.

But It's a Dry Heat

Thank God I still have a stash of hash—

I've saved it since Montreal in case of emergency. And, hidden behind the legal plants on the porch, is a petite pot plant, a scrimpy little thing but it has potential. I'm growing it for medicinal purposes. Without it, life would be too sickening; I have spasms. My neck clenches my shoulders to make sure my arms don't fall off.

Never has so much been expected of such a small shrub. It has two branches and twelve leaves—I have high hopes. But the weeks pass and because of over-farming the plant is down to a twig and one leaf. One sad leaf that shakes as I come near.

My Monday-through-Friday ritual is as follows: Wait till Lewis is out the door;, put on mascara until he's left the garage, go to the balcony to make sure the coast is clear. I sneak out on the porch and sheltered by bougainvillaea, pluck a tip off a leaf and run back into the apartment.

I sit legs crossed hippy-style on the floor, tenderly place the leaf in my pipe and suck in hard for twenty seconds. Then I hold the smoke in for another twenty. It's my only toke of the day—I must make it last.

Ahhh . . . I relax—probably because this is the first deep breath I've had since I woke up. There's enough marijuana to get high, if you weigh six pounds. The injection of *oxygen* into my blood-drained appendages—and the placebo effect—brings on the buzz.

I later find out that a *real* marijuana grower dries the plants by hanging them upside down in a dark closet for two weeks. Who had time to hang my leaf upside down?

If a Tidal Wave Comes, I'll Drive

I'm at the pool with my sketchbook.

Dennis, the guy who lives next door, asks to see my drawings. He's an interior designer who looks like Bill Bixby from *My Favorite Martian*. Then he asks if I'd like to work for him doing renderings. (That's the way to find work—find a pool stocked with TV executives!) Dennis assures me I will never have to count money, and I can wear any shoes I want.

Armando, Dennis' carpenter, is a tanned surfer with big white teeth and long yellow hair. He's surfed with the actual real-life *Gidget*. "Yeah, man, she was a short Jewish girl from Tarzana. Real cool." Sure, I know, Sally Field.

Armando has the best pot and is always happy to share a roach.

> *For the drug-illiterate: The roaches I'm talking about don't creep around the kitchen in the dark; they don't check into The Bates Bug Motel from which they don't check out. We potheads keep our roaches in a shoebox lid—and **we** check out. The roach—a "joint" smoked down to its end—is believed to be the most potent part. I want to believe that, especially if it's all I have. A roach clip is used to avoid burning fingers. Sometimes I use my fingernails. The tips on my right thumb and index finger are brown. Before I figured out why, I worried I had a disease. I do, but not the kind I think.*

Lewis hates Armando. But he likes Dennis, the capitalist.

Dennis and I are working alone in the shop late one night, smoking grass, when right in the middle of showing me a swatch, he grabs my shoulders and kisses me. The one straight designer in Los Angeles. I thank him profusely, but just because I'm a drug addict doesn't mean I'm loose. I do, however, appreciate the attention. Armando's never tried any funny business, and he's had plenty of opportunities.

Lewis gets a better job . . .

He travels the country inspiring car salesman with his motivational pitches. He's less inspirational at home. One night, after the news and before *Johnny*, Lewis and I are drinking and he punches me. I punch him back. We tussle till we're worn out. I fall asleep on the floor feeling bruised and confused. But the next morning, I figure out the problem. We need a bigger apartment. After all, even rats go nuts when they're crowded.

We move to Marina del Rey—the gold-chain-wearing, Porsche-driving, newly-divorced-man capital of the world.

Getting to work now means getting on the 405 Freeway—

I'm cruising along on my way to Dennis' workshop in Van Nuys, and a thought pops into my head—what if some poltergeist in me takes over and spazzes out my arms, and the steering wheel jerks and I find myself facing oncoming traffic. (I hadn't heard of a panic attack, I just thought it was part of the weirdo package.)

I get off the freeway and take surface streets back to the Marina.

I quit Dennis and set a no-drive policy. If I hear on the news that a tidal wave is heading toward the Marina, then I'll drive. East. It's a plan.

Mariners' Village is great for someone who doesn't drive. There's a video rental, grocery store, five pools, and a dry cleaners. (And what am I going to dry clean? My *good* shorts?) The main pool is where the action is, but gearing up to go there means attaining that not-made-up look, which takes hours.

Going to the pool from the apartment is hard. But not as hard as going to the pool from the chaise. The Earth's center tugs on my butt, making ripples. Direct overhead sunlight makes a little cellulite look like corn chowder.

I grope my bathing-suit bottoms when I think no one's watching. I don't know if underwear slippage is exclusive to my butt, but I'm forever discreetly yanking bottoms out of my bottom. I haven't learned the beauty pageant trick. When Miss America is strutting down the runway and her suit is staying put, it's because the thing's glued to her ass. *That's* magic tape.

Armando takes me to Malibu, he's surfing, I decide to take a dip . . .

I adjust my bikini, take another hit off a joint, and dash to the water so people can't see my thighs long enough to make judgments. Cellulite in motion. I know everyone's eyes are riveted on my corn chowder, *"Oy! Gib a kik! A grobeh tuches!"*

And they say landing at Normandy was stressful.

I stop dead at the shoreline. Waves.

This is my first time in the Pacific. I'd gone to the Caribbean on Christmas break when I lived in Montreal—met an airline pilot and a cruise director, don't ask—the ocean was flat. Easy entry. But waves? If I didn't *have* to get in to hide my thighs, the waves would be a deal breaker. Maybe I can bury myself in sand instead.

But then the waves stop. Oh good, the ocean has calmed down. I go in.

Okay, *brrr,* my toes froze, my arms are tired and my head keeps rerunning scenes from *Jaws.* Enough with the fun. I paddle back to shore, unaware of the wave following me. It crashes on my head. Gulp. I'm pushed underwater.

Must get head above water, must breathe. I scramble and my head pokes up above the surface; I'm about to breathe when—*crash!* Another wave hits and I'm thrust back down. I flap my arms and kick my legs and I'm up, spitting out water, about to inhale, when I see it. The wave that ate Alaska.

Shit! CRASH. I'm rolling and submersed. I'm determined to push up, high out of the water, and snatch a breath. With all my might, I kick, hands overhead, expecting to feel air. Instead I feel sand. I'm upside down. Up is down! I somersault and grab a moment on the surface. I see sunbathers on the beach. They have no idea a girl is drowning twenty yards from them. I can't call for help. I can barely catch a breath.

I turn my head to check if I have time to get any air in, when another monster wall of water plows me under, engulfing me again. I'm tossed into a spin. I'm going to drown, right *next* to people, and they're oblivious. They don't recognize how much I need their help. *Why does this seem familiar?*

NO! I refuse to die like this! The waves keep pushing me down, so that's where I'll stay, dammit. Down. Air? It's overrated. I grab rocks on the ocean floor to keep me from rolling, and I drag myself to shore.

I cough up ocean, and pass out. I come back to consciousness. My face is sand-embedded. I look at the wicked water, Armando is merrily surfing, clueless of my Poseidon adventure. My body stings. I look down. Blood. For once, my thighs are not my primary concern. I sliced the front of me open on the sharp rocks and salt water is entering the ripped skin. I hope nobody notices. They do. The once oblivious sunbathers are rushing to help. *A little late, aren't you?* I'm embarrassed. These wounds are my own fault; most of the people who drown are intoxicated.

◆ ◆ ◆

Armando sneaks over to the apartment when you-know-who is away. He's mellow, respectful, and kind enough to provide me with Thai sticks. He's the anti-Lewis.

The richer Lewis gets, the more he drinks; the more he drinks, the ornerier he gets. This makes me withdraw, and the more I pull away, the more possessive he grows. This push-pull relationship is familiar. "I want you, I need you." "What? You want me? Well, I don't want you that much. Besides, if you want me, what's wrong with you?"

The more I know about Lewis, the more frightened I get. The guy campaigned for Nixon, even though he thought Nixon leaned too much to the left. The joke's on Lewis. He's harboring, aiding, and abetting a drug-importing illegal alien, who's been working under the table. Lefty-loosey meets righty-tighty. If he ever runs for office, I'm calling the *Enquirer.*

How Does a Nice Jewish Girl
Get Busted at Disneyland for Possession?
Practice, Practice, Practice!

Sylvia sends my nieces out to visit; they're eight.

I have purpose. Pam, Shelley and I shop and play. I hear myself laughing again. We put bubble bath in the outdoor Jacuzzi and run screaming when bubbles overflow onto surrounding patios.

They want to go to Disneyland. Sure, *they* don't have to worry about *Thomas Guides,* missing exits, and sudden sideswiping. I put on my most comfortable platforms, pack Thai stick in child-size Tupperware, and we head to the Magic Kingdom. It's magical how they can lure so many people into one place on a Thursday.

The girls are spinning in bright-colored teacups when I sneak off behind some bushes with my portable pipe and light up. That's when Goofy—who I thought was a statue—busts me. He confiscates the Tupperware and when the girls' ride is over, escorts us to an office deep in the bowels of Disneyland. I sit in a hard chair as three park narcs, my age, grill me and paw through my belongings. When they find out I'm Canadian, they up the ante, threatening to have me deported. SEE! I *knew* it was bad to leave the house!

Snow White is sitting on a desk in the corner watching the inquisition and smoking a Marlboro. She's come a long way, baby. I'm given a lecture by Goofy, a kid with cystic acne and a badge. I swear to never do drugs at Disneyland again and I'm released. They keep the Tupperware. I'm so relieved they're not kicking me out of America, I don't argue.

I swear the girls to secrecy, "Lewis will get really angry if he finds out." None of us want Lewis any angrier. Desperate to cop a buzz, I make the girls ride the Matterhorn. Twice. Snow White's probably back in the bowels with my Thai, toking up with the pimply dwarves. As we plummet toward

Earth, I wonder if they can hear my long-awaited piercing scream far off in Never-Never (go-to-again) Land.

The next day, Lewis is jealous when I play with the girls . . .

"Suzan, get over here, sit next to me on the couch!" I cut the girls' stay short not wanting them overexposed to his Royal Assholiness. I drive my nieces to the airport, my heart in two pieces—one in the passenger seat, the other in the backseat. I pull in front of the terminal and start unpacking the trunk. Pam gets out of the car and slams the door shut, locking us out with the motor running in the white zone—which is for loading and unloading only.

I start screaming. "WHAT DID YOU DO!?" Not a question. I watch Pammie's scared little face go into pre-cry. Tears begin flowing from eyes the size of pies. Oh, God, what have I done!

I'm frantically kissing her chubby wet cheeks, "I'm sorry. It's okay, you didn't do anything wrong!" Subtext, "Don't leave! I'll die without you!"

Pam and Lana take off on time, thanks to a professional criminal—also parked in the white zone—who uses a tool to jimmy open the door.

Lewis is still at work when I return from LAX. I can't imagine being alone with him. Not sober at least. I must get a drink down before his angry posture comes in and deflates my core even more. But the rule—it's only 4:30. I look at the front door. Do I have time to get over to the wet bar, pour myself a drink, brush my teeth and get busy cooking before Lewis opens the door? No. I'll have to chug from the bottle.

At the bar, eyeing the door, I twist off the top of the Jack Daniel's, guzzle down the liquid medicine, and it hits me—*wow, if I ever play an alcoholic on stage, this will be how to do it; this is just like an alcoholic drinks!* Just like. I make a mental note to store the feelings so I can draw on them in the future.

Who *wouldn't* drink living here, I ask you? Not really a question.

I know the icky liquid sliding down my throat will soon be followed by a calm, everything-will-be-dandy feeling. Hurry! I cap the Jack, go gargle with Listerine, grab an apron, and rip open the Hamburger Helper with my teeth. Noodles fly.

I'm scooping my Helper off the floor and into the skillet when Lewis opens the door. Tying the apron behind my back, I'm Donna Reed! "Hi, honey, how was your day?"

It's five o'clock. I'm back to the bar, this time using glasses. Tumblers. I pour. We drink. I pour again. And again. And everything is dandy for several hours, until the pleasant alcohol buzz turns mean.

"Did you get the mail?" Fighting words. He knows I'm too scared to go to the mailboxes.

"Uh, no, I didn't . . . have time."

His face is inches from mine, "Why? What the hell do you do all day?"

"Stuff."

"What stuff? Watching *Geraldo*?"

"*Geraldo* happens to be informative. And he's half Jewish." Lewis throws me a dirty look.

Hating myself for defending Geraldo, hating Lewis for not understanding what I can't explain, I slap his shoulder. The next thing I see is his fist coming in for my close-up. Crunch. I'm on the floor. Chevy Chase didn't fall down this much. The left side of my head throbs.

I jump up and start kicking like a Bond chick. Then I run for the bathroom. Like in Cote Saint Luc, the only door with a lock.

He's banging against the door, "You better open up!" The door shakes with each BANG! I'm in the corner on the floor, whimpering, wondering how I can kill him and get away with it. I can kill him, I just can't *leave* him.

It turns quiet. Is he out there? I look under the door. No feet. But I'm not going to fall into his trap. I can sleep in the bathtub. Damn, it's cold! I grab a towel for a blankie, another for a pillow. Still cold. I think of Ma in the forest. At least I'll be alive in the morning.

Why the hell am I with this guy? If I stop drinking, I could start thinking. But thinking causes drinking. See the problem? Anyone can avoid taking the obvious steps for *years* if they have help from Seagram's, cable TV and Frito-Lay.

◆ ◆ ◆

I heard Carol Burnett say, "You can't get on TV by *watching* it." How depressing.

I need Mary Tyler Moore. She's never irritated with me. Lou Grant doesn't say I'm too sensitive. And Rhoda makes me feel better about my thighs. Murray doesn't tell me I should get married, he just picks on Ted. I relate to Ted, a puffed-up, pompous fool, a fool only the sweet, kind Georgette can love. What's *her* story?

The people on TV are my friends, my family, my quiet family. They're so pretty. And they visit each other all the time. Phones are used only to say, "I'm coming over." (Scenes work better face to face.)

◆ ◆ ◆

One morning I wake up to find nothing on the screen but snow. In withdrawal, I scream at customer service (service?), "What the hell do you mean you'll come out Thursday between eight and five?! Do you expect me to stay home, waiting all day?!" I'm agoraphobic, where do I think I'm going?

Finally, on Thursday, the doorbell rings. A large man wearing a tool belt announces in a Southern drawl, "Cable repair."

My eyes drop in a Southern coyness, "Enchanted, I'm sure."

I notice, on the mat at cable-man's size fourteen feet, a thing lying on its back. It's moving its arms and legs. It's pinkish. It looks like a . . . skinny fetus . . . with the head of a big-beaked prehistoric bird. It's got claws. And they're snapping. It's squirming on its slimy bug back, waving its curly arms and legs, twisting its bird head. Like Regan in *The Exorcist*. It's looking up at me. Is it *squealing*?

Do I call the CDC? NASA? I'm thinking Roswell.

"That there's a potato bug," drawls the cable-man-botanist. "We got 'em back on the farm."

This should be taught in school: "Class, here's a photo of Earth's ugliest creature. Should you ever encounter one, do not be alarmed. And class—you are bigger than this bug."

Again, an Exodus

One guilt-filled month after Omar at the pool —

Ma said one day Lewis would call me a "Jew" and not as a compliment. She was right—even a stopped clock is right twice a day. The day comes. He calls me *Jew* as he's punching me in the face. He loosens a front tooth. This is serious. We're talking about my *looks*. I may need them later.

I call her. "Ma, can you come to L.A.? I'm leaving the *goy*." For a weekend trip to the Catskills, Ma takes two weeks to pack. To help me move out of *da goyfriend's* apartment, she's at Dorval airport in an hour. And she pays full fare.

I bring her home to the Marina and Lewis is pissed. She's telling him how lucky he is to have a girl like me.

"Back off, you meddling old Jew!" is his response.

"Hitler! *Oy!* You're a *Hitler!*" Lewis seems flattered.

Lewis goes to Oklahoma knowing nothing of my plot to escape. I find an apartment in Venice and go from Mariners' Village to Windward Village. *Shtetl* living may be genetic. I'm moved out by the time Lewis gets home.

The Venice Village . . .

Ma and I are unpacking, the TV's turned to *Wheel of Fortune*. "Hanala, you should go on dis show, you know all da answers!"

Suddenly BOOM, BOOM, BOOM. There's a banging on the door. I know Lewis' bang.

"Let me in, I know you're in there." He's been drinking.

Ma yells, "Don't let dat Nazi in!"

"Don't worry, Ma." But I am worried. He's raising a ruckus, and I'm afraid the neighbors will call the cops.

I open the door when I see the LAPD badge through the peephole. Lewis tells the police I'm in the U.S. illegally. I freak out. I'll be deported!

A nice Joe Friday says, "That's not our department, Sir."

The officers escort Lewis out of the building. I peek from behind the curtain and watch as Lewis gets in his car. I'm surprised the cops let him drive. Maybe the experience sobered him up. He drives off. And that's the end of Lewis.

Ma and I return to the TV, which had been muted, but not turned off.

Ahhh . . . *Knot's Landing* . . . I open the cornflakes box filled with Ma's homemade almond cookies. There now . . . there now . . .

Six Cheeses of Separation

We're at Ralphs Market when Ma's bladder attacks!

We're rushing down the cold-cut and cottage cheese aisle trying to find the bathroom, when Ma almost bumps into an old man. Permanently bent, he's even shorter than she is.

She says,"*Oy gevalt*, it's Ralph!"

"Yeah, Ma, this is Ralphs."

"No. It's Ralph, from da forest!" she says, pointing at the strange little man.

Opening his arms he says, "M-M-Mania . . . Mania! Is dat you?"

Wow, he sounds like Ma. He starts to cry, "MANIA!"

"I can't talk now!" she says, and dashes off.

"Uh, my mother had to go to the bathroom."

The little man is explaining how Ma sewed underwear for his wife, Ann, from an old shirt in *da forest,* when a relieved Ma returns. The two embrace. We go out for a glass of tea, and they spend hours reminiscing about the good old days, sleeping ten to a hole with Germans stomping overhead.

Ralph says, "First vee came to New York, but Mania, I didn't survive Nazis to freeze my *tuches* off! Too bad you and Fishel didn't come mit me to California. I bought buildings cheap in da 1950s; I have many now. I vant to take you around to see dem." This overripe midget is a multimillionaire.

"I have two sons and a daughter—not one of dem *any* good. I don't talk to dem." His lips curve down in the corners, like he's been angry since the war. And of Ann, his wife, "Ach, I had enough from her a'ready! Da head stopped vorking, she remembers nuting. She's no vife to me! Da doctors say it's *old-timers.*" If I were his wife, I'd want to forget, too.

A week later Ma leaves for Montreal. I sit on my single bed, in my single room in Venice, one block from the beach. Ma gave me $2,000! I have to make it stretch. I light a joint, take a deep toke and the words ring in my head: "Free! Free! Free at last."

Suzan, Coke—Coke, Suzan,
It Was Love at First Snort

Three months later—

Money's thin, I'm fat—L.A.'s definition of a loser. I've got to find a new job; I'm quitting the one I have; it isn't satisfying. (If you bought Arrid Extra Dry roll-on deodorant in 1978, *I* may have placed it in the box.) Working on an assembly line isn't as exciting as Lucy made it seem.

The job before that was handing out free disposable razors to shoppers as they entered the supermarket. They acted like I was attacking them, which did nothing for my social phobia.

The longest job I kept was getting hung up on by people who didn't care about saving money on long distance. I was in a florescent office with fifty cubicles and a manager who conducted sales meetings from behind his desk. We suspected he didn't have pants on, but nobody wanted to check. At the end of each day, the sales force would gather in his office where he'd pull a bottle of gin out of a drawer—like Lou Grant.

And now, I'm going to see if The May Company will hire me to shpritz perfume on women as they try to get through the makeup department. I'm allergic to perfume, but the job doesn't require working a cash register.

Tuck, tease, and camouflage, it's been a morning of primping. I finally make it to the elevator, a problem area—what if someone's there?

Elevator doors open and, I could *plutz*. Sunglasses, messy hair, and a leather jacket in the middle of August—I've seen him in the parking lot, getting into his Porsche. The tag on the bumper says, "Capitol Records, Executive Parking."

Just the previous week—

I finally get it together enough to get to the mailboxes. Two teenage girls, four thin thighs, are picking up their mail. They're in dental floss bikinis. I'm in a mumu. I check them for cellulite. One has a little; I'm happy.

Thin and Thinner are giggling and opening mail. I don't giggle when opening mail; I prepare to experience catastrophe. They gossip about Bruce, the hot music producer who lives in the penthouse. I'm not even a music wannabe, and I wonder if he can help me break into the biz. His is not *my* biz, and yet, you never know who knows who.

And—here he is . . .

The big shot who lives upstairs is holding the elevator door for me. Betty and Veronica were right—he's hot.

I want to say, "Oh! I just remembered, I forgot something, keep going down to your Porsche." But it's too late. My high-heel flip-flops have started walking forward.

Doors close. We both look up and do the *don't-talk-to-me-I'm-in-an-elevator* posture.

The words spring out of my mouth, "My! Those floor numbers are riveting!"

He laughs. Victory! He asks me out, which means *in* for Quaaludes and sex.

I never make it to the job interview.

The next morning, new boyfriend Bruce suggests, "Let's go to Vegas for the weekend." The Paris police car alarm sounds off in my head and the committee calls a meeting. Caution cautions, "Wait! See who Bruce *is*—not who you *want* him to be." The adventurer interrupts, "We've never been to Vegas! Never flown first class!" A *pisher* from the back demands, "So, is he Jewish? Did you even look?" The backup singers drown everybody out with choruses of "If They Could See Me Now" and "We're Movin' on Up!"

Las Vegas is the Catskills with slot machines, and fewer Jews.

The Strip's like a Christmas tree with a broader range of colors and no Jesus paraphernalia.

Bruce gets a suite comped at Caesar's. Our luggage is whisked away by little men in little caps, and we hit the casino. Bruce gets me a bucket of money and stows me at a slot machine. My loot's gone in ten minutes. So is Bruce.

I'm Shirley Temple, the lost waif roaming battlegrounds in search of her Daddy. I make my way through lounge acts, polyestered Americans, and cocktail waitresses in Bunny outfits altered to look like togas. I'm in awe of the wrinkly women, cigarettes dangling from thin red lips, feeding coins into two slot machines at once. They scare me with their I-mean-business looks. Did Bruce leave me here forever? Will I become one of them? Has Bruce become a victim of foul play? What should I do? Report him missing? Go to the police? And what is keno?

The bells, lights, and free vodka get me dizzy. Hours later, starved and defeated, I retreat to our room. I stand at the floor-to-ceiling windows, mesmerized by the lights below. Is he down there somewhere? I'm halfway delirious when Bruce walks in. He seems surprised I'm still around. He mumbles about a private blackjack room, but I know it's just filler; something else is on his mind. Plunking down on an orange velour settee, he looks at his lap.

I look at his lap.

"Here's the thing," he says. Oh God, there's a thing! These things never work in my favor. I've learned to hate *things*. "You're a nice girl, but . . ." Oh no! This is going to be worse than I thought. I've learned that when *but* follows a compliment, whatever's after the *but* reduces the compliment into a condescending, humiliating shit pile.

Psychologists call this "fragmenting." A bomb explodes in your face, and POW! Only bits of you are left standing; well, leaning. Your adult words have been blasted far away, and you do your best not to say something too unbelievably stupid. Later

*your bits come back and you think of what you should have
said . . . things you'd have said if your good brain bits hadn't
sped off to Easter Island.*

I brace for the tidal wave. Will what comes after, "nice girl but . . ." blow
me to smithereens? I've been blown there, and it's a rotten place. Hurry up,
Bruce, get the assassination over with, I have a depression waiting. I need to
start eating so I can be a size sixteen by summer.

Time slows as his words drip like hot tar in through my ear canal and
down into my belly, "I like *skinny* girls. It's not like you're *fat,* it's just that I
like women who are, uh, skinny . . . like super-model skinny." If he says
skinny one more time, I'm going to raise my pudgy arm and slam him with it.
But what am I so mad about? He's right. In America, if you're not skinny, you're
fat. I'm a *zaftig shlub* off the boat. How can I blame Bruce for ditching me when
he can easily rent an anorexic in the lobby?

He puts a plane ticket on the bed with some cash. I'm too wobbly to get
up and leave. I haven't eaten all day. I remember the $7.99 all-you-can-eat
trough downstairs.

"Can I stay just a little longer . . . to eat?"

Bruce pulls a vial of white powder out of his pants pocket. "Here. Take
this." I examine it. Mmm . . . pretty powder.

"Baby, don't tell me you haven't done coke before." Coke? Drink, yes; *do,*
no.

Oh, Vanna, let's show Suzan what she's won! Bruce scoops out some
powder with a tiny silver spoon, squeezes one of my nostrils and tells me
to sniff in hard with the other. (The last time a man told me to sniff a drug,
I had a God-like experience in my pants, *in where my pants would have
been.*) My nose burns for a moment and then—I'm electrified. I have an
urge to go vacuum the casino.

Everything's sharper, cleaner, brighter. Is this Ajax? And, the funniest
thing, I'm not hungry anymore. I don't ever need to eat again. Bruce tells
me to keep the bottle—and the spoon!

The good thing about being dumped by rich guys? Lovely parting gifts.

I vow to never date men from the building again.

I force myself to go for a walk on the beach. Two minutes from my apartment is a big boxing ring on the sand filled with weights and Nautilus equipment. It's called Muscle Beach.

So here I am, watching the weight-lifting weirdos in their natural habitat when a bronzed, blonde, six-foot-tall bodybuilder approaches.

He sits. "I've never seen you here."

"No, my TV cord doesn't reach this far."

"You mean, you watch a lot of television?"

"Yes. I like to watch." Muscleman doesn't get the Chauncy Gardener reference. What he lacks in Hollywood trivia he makes up for in warmth. In one hour I tell him more about me than I told Lewis in the year and a half we lived together. This man who looks like Adonis makes me an offer. He'll help me become fit. Why? He needs a cause. The case of the steroid case and the charity case? Or does he want sex? And would that be so awful? Whatever the motive, I become his mission.

I've committed to work with him every day no matter how scared I am. I *have* to show up; there's no phone on the beach; I can't call to cancel. Adonis buys me books by Dale Carnegie and Earl Nightingale. "What the mind can conceive, and believe, it can achieve." I want to believe. He introduces me to the world of dark green lettuces. And to his oiled friends in the playpen.

Turns out Adonis is a celebrity in the world of muscles. Everyone knows him. I feel like I belong. (As much as I can, being the only lard bucket in a land of lean.) The regulars work out in bathing suits. I'm in a long pair of shorts and loose fitting T-shirt. A month into my mind/muscle/menu makeover, I'm sore all over, but feeling hopeful.

After a few months my body shows the visible signs of aching. I'm creating lean muscle mass. I invite Adonis to my place for a thank you dinner. He sits on my couch/bed explaining the concept of higher self. I'm confused. There's more than *one* self? I'd be happy having *one*.

I finish my third glass of wine. He's hardly touched his first. How do people do that? I sit on the floor, watching as he reads passages from *How to Win Friends and Influence People*, wondering if he's a natural blonde. I'm glad he's reading even though I'm not listening. I bet I can influence my friend without having read that book. I pour more wine, organic, of course, and ask him if he ever smokes pot. No, he hasn't. Oh good! I can teach *him* something. I want to give back.

I show him how to inhale. He doesn't hear ants marching, but the platinum locks on his forehead relax. The more we inhale, the messier his hair gets and the better he looks. I don't know if he's as lonely as I feel, but we stretch out to each other. We work new muscle groups. Then, it's over.

I still don't know if he's a natural blonde—Adonis had me keep the lights off. Why I don't know, he's practically naked on the beach. Is his pecker purple? Oh well, it worked fine. With sexual tension out of the way, we resume our platonic buddy system.

Along Comes Arnold

To tell the Arnold story, I have to begin with Neil.

Ma's bugging me every day from Montreal, "Call Ralph! He has *two sons*! Vhat are you vaiting for?" The next *Dallas* episode.

Adonis is a day gig, and I have lonely nights. A bad bout of void persuades me to call the sons. Neil, the older, is a student and a nice guy. Henry, the younger, raises lizards. He poses them in professional outfits, takes pictures and turns them into postcards and calendars. I pick the son without lizards.

There are two types of guys: chocolate men or broccoli boys. I've had the chocolate man, who's left me with zits and a cavity, one I filled with another chocolate man. I figure it's time for a broccoli boy. The worst he can do is give me gas. Neil is broccoli; steamed, no butter. We date for a few months.

One night we're in bed at my place, and again I find myself trying to get a guy to smoke dope. Poor Neil, he coughs and gives up.

I take a hit and turn to him. "So, Neil, do you know anyone interesting to fix me up with?" Apparently, I'm a sensitive person only when *my* feelings are concerned.

And perhaps for revenge, Neil introduces me to Arnold—

Arnold is two hours late for our first date. I'm about to burst into flames. I prepared all afternoon! Every zit is hidden—I used spackle. Every eyelash is sculpted in Maybelline tar.

The bell finally rings. I open the door, but I'm not letting the hoodlum in. He can't do this to me! (Sure he can. He ends up doing much worse.)

A Jewish elf stands looking apologetic. "Wow, you're beautiful. I mean, in a pretty kind of way. The good-looking beautiful, not the unattractive kind." I forgive him.

Arnold has a big nose, tinted prescription aviator glasses, curly black hair and beard, and is five-foot-five, but he meets my three top prerequisites. He's funny, complimentary, and comes with drugs.

He whips out a vial of cocaine. "Had to stop at the dealer's."

"Where does your dealer live, Colombia?"

"Worse, the Valley." I understand. I show him to the couch.

Arnold is Arnold, never Arn. We have a lot in common. We love old movies, pizza, and Quaaludes. Quaaludes: God's gift to the nervous and insecure. He has the little-boy quality that makes me melt, and he's *smart*. He teaches me that pills work faster on an empty stomach. So instead of heading out to Hamburger Hamlet, we pop a 'lude each and line up some coke. Half-a-gram later, I'm in love. A week later, I move into his high-rise in Brentwood.

Another thing we've got in common: Arnold's had a lifelong fat fight. Cocaine conquers food obsessing. We're living on coke, pills, pot and Jim Beam, and the occasional pizza from Pizza Man (he delivers).

Arnold and I couldn't eat if we wanted to. No clean dishes. It's been months since I've seen the sink. "I'll wash this later." Later turns into never. The man of my dreams is supposed to come with the *maid* of my dreams. It's too dirty to have a maid come. I'd be ashamed. Besides, I have no right to ask for a maid. Not contributing in a financial way, I really should be contributing in a Windex way. But, the laundry sits in borrowed supermarket shopping carts. Every three months I wash the sheets. I'm a homeless person who has an apartment. Arnold has a resentment. He wants me to work.

But how can I? My wardrobe is two pairs of shorts, my good pair and my everyday pair, which I hand wash once a week. Or so. I have a bra. Five bathing suits. Two sundresses, bikini bottoms serve as underwear. I have a sweatshirt, black jeans, and a jacket. My terry robe doubles as a beach coverup. And my platform shoes. My entire wardrobe fits in a carry-on.

None of my fat clothes fit anymore. I'm ninety pounds. I now wear a size zero. Size one on a fat day.

Thanks to my snort-and-starve diet, I have the bony *shiksa* butt of my dreams. I decide to get me a portfolio, an agent, and do them TV commercials. I book a photo shoot using the last of the money Ma gave me before she left.

I buy a "who's casting in Hollywood" book, make appointments, and even though I actually show up to half the appointments, *who* is casting me in nothing. I can't get an agent. I can only get more coke from Arnold.

My skinny neck barely supports the weight of my skull, and I wonder, "What the hell is wrong with these agents?" (Nothing, it's just that this is twenty years before *Ally McBeal* and heroin chic. Twiggy is thin for the seventies; these days, she's average sitcom-star weight. So while I think I look hot, agents think I looked like *E.T.*)

I'm persistent. I sign with an agent in Hollywood, a Vegas sort, in his fifties. Dick Clark hair, Groucho glasses, and a diamond watch the size of a clock. He's in an old building, four flights up, no elevator, it's 98° in his office. I need cooler clothes.

I phone home, "Ma, can you send my birthday check early?" Arnold doesn't share his money. He barely shares his Quaaludes. The only clothes he's bought me are T-shirts with slogans, like "Hang in there, Baby." Hanging in there is getting harder. Arnold's rapier wit cuts and hurts me like a sharp rusty knife. But I can handle it.

❖ ❖ ❖

One day Ma says, "I'll come for a visit, I vant to see how you live." No she doesn't.

Arnold is like Arnold Ziffle, the pig on *Green Acres*. We're two pigs in a pod. I need to clean the apartment before Ma comes. I could clean faster if I had some black beauties. But they'd make me too speedy, I'd need a Valium. The Valium would make me tired. I'd have to do some coke. And then I'd need a Quaalude to take the edge off the coke. Just thinking about the drugs required is overwhelming. So I put down the sponge and pick up the remote control. I'll clean up later.

At LAX . . .

Rosy-cheeked little Ma waddles happily from the jetway but when she sees me, the rose drains from her face. Huh? Crying usually happens only during drop-off, not pickup! She hasn't visited since I became a full-time cocaine addict.

"*Oy a broch!* You look like da people vhen dey came out from Auschwitz!" I take it as a compliment.

Ma takes an immediate dislike to Arnold. "*Feh!* Ug-a-ly!" And she doesn't like how sarcastic and hostile he is to me. Ma likes his business partners better. Gary and Pete. "Dey're nice, you couldn't take one of dem?"

Two weeks fly by like twelve. Ma leaves. There's no crying.

Pete—the Kind of Guy
Who'd Give You His Last Quaalude

Arnold has a small advertising business that he started with Gary and Pete, his friends since junior high. Gary doesn't do drugs. His high is watching others do them. He throws wild parties. The guests get naked, not all of them, but those who do, are invited back. Gary is ring leader of *Cirque du Seventies*. He knows alternative people, like from the music business. He probably knows them because he's Bob Dylan's road manager. When he's not on the road with Dylan, he's at the office with Arnold and Pete.

Gary's parents are also Polish Holocaust survivors. And, like me, he has a short attention span. Three seconds. In mid-sentence his eyes drift to someone he'd rather be talking to. I try talking to him, but my words aren't getting in. And they're sure not landing anywhere. Reminiscent of childhood.

Pete, the other partner, speaks rapidly, like you'll go away before he can finish. I think he talks *a lot*, till I meet Pete's father. Mr. Babble-on. His words build a wall around him; feelings don't get in or out.

Poor Pete. His mother just died of breast cancer. His girlfriend cheats on him with other men—and women. And he's losing his hair. He has a cherub face and reminds me of the Gerber baby. He does a hundred push-ups a day. His chest and shoulders are wide. A girl could rest her head on them comfortably. And he has a good ass. Especially in jeans.

I like Pete. Even though his girlfriend cheated on him, he has never cheated on her.

When Pete was over one night, and Arnold was in the bathroom—where he spends hours—Pete said, "I'm sorry Arnold is so awful to you." I didn't know what he meant. Arnold insults me, orders me around, and won't buy me anything more than a T-shirt, but he pays the rent. I did like Pete saying that, though.

◆　◆　◆

Arnold wakes me early one morning (10:00 a.m.), saying, "Get up, Pete's leaving Nicole, we're going to move him out of his apartment."

I'm upset when the move is over, and I have to leave with Arnold. Sweet Pete could use company, and I could use Pete.

Arnold is getting the car. I linger. Pete reaches into a drawer in his night stand, pulls out a sock, unrolls it and a few Quaaludes fall onto the bed.

"Here," he says, "have a couple." He asks for nothing in return, just to make my afternoon with Arnold a bit more pleasant. What a nice guy!

I decide Pete needs a girlfriend. I suggest to Arnold that Pete might like Roxanne, the coke-whore from next door. She's a part-time stylist for TV, and has pink hair and is a dancing machine. She and I play when Arnold's away.

Arnold and I have Pete and Roxanne over for pizza. And whatever. Mostly whatever. Six days later, the four of us are driving, in two cars, to the Grand Canyon, escaping from Roxanne's ex who shows up at the building with one big shotgun. Pete and Rox escaped out the garage while Arnold and I distracted the ex.

Going eighty miles an hour, we're passing Quaaludes and a bottle of Jack Daniel's between the Alfa Romeo and the Camaro. We finally get to the Grand Canyon, and when we do, we all throw up in it.

God Help Is Hard to Find

A year goes by, I'm still with Arnold, and dealing with a dreaded passing-out disease.

Whenever I get up from the couch, a tingly dizziness comes on, everything goes black. I teeter. I'm usually able to stay on my feet. If I do fall, I'm on the floor for only a minute. I get up and continue on to wherever I'm going. I don't think much of it.

Armando comes by to take me to Malibu. We sit on the couch to smoke a bongful first. I'm up and on my way to the bathroom when the dizzy hits, all goes black, and I fall down in the hallway. My ability to focus returns, and I see big toes in flip-flops in my face. Like Ma in the forest, only the feet in her story had shiny black boots.

Armando's staring down at me. "Man, are you all right?!"

"It's okay," I say, getting up. "I have low blood pressure."

He says, "Girl, that's not normal!" It isn't? Before I can say *cowabunga*, Armando is rushing me to UCLA hospital. Cool, that's where *Medical Center* was shot! A bunch of blood is taken and then a doctor, using Chad Everett's serious-scene-face, says, "Your bloodwork indicates that you are suffering from malnutrition."

I say, "That's impossible. I live in Brentwood!"

"Yes, well, you have a liver panel that says you're in the early stages of liver disease."

"Liver disease? That's something Dean Martin has, not me, I'm twenty-three years old!" Poor Ma, I'm gonna die *before* she does. That's gonna kill her. Bummer. I get scared straight. Until I get home. Armando drops me off with a baggie of pot, some food, and twenty bucks. "Here, man, get to the grocery store, buy some fruit!"

Must get to bong. Must not think. I'll have the remote control in my hand in a minute. Hang on, sing a song, don't think! Hang in there, baby.

But *Three's Company* and Thai stick don't drown out the images. *Liver disease*? I can't get the scene of Ma at my grave out of my head. I need a more serious chemistry formulation.

I call Dealer Danny in the Valley; Arnold and I get good stuff from him. "Do you have any *real* 'ludes, not boots?" Yes, he does. I can get two for my twenty.

I take a hit of pot for the 405. Drugs help me merge. I don't know why I worry about liver meltdown when driving under the influence is more likely to kill me first.

I walk through the door of Danny's darkened apartment, telling him I must pop a 'lude immediately. He's holding an envelope. *The* envelope. Good things come in these envelopes. I follow him through the living room—blinds are drawn, how seedy—and I'm thinking, "Where's he going? Why doesn't he take a pill out *now*?" He takes me to the kitchen. A kitchen with crud in corners and avocado-colored appliances in need of Ajax. But who am I to talk. Anyway, my focus is really on the envelope. I look at it anxiously.

Danny smiles, opens it, and hands me a white pill that will make all anxiety disappear. "You want vodka with that?" I nod.

The next thing I know, it's night . . .

I've left Danny's and have absolutely no memory of the hours that passed. I think maybe we had sex. I'll go home and check.

It's so dark out I can't see, which wouldn't bother me so much but I think I'm driving. And I think I'm on the freeway because I see a green sign passing fast that reads *Mulholland Drive*. And then everything goes black. My eyes are open, I'm aware of traffic around me and the steering wheel in my hands. I know I'm moving fast, but I can't see! Is *this* what they mean by *blind drunk*? For a second I see the lane lines, curvy and blurred. I can see cars whiz by and then everything goes dark again. Horns are blowing, I get patches of vision, streaks of lights.

"God, get me to the off-ramp safely and I swear I'll never have another drink again as long as I live!" Why am I in the left lane? I put on my flasher . . . or the wipers . . . whatever, and turn the steering wheel to the right. Bump-bada-bump. Good, an indication I'm one lane over. Out of the blackness I make out the words *Sunset Boulevard*. "Oh, hurry, God, please, please get me over before I miss the exit and have to drive to Wilshire. I can't cope with Westwood right now!"

And with that plea, my vision returns. Whew. I make the exit and say, "Thank you, God." As I pull on to Sunset, "That's right, God, I've learned my lesson. No more hard liquor for me! Wine only, from now on." I approach Barrington, "Just wine, and a little grass, God. Maybe a few lines on weekends to keep my weight down, but I've learned my lesson on how *not* to drive."

Approaching an intersection, I think, "Well, that light hasn't been red *that* long, and I really need to get home." I floor it and BOOM! I'm hit on both sides by cars. I'm too wasted to hang around for the cops; I speed off to the sound of angry yelling. Heart pounding, I pull into my driveway, turn off the motor and sit shaking. I've left the scene of a crime.

I get upstairs, plop on the couch, the platform wedgies fall off and I say, "Arnold, pass the vial. I just had a drive home—don't ask!" Then I go into the bathroom to check for telltail signs of sex.

Oh goody, more to feel guilty about. The guiltier I feel, the more drugs I use. The more drugs, the guiltier . . . .

I didn't drink to have a good time, I drank to stop having a terrible one.

When sober, I think of ways to take care of others. Drunk, I get in the driver's seat in danger of annihilating others. Am I against drunk driving? Yes! Do I drive drunk? Well, I can't drive sober. It's too scary. Fortunately my periodic agoraphobia limits my opportunities to run people down.

Using the pizza money Arnold gives me, I drive to Dealer Dan's twice a week and buy my stuff. Sometimes I go without money, but I leave with pot, pills, and cocaine anyhow. Normally, I can remember the drive *to* Dealer Dan, but not the drive back home. I know I drive back because the car is always in the carport, straddled diagonally across two spaces maybe, but it's in the carport.

Other than to purchase chemicals, I don't leave the house much anymore. There's really no point in going out. I'll be dead soon. Might as well watch TV until it's over. Poor Ma. I'm sorry to make you bury me.

The other reason I drive—

Arnold has a son. Mikey, like the kid in the commercial who'll eat anything, except *this* Mikey won't eat *anything* and I'm petrified that he'll starve to death on my watch.

Ex-wife, 180-pound Mona, kicked Arnold out when Mikey was two and Arnold gets visitation every other weekend. A lot of times Arnold forfeits his turn so he can be free to do—whatever.

I do the picking up of Mikey on Fridays. Encino. *Oy,* the Valley again. I schedule my drugs around the drive. I need to be sober enough to drive, yet, I need to anaesthetize before seeing Big Mona. The first time I met Mona I was on a 'lude, but other than a slurring, laid-back Dean Martin quality, I don't think she could tell.

She smiled, "How *cute,* Arnold. Suzan reminds me of *me!*"

"Not even on a thin day, you fat bitch," is what I want to say, but I'm not gonna mess with Big Mona, *BM* as I like to call her. At 180 pounds, she can sit on me and break me. So I take a few tokes to gear up for the drive—but I don't drink. It's my new civic duty.

Four-year-old Mikey likes Legos and hates me. I take this personally. The rotten kid should like me, I'm nice to him goddamn it! But I realize he just wants his dad to himself. I feel sorry for him.

One Saturday Arnold is passed out on the couch. The little tyke tries to wake him. Arnold has taken Tuenols (horse tranquilizers). Arnold looks dead. The frantic four-year-old shakes his daddy, pounds on him, he becomes hysterical. Arnold doesn't stir.

I try to reassure him, "Your daddy's okay, he's just *very* tired." I cook his favorite meal, cocktail hot dogs wrapped in Wonder Bread. He won't eat. He keeps crying and screaming. I don't know what to do. It's the night with the kitten all over again.

Mikey is over thirty now. I hope he's found a good shrink.

Ten Quaaludes a Dance

Arnold wants me to get a job.

He says, "I'll have more respect for you." Good, because he couldn't have less.

Me work? Yikes! I can't pull the "but-I-don't-have-a-green-card" excuse, because I got one. (Sylvia became a U.S. citizen and petitioned for me to get permanent alien status.) Then, I see the ad in the paper—GIRLS WANTED! Make EASY money dancing. I'm a girl. I can dance.

The dance hall is downtown. *Down* town as in *low*. I get a flat fee per man, per dance, plus tips. The idea is to make the men buy drinks. But the manager/head derelict tells me that *I'm* not allowed any drinks. Luckily, he doesn't mention Quaaludes. The money's meager, and there's nothing EASY about any of it. I have one clear thought and it's in Cockney, "I'm a good girl, I am!"

I don't see the supposed job-related respect exactly flying out Arnold's mouth. He's getting more selfish, hoarding coke and Quaaludes. He stashes them, and when I ask for some coke or a 'lude, he says he's out, but then is mysteriously wasted later on. After a week of dancing downtown—more like peeling probing paws off my torso—I quit.

Arnold announces he needs "space" and drops me off at a hotel. I formulate great plans. This event will force me to get out to pursue my career. Unfortunately, I can't get out the hotel room door. If it weren't for room service and Armando, who sleeps on the floor next to the bed now and then, I'd starve.

"Space" is never empty. When people tell their lovers they want "space," you'd better believe it's because they're ready to put something or someone in it. Arnold's "space" would be filled with drugs. Maybe he figured it would be cheaper to put me in a hotel than share his drugs with me. Or maybe it's something else . . .

Arnold calls after two weeks, slurring something about not knowing how much he loved me until now. Flexing my new position of power, I insist he marry me. I'm twenty-four. The engagement is announced. Good. My agenda had been: be married by twenty-five.

Two weeks before the wedding . . .

The invitations have gone out, presents have come in, caterers are paid, I have the princess dress, and Arnold says, "Suzan, we have to go see the rabbi." As much as I like Rabbi Freehling, I don't want to go see him.

So we are in the rabbi's study. He looks at me, then at Arnold, and says, "Tell her, Arnold."

The Sunday-night-and-I-haven't-done-my-homework-yet dread hits. "Please *don't* tell me, Arnold. I don't want to know. Please don't tell me."

But Arnold tells me. "Mona wants to give it another try." I'd been wondering who Arnold was talking to when he'd take the phone into the bathroom for hours.

We're in the car going home, and Arnold says, "You can take a couple of weeks to move out." No bank account, no credit cards, no income, and now no home. An agoraphobic who can't go home.

Arnold needs to take the edge off. He lights a joint. The car in front of us stops. Arnold doesn't. I see what's coming. And I realize that I don't have my seat belt on.

Crash! Crack! Holy shit, Batman! My head smashes the windshield of the Alfa. Two months later, while undergoing treatment for injuries sustained in the accident, I marry my chiropractor.

How to Marry a Chiropractor

But before I explain, let me explain.

I stay at Roxanne's while recovering from the jolt of being jilted and thrown through glass. We're lighting up when Roxanne announces, "I'm having my first homosexual experience!" She tells me all about it, and at 3:00 a.m. says I can bunk with her in the queen-size bed or take the couch. I choose couch.

Roxanne still likes men, especially ones with cocaine, and she brings them home at 2:00 a.m. after the clubs close every night. She clubs, I watch old movies on TV. I fall asleep watching Cary Grant and Irene Dunne, and Roxanne breezes in, fresh as the women in the Summer's Eve douche commercials. One or two men, with drugs and foreign accents, follow her in the door. My wake-up call. And I'm up all night. I'm not recovering from anything here.

There are also double "dates." Men in limos. A girl will sometimes do things she wouldn't do if she had any sense of self. After a date, girls with high self-esteem say, "Thank you." Girls with low self-esteem say, "Can it just be a hand job?" Girls without *any* self-esteem, close eyes and open mouths. And that's all I want to say about this, for now.

Ma sent money and I got an apartment of my own, right up the street from Arnold just in case he wants me back. It's a Spanish building, mostly singles, mostly Jewish. La Casa Hadasa.

Arnold's lawyer assures us a nice cash settlement from the accident if we run up the doctor's bills. I need cash. And I need a doctor—a nice Jewish one, I'm hoping. Everything from my neck to my belly feels broken.

Arnold's lawyer, Herb, sends me to a specialist. His specialty: women and manipulation. I lie on an exam table, in a big napkin that opens at the back. The doctor walks in the room, and I think I'm hallucinating. It's Richard Chamberlain. I'm on a *Dr. Kildare* rerun. I figure out he isn't *really* Dr. Kildare. Some will argue that he isn't *really* a doctor. He's a chiropractor.

The sun streams in the transom window and creates a halo around his blond head. He asks me a few questions, but I haven't been able to think since the rabbi meeting. Then Dr. Kildare starts checking my spine. I'm on my stomach, he's touching my neck. Then he inches down . . . and down. On one hand, I'm glad someone's touching me. On the other, why is he rubbing my thigh for whiplash? I don't voice an objection, he's in the lab coat, I'm in the Kleenex.

Why don't I have my good panties on? Or *any* panties on. I cannot permit panty lines, so there is never anything between me and my Calvin Klein knockoffs. I didn't think I'd have to undress. My *neck* hurts, not my ass. Suddenly, his hand brushes briefly against an area not related to the spine. I squirm. His attention returns to my neck.

I'm tortured in thought. Was it a *deliberate* brush? Has he taken the absence of underwear as a signal? Is he really Dr. Shmuck? I make a feeble attempt at rescue humor.

"So, Doctor, can it be fixed or do I need to get a new one?" He crosses the room and picks up a plastic spine. I sit up, clenching the rear of the napkin. As he says words like *subluxated* and *degenerating*, I'm trying to figure out which cervical area he's more interested in.

He's going on, ". . . soft tissue . . . disc . . . pinched . . . you need to come back three times a week for the next twelve weeks, and do you want to go out for dinner?"

"To discuss my soft tissue?" Now this is a treatment! I almost fall off the table. This is a professional grown-up college graduate—I'm not worthy. But he's so cute. Can I get an adjustment on my brain? Will he help me recover from Arnold?

I say, "You're the doctor . . . ."

Yes, I Marry My Chiropractor—
I Don't Like to Drive

Sunday morning, Dr. Kildare and I are in bed—

I wake him up. "Let's get married." Dr. K's nutso for me, he'd knock over a liquor store if I asked—especially with all the narcotics still in his blood from the night before. But what I really want is to marry Arnold. So I send Dr. K to the liquor store for Kahlua—he's already made the coffee—and I call Arnold. "Marry me or I'm eloping with my chiropractor."

"Uh, wha . . . ?" It's ten in the morning, and already he's stoned!

"Arnold! Tell me you made a mistake and you want me back—or else—I'm flying to Vegas to be married by an Elvis impersonator."

Arnold declines the proposal/ultimatum, but tells me not to do something I'll regret. Suddenly Arnold cares?

"Okay, this is goodbye, Arnold. I'll *never* see you again. And when I do, you'll be looking at a married me." I hang up and call American Airlines. I've just hung up with them when the phone rings. It's Ma and Daddy. Arnold called them. He told on me!

But Ma says, "*Oy,* he vas crazy. He vas talking like a *shicker.* You can't understand a vord. *Oy,* a *meshugeneh,* he says you ver going to marry Elvis Presley! So I hanged up on him. Finished mit da Arnold."

Finished? I don't know, but Kildare comes back, I've packed for us, and I grab the Kahlua and a sock full of 'ludes. "Come on, we've got time before the flight." I've always wanted to go to Trashy Lingerie, an upscale Frederick's of Hollywood. Thanks to my endless coke-inspired mid-night laps in the pool, I'm thin enough to look good in the skimpy lingerie. Even in the dressing room! I can't understand why women's dressing rooms have three-way mirrors and direct overhead lighting. Aren't stores *interested* in selling their merchandise?

My chronic fatigue, along with any modesty, has lifted and I strut out of the dressing room modeling teddies and nighties for Dr. K. I buy a few items, including a pair of edible panties—in red licorice—in case we need a snack on the way to LAX.

Exactly nine weeks after rabbi Sunday, the (not-so-good) doctor and I are married at the Silver Bells Wedding Chapel. I'm on five Quaaludes. Some guy, not Elvis, officiates, and we say "I do" at some point. Like in class, I hadn't been listening. I'm reliving Arnold's slurred last words, "Don't marry the chiropractor . . . ." Or maybe he said, "Don Murray, the carob actor."

I remember The Desert Inn pit boss from the Bruce trip, and he remembers me. He gives us, the newlyweds, Wayne Newton's suite! For the price of a standard room, we score a four-person Jacuzzi, a magnificent view of the Strip, and mirrors. Many mirrors. No matter where you stand or lie, you can fix your hair.

I'm fulfilling my potential as an up-grader. Not that I can afford even a standard room, but I'm still in possession of Arnold's "just-in-case credit card." I don't leave his home without it.

I never used it when we were living together (felt too unworthy), but you have to start somewhere. I put every expense: Trashy Lingerie, plane tickets, Silver Bells, and the hotel—on Arnold's MasterCard.

◆ ◆ ◆

Dr. Kildare—the poster child for the Third Reich—and I live together for a month or six. It was the seventies, who remembers anything? Poor Ma doesn't know what to think. He isn't Jewish but—his patients do call him *Dr. Kildare*. It's like the Yiddish dilemma of ham on sale. So we play house. He likes me more than I like him, and I like it that way. On a good day, Kildare looks like Richard Chamberlain; after a coke weekend, he looks like Mick Jagger.

One morning the phone rings. It's Arnold. Mona's kicked him out, and he wants me back. We meet at Dan Tana's, a dark Italian restaurant where lots of cheaters eat. As I drive up Santa Monica Boulevard, I begin noticing signs posted on each telephone pole. They're pink hearts that say, "I Love You, Sue." Arnold calls me Sue when he isn't calling me Floozen. I almost rear-end the car in front of me. Arnold has posted these signs! He paid for printing and ink, and a crew to distribute . . . all for *me*?!

Walking into the restaurant, all I can think is, "Do I look okay?" I try to focus outward. Arnold is sitting at the end of the bar with a bouquet of pink roses. Yeah, *that'll* make us even. I'm holding my stomach in, while six months of fast food hangs shamelessly over his belt.

He fills me in on his current events. He was lighting a joint on the stove, and through a series of goofs, boiled Mikey's pet goldfish to death. Mona gave him one day to move.

And Pete and Gary kicked him out of the business. He wasn't showing up anyway. Arnold's downsized in every way except in the stomach. He's living in an apartment in Van Nuys and wants me to move in. I leave Dan Tana's excited, but . . . leave Kildare? I'm up all night thinking.

Kildare goes to work in the morning, clueless to my plotting. At noon I call him at the office. "I'm not going to be here when you get home." He asks me to hold on. After a few minutes, I realize he's on his way over. There is no way I can get out before he arrives.

Will he hit me, or hit Arnold who's throwing my stuff into boxes. What Kildare does hurts more. He sits on the couch, his big puppy-dog eyes looking at me, the long lashes batting slowly. Why do men always have great furry eyelashes? Women would smear fertilizer on their lids if it would grow half the crop.

K looks like Bambi after they killed Bambi's mother. He's begging, "Please stay, little honey." His eyes look backlit. As he begs, I think, "Hey! My eyes get like that when I tear up," which they are now doing. Our eyes become patriotic glowing spheres of red, white, and blue.

"I'm sorry," I say. I pick up a box and leave with Arnold. I turn back to get a last look. Kildare's at the window. Puppy watching master leave.

I'm back in the hot smog of the Valley; at least it's a shorter drive to Dealer Danny.

Once more life is cocktail hot dogs, the Miami Dolphins and sunflower seeds in Arnold's beard. He's stopped talking to me. He's pissy. Coos of love have turned to *The Big Chill*. Yell at me! Slap me! But say something!

"Please talk to me . . . pleeeze!" I'm back in Montreal—different characters, same plot. Mean Arnold, like Mean Ma, has shown up and will not leave!

So I put in an SOS to Dr. K. "I made a big mistake. I'm so sorry. Is there any way you . . . you . . ."

"Where are you? I'll be right there." Kildare shows up with his best friend, Leroy.

Leroy Washington. He's Caucasian. He was Leo Witoslava until his parents arrived at Ellis Island. Leroy does have an Afro and dark skin, but that's because the white Russian Jew has sat by the pool so long, his freckles merged. His Jew-fro is interrupted by a sweatband. He takes aerobics. He's "a producer." He had the phone company hook up an extension from his apartment to the pool so he can one day actually, maybe, get a movie produced. If I'm ever *broke* broke, and have to phone home for money I can hook my phone up at Leroy's pool. I auditioned for Leroy once. His opinion was, "You're no Meryl Streep."

Life with Kildare resumes as if nothing happened. Except for one important change. Arnold no longer holds any appeal for me. The spell is broken. Or rather *transferred*.

A Day Without Downers Is Like a Day Without Sunshine

I become an urban hermit . . .

A typical day goes like this—I get up in the morning. Technically 11:30 is still morning. I never sleep past noon. Bad people get out of bed after noon.

I slip into consciousness. Oh no, another day of not living up to my potential and not moving toward my goals. How am I going to be *on* TV by sitting home watching it? And then the shift. Yippee! I remember I have a Quaalude stashed in a sock in the nightstand! The pill is in my mouth before the toothbrush. How can I stand at the bathroom mirror without medication? I blast my Eagles tape on the stereo and begin an endorphinating prance around the house. *Peaceful, Easy Feeling.*

Or—if it's a morning after a night of coke, the pill cache will be exhausted. I have to get out of bed without booster rockets. *Desperado.* I dig through every ashtray. Sometimes I find a bong stuffed with Thai stick from the night before, again yippee! I inhale like I'm preparing to swim under-water to Catalina.

There's nothing like the first buzz of the day. After a good night's detox, my body is as clean as it gets and the bong buzz is its most intense. I won't be able to re-create the same mind-altering effect again in the same day, but I'll try.

Breakfast: Kahlua and coffee.

Then I Marine-maneuver onto the balcony. Careful not to let neighbors see me, I strip, apply oil, and work at my perfect tan. I turn with the sun, occa-sionally flipping like bacon. I tan for who? The UPS guy? Kildare is too drunk at night to care about my naked body. Wiggling my tanned tush around the apartment seductively is wasted on the wasted.

Brunch: Pringles.

Some days, I dress in the morning like I'm leaving. I put on mascara and platform wedgies, trying to think of something to do that'll make me feel like I'm not wasting my life. On the way out the door, the dread hits. *It's Sunday night, the essay's due in the morning.* I must take a hit off the bong. And so I sit. Needing to avoid any accidental thinking, I turn on the TV. If a romantic comedy is on, I smoke more pot. My wedgies are now footrests. I might as well eat a little something. The pot-induced insulin drop inspires me. I melt marshmallows on Pringles in the toaster oven to simulate the thing I saw on a commercial. *Chipped Mush a la Pothead.* Then I smoke some more pot so I can back out of the garage without anxiety. This leads to another snack and a *Star Trek* rerun. By now it's dark and too late to go anywhere.

Kildare comes home with a new kind of Russian vodka.

He says we have to keep it in the freezer. The next day Kildare goes to work, and I go to work on the vodka. As hard as I try to conserve, a quarter of the bottle is gone by four o'clock. Not to worry. I refill the bottle thinking, "Perfect! Vodka's clear—like water." A vital detail eludes me in my brilliant scheming. Vodka doesn't freeze. Water *does*.

That night K walks into the bedroom with a puzzled look on his face and the bottle in his hand. He shows it to me. And there it is—a vodka popsicle. Kildare is staring at it, and I exclaim confidently, "A *defective* bottle! You better take it back to the store, honey. It's not supposed to freeze!" Luckily, wine and weed have warped his thinking. He puts the bottle back in the freezer. Whew!

I Want to Feel Better—
Even if It Makes Me Feel Worse

I hate cocaine, but I do it every chance I get.

I know everybody has their burden to bear, but I can't even find an honest drug dealer. Danny DaGoniff cuts my coke to stretch profits. He grinds the Peruvian powder with baby laxative, amphetamines, and I suspect, Ajax. My nasal cavities burn, but they're clean!

Dr. Kildare says, "Danny's coming over tonight." Goody!

I'm in my nightie filing my nails when the buzzer rings. The game's about to begin.

Dr. K says, "Go to the garage and meet Danny. Here's three hundred bucks."

Normally, I don't wear a negligee in a subterranean parking lot, so I look for something to put on. I jump into my bikini bottom, slip on my Bugs Bunny mules, and stride to the elevator, indignant. *Is it too much to ask for a husband who deals with the dealer himself?!* K says *he* pays, so *I* should go. *Some provider!* Well, I've spent the day in front of the TV eating, it'll be good to get out.

I take the elevator to P4, the bowels of the building. It even smells turdy. It's not like I meet my dealers at sunny Farmers Market. I wait and wait, like Woodward or Bernstein, wondering, what's he got for me? Please God, make it high-caliber shit . . . am I on the right floor? I hear a match strike. I turn to see the burning end of a cigarette. Danny is leaning against the wall in the shadows—Fonzie with black teeth. He's not moving. I go to him, my mules clunking, quietly.

He exhales a cloud of smoke, "Hey, blue eyes. You got it?"

"*You* got it?" I'm no fool.

He steps toward me, grinning, "Gimme a kiss."

"Nuh-uh." I need this? I have a *doctor* upstairs.

"C'mon, gorgeous!" his finger strokes my collar bone, "You sexy little thing, I could just . . ."

Oooo, all this intrigue and attention, how *Bogart!* . . . I could too . . . But mercifully, his black teeth snap me out of it.

"Danny! Put that thing back in your pants!"

"Okay, okay, cutie pie. You're gonna looove this shit." Thank you, God, for quality shit. He places a white envelope in my hand. Not the kind you buy at Staples. This is a special Colombian cartel coke container called a bindle. It's designed to open flat so it can be scraped clean with a razor blade. Any remaining powder can be wiped up by your just-licked finger and rubbed on your gums.

He also hands me a regular envelope filled with Quaaludes. It's impossible to do a night of cocaine without the periodic pill to soften the edge. Cocaine makes me nervous, but not as nervous as running *out* of cocaine. I try to buy enough to avoid coming down, but I'm no rock star with flunkies and fans dangling drugs in front of me. I buffer come-down-panic with any sedative I can find. I rummage through purses, popping pills with the purse lint still on them. I steal horse tranquilizers from friends—not that they have horses—they just like to relax. I use bongfuls of pot, or shots of Jim Beam, but I prefer Quaaludes.

At the beginning of the night, I count the Quaaludes, over and over, calculating how many I can do throughout the night and still have a couple left for sleep after the coke is gone. My calculations depend on the quantity of coke, the number of Quaaludes, and how many addicts are visiting. Unfortunately, I have no self-control. By 3:00 a.m., I've run out of 'ludes despite the pile of coke still on the mirror. I spend the next few hours grinding my molars and trying to keep my eyes in their sockets. This love/hate relationship with coke is time-consuming—the getting, the grinding, the guilt. And it's a three-minute buzz with an eight-hour come-down. And we pay $100 a gram for this.

But this time it'll be different. I take the stash, Danny gets the loot, and I'm back upstairs with my head hanging over the coffee table.

I make it my business to know *exactly* how much coke is on the table, *and* when it's my turn. When coke and I are in the same room, I do it. I share only because it's drug-user etiquette. And because *he's* paid for it.

Snort. Zing! WOWZAH! I pass the straw and watch as it travels to Dr. K, to the mirror, back to me—No! he's got it again. My turn—yes! No!—he's intercepted, he scores—and my *have-to-have-it-now* mounts. Finally, he hands off the crusty conduit and I do, *not the fattest*, but the *two* fattest lines on the mirror. Power lines. And it's goood!

It's 4:00 a.m.

I'm not zinging anymore. I feel icky. Grease is squiggling out my pores like slimy snakes that wind around my chest, bind my arms, and knot my jaw shut. I can't speak.

A chunk of my brain flatlines while other parts cling to a rocketing roller coaster. Half-thoughts come so quick, they're a blur. Movement is limited to pacing, chain-smoking, playing solitaire, and snorting more and more coke, desperate to reexperience that initial ZING! It's like going 100 mph with your feet nailed to the floor.

I must take a Quaalude. But . . . I can't move . . . can't turn head . . . can't lift ass off sofa. I'm Lot's wife.

Why do I *do* this again and again? I have no choice—the powder has the power. I don't think, should I do coke anymore than I think should I breathe. I do it to survive. As Ma would say, "Dat's—surviving? Dat sounds like hell!" Yeah, but it's a hell I picked.

Why pick hell? It's a good distraction. Coke, gross as it is, creates white noise that overpowers *the attack of the killer thoughts*. I need to get an agent, I want to be on a soap, I should write a book, I don't have the nose for a soap, I have to get a nose job, I have to get the mail—oh, who's kidding who? Like I'll do anything other than hide at home holding the remote, making friends with people in the soaps, who won't laugh at me behind my back. My near-life is exhausting. Coke wakes me up. At midnight. My energy is all dressed up with nowhere to go and nothing to do. What would I do anyhow? Play Twister with myself?

We're having our normal Friday night: K with his paranoia and me with my panic.

At least we have structure. It's 5:00 a.m., I'm circling the coffee table, wearing down the living room rug. I notice its worn state because I'm on all fours hunting for the rock that may have dropped at 2:00 a.m., when I was less careful.

Kildare, now naked, is crawling by the window, staring outside. He beckons me over. "Shh. Stay down. Look!"

"At . . . the bushes?"

"No! Shh! The *people!* The people *in* the bushes."

"The bush people."

"Yeah! Look!" He points, keeping his gestures small so as to not alert the bush people. I try to figure out if the problem is his coke-induced psychosis or my poor night vision. I've decided: *His* DEA agents are hallucinations. *My* dropped rocks are real.

Holy cow! I spot a white speck on the carpet. I assume the downward-facing drug addict pose, then carefully transport the speck to the coffee table I just licked. I chop the bit into powder and suck the grainy particles up my nose. I've snorted stucco. Well, there's no proof that stucco *doesn't* get you high. It's California's cottage cheese—ceiling crumble. Earthquakes could have shaken them loose; I haven't vacuumed since the last one. My nostril's stinging and bleeding, and I'm wondering, "Have I torn my nose?"

A bird chirps. I shudder. "It *can't* be morning already!"

I watch the sun rise. How lovely, *isn't* what I'm thinking. Fuck, Fuck, FUCK! I did it *again*. And what am I supposed to do with this day? Look for a job? Kildare walks back into the room, dressed. Apparently, his bush men have left, and left him hungry, "Let's go eat."

Our fourteen-year-old waitress Rollerblades over to our table as Dr. K whips out the vitamin B. Wired, tired, my brain's running a marathon but my jaw's hardened into cement. My lips barely move, "Pancakes . . . decaf . . . orange juice, fresh-squeezed, please." Who said that? It's a ventriloquist act— I'm the dummy, K's hand is up my ass, we're both groping for sanity.

He's My Six-Foot Quaalude

I start liking him more than he likes me—

I don't know exactly when it happened, but somehow, Kildare's infatuation with me turned into my obsession with him. The tide has turned. I'm drowning in the surf and can't catch my breath, again. I'm addicted to him. He's like a powerful drug. I want to stay home all day and *do* him. Turns out, he's doing someone else. But I'm practicing denial, so don't ask me questions.

What do I do? Become frantic with fear of losing him, of course. "Where are you going, what are you doing, when will you be back?" My separation anxiety causes clingyness. He runs to escape. The faster he runs, the more desperately I cling.

◆ ◆ ◆

We really have only two things in common:

(1) We're both obsessed with him. (Within a minute of meeting him, Ma pulled me aside, "He loves himself too much to love you." Dulled by a lifetime of Ma's put-downs, I ignore what she says. Again, a stopped clock may be right twice a day, but you don't look to it for the right time.)

(2) We share a mission to get healthy without giving up drugs. We use niacin and saunas, high-colonics and high-impact aerobics to detox from our lost weekends.

We're trying to be good. Kildare drives us to the Self-Realization Center where gurus hand out mantras. But I don't want my own mantra, I want *his* so I can chant it. I have no life, I want to live his.

The Vitamin Thief

Dr. Kildare wants me healthy, but not too healthy.

He says I need to be taking nutritional supplements. After all, I have Dean Martin's liver. So he brings home vitamins from the office and gives them to me—at cost. They're expensive, *high quality*—so high I can't afford to buy them. So he brings home enough for himself.

What's a girl supposed to do? Steal them from him. *Carefully*. I figure out how many I can pilfer without his catching on. And I skip days, like old, poor people who cut their meds and die. I sneak vitamin B-12s like they're heroin. I'm trying to stay ahead of the game. But odds are against me. We party too hard.

Our lives are designed around drinking. For example, we don't select our wine according to the food we're eating. If K feels like drinking red wine, we have red food.

Back to the beach, only it's a nude beach . . .

We decide we'll do something outdoorsy. Kildare likes to walk around naked. He's *so* not Jewish! So he takes us where he can walk outside, naked. I don't like the beaches of the Pacific. Waves. Drowning. And the beach is big. The water is so *far* from the parking lot. The bathing-suit-optional cove is hidden just north of Malibu. I keep my suit on, and my eyes on everyone around me. But after the wine is gone and the Quaaludes have kicked in, my suit's off.

I get up the courage to walk to the water when two LAPD officers approach. All I know is, at some point, the police must have triggered something in me, because I'm yelling at them. They call it resisting arrest.

So Kildare and I are handcuffed (clothes on) and sitting in the back of the police car on our way to the Malibu jail. A nice jail to be booked in. We stay the night. Separate rooms. The following morning, Kildare's lawyer gets us released, and I swear to never take my clothes off again.

Friday night, Kildare's patient's Bel-Air mansion—

The estate is perched on top of Mulholland Drive with a view of the Valley. But it's the view *inside* the house that's breathtaking. Mountains of cocaine, bowls of pills, and shoe boxes of marijuana are conveniently arranged for guests' brain-cell-destroying pleasure. I put powder up my nose, smoke into my lungs, and wash down vodka with a multiplicity of pills.

Dr. K has disappeared. I hunt through the rooms, calling his name. Laughter is coming from the master bedroom closet. I swing open the door only to have it slammed shut by someone on the other side. I pull the knob to open the door again, but it's held shut. With the strength that fortifies grandmothers who lift trucks off children, I swing the door open to find my man zipping up his pants. A woman with messy hair is kneeling before him. She isn't worshiping.

I've entered a warped movie of the weak! What would Lindsay Wagner or Meredith Baxter do? I grab my bag and my husband, and head to the door. I go "waaa" all the way home. K whimpers, "I'm sorry." It's Lana Liebman and Leonard all over again.

Imagine my shock to realize it's Monday noon. But it was just *Friday*! Three days ago. Where did the time go? I see the light flashing on the answering machine. I play the message. It's the one I've been waiting to hear. My agent is saying I have an audition with Barbara Miller, head of casting for Lorimar Television—in three hours!

Oh good, another opportunity to blow another opportunity.

L.A.'s having a heat wave. It's 105°—160° in the Valley. I decide to wear my slenderizing jumpsuit. It's black. I'll look ninety-eight pounds, instead of 102. I layer on the Cover Girl to hide zits and puffy eyes, and work furiously to fix the clumps of mascara on the tips of my lashes. But the more I fix, the clumpier they get. I use tweezers to shmush together the black balls of Maybelline, trying to form them into longer lashes, but they bend at the ends, making right angles. I think of Linda's spider legs. Should I just wash my face and start over? No, I have to give myself extra time to get to the appointment, I always get lost in Burbank. The Lankershim/Barham Triangle defies *Thomas*

Guide sensibilities. It's the Decarie Circle. I grab coffee, keys, and slip on the six-inch wedgies.

My Pontiac doesn't have air conditioning. The sweat frizzes my black hair. The makeup that was on my face is gliding into my cleavage, which I've cleverly enhanced with blusher. The v-neck trim of the black jumpsuit is turning orange. I'm Elvira, Anorexic Mistress of the Dank, on the last leg of a 10K.

Driving through the gates of the studio, Leroy's voice echoes in my head, "You're no Meryl Streep." Who does Meryl Streep get compared to? The parking space given to actresses auditioning is practically back at the beach. By the time I get to the casting office, I've got blisters on my feet and sunstroke. I'm three pounds lighter. (So there's some good in everything.)

I pick up the script from the receptionist and go into the bathroom to go over the lines. What I need is a few lines. Of coke. I stole a gram from the party. Shoot me, I took a doggy vial. I whip it out and snort maybe an eighth of a gram, just to gear up.

I strut into the audition room, my head high, probably high enough to display a residue of white powder around the nostrils. Four men and a woman sit behind a table. The assistant introduces us. For all I know, she's saying, "This is Tweedle-Dum, Tweedle-Dee, Daryl, and his other brother Daryl." I try to smile without a lip twitch. (This type of situation causes my upper lip to dance around, making a fool of the rest of my features.)

Teeth grinding, limbs in rigor mortis, I sit to read. And then it happens. I leave my body. I've floated up to a corner of the room. As a disgusted Endora observing poor bumbling Derwood, I watch myself *act*. We've established I'm no Meryl Streep, but I might as well be reading from the yellow pages. It isn't going well. Is the nylon stocking I stuffed in my bra creeping out the top of my jumpsuit?

The tension is too great, even for me, who can normally discount my feelings and steamroller through anything. With clammy, trembling hands, sweat trickling down my face, I stop in the middle of a line and look at the executive firing squad. "Would it be possible for me to start over?" Normally, I don't feel entitled to ask. Who am I to waste the important people's time? My audition strategy has always been: Read fast, get rejected, and get out. Plow ahead, sputter, never take a minute to regroup. Get out of the room and let the grown ups get back to work.

Barbara Miller suggests I take ten minutes. I leave the room and take two Quaaludes. I slip into a blackout. Did I go back? I don't think so. One thing for sure, I didn't get the job.

Many auditions follow. I get a bit here and there, nothing to call home about. *Oy.* I'm getting rejected for a living.

Another dream: I'm an actress working as a waitress. Serving mankind. "We are the world, we are Denny's." Every so often, a gunman comes in and shoots the employees. He always shoots me in the face. The bullets don't kill me. They go in and leave me scarred. I think, "Hmmm, if this keeps up, I'm going to be too scarred to be cast in anything." I come up with a solution. When the gunman comes in, I'll bow my head.

He comes back and I drop my head, the bullets go in under the scalp. No one can see my injuries or the scars now. A doctor is stitching up my head. He looks like Harvey Keitel, which, in itself, is scary, but what kind of doctor eats at Denny's?! The man I hope will put me together is a loser.

I ask, "Doctor? Will the scars leave me bald?" Bald women don't find much work in television. Unless you count Star Trek.

Dr. Keitel says, "You can get a scalp reduction." Reduction?

"Is my head too big?" He doesn't bother to answer. Dammit! At least tell me how bad it will be so I can prepare! I'm really annoyed. I catch our reflection in a mirror and realize, as he's stitching up my head, he's watching television. Bastard! In my time of greatest need, I'm not important enough to the one person who can help me. I need his attention! Otherwise, my head will be all fucked up!

*Also annoying, someone **else** is on TV, not ME. They're not working at Denny's! I know if I quit Denny's, I won't get shot anymore. I wake up, call my agent, and tell him to throw away my pictures and résumés. The casting directors will, anyway.*

Two months later, we're at Leroy's, my cocaine use is down, my weight is up.

Leroy's parties bring Brentwood residents together to get wasted in a cozy private environment. Always dark and crowded, with music, drugs, and BBQ.

I'm in the living room lifting a burger to my mouth when Leroy broadcasts from the kitchen doorway, "Hey, Suzan, you better not eat that, Hollywood isn't hiring chubby actresses!" He sure knows how to grab everybody's attention.

He doesn't stop. "Not that you're *chubby*. You're stocky. Muscular. You know what you need?"

I tilt my head, "Heroin and a razor blade?"

"You're taking this personally. All I said was—"

"Yeah, I got it. *Hollywoodn't.* No fat, low fat. I'm half and half, they're hiring skim. Got it."

I'd been thinking about moving on to heroin. The Big H, the odd nod, the top of the addict's food chain. I'm aware of the downside of heroin: You lose your health, your soul, and your teeth. Heroin addicts don't shower, let alone floss. Yet, I've asked K to score some. I asked Danny, I asked Leroy, I asked the dry cleaner. They all said they'd get back to me, they never have. Are they lazy, or maybe they don't want to be the one to help me O.D.

Overdosing right now would be welcome.

Leroy continues, "*You* need to do aerobics."

"Yes, I see your point. With the chubby-stocky-muscular, and all."

He's excited. "Take Beverly's class. You'll *love* it." A person could *love* an exercise class? He may be right about chubby actresses, but about this? His sweatband must be crushing his brain.

Next day, he's pulling me through the door of Brentwood Nautilus. I had run out of Quaaludes and had to go to the gym on only vodka.

He shows me a room with people jumping around to music. That's what I used to do in the basement—dance to Tom Jones' "Delilah." I watch for a while. I can do that.

Leroy says, "I bought you a six-month membership." Amends for chubby-stocky-muscular?

I decide I'll take Beverly's next class. Kildare takes me to SportsMart. I buy a brown spandex leotard, brown tights, white ankle warmers and sneakers made by a new shoe company called Reebok.

I walk into the aerobics room and catch my reflection in the mirror. I look like a Twinkie. But I stay. And drown in sweat. My lungs wonder, where's the pot that goes with all this deep breathing? My shins catch fire, but I keep bouncing.

Beverly is my favorite aerobics instructor. She looks the part—blond hair, no fat. After demonstrating gravity-defying leg lifts, Bev walks around the room correcting people's form. But what she's telling us to do is humanly impossible; people can't keep their legs up that long. Maybe a dog. I tell her *she* can't even do her own routine, that's why she walks around correcting us.

She smiles, "Yeah, I can." I bet her a bottle of vodka she can't.

Two days later, I buy her a bottle of vodka.

The Enemy's at the Gate

I'm home watching "All My Children" and grazing.

The phone rings. The phone is frightening—especially when it *rings*. It's the bugler rousing each cell to come to arms. Goose-bumped arms.

I look at the loud, intrusive thing like it's a rapist. Or a telemarketer. Who can it be?! What can they want?! Do I have time to take a toke before picking up?

I exhale as I say, "Hel-lo."

"Is Kildare in? Tell him it's Brenda." It's K's ex-wife. He said he had one in Wisconsin. We chat about weather as I try not to faint. Ex-wives spell danger. Breathe, but don't let her hear you *trying* to relax, pretend you're a grown-up.

I wish I could say, "I'm not comfortable speaking with you. I'll tell K you called." But what's to be uncomfortable? Is a Nazi chasing me I should be uncomfortable?

I panic quietly and continue acting like the I'm-fine woman. *Eleanor Rigby keeps her face in a jar by the door, who is it for?*

So, I have two conversations going: One with Brenda, and the one in my head that sounds like Dino, the Flintstones' dinosaur, locked outside.

Finally, I fess up and mention my fear of ex-wives.

"Well, Suzan—it *is* Suzan, right?—I'm not technically his *ex*-wife until we finalize the divorce."

"Oh, well, yeah, right." *WHAT?!*

Brenda breezes along, "I think it's about time he sees his lawyer, what with the 'big' birthday coming up. Turning forty, I bet he *hates* that!"

I gasp. At least it gets air to my brain. "But, he's twenty-nine."

She's laughing so hard, she can hardly speak. "He said he was twenty-nine? Oh, that's hysterical!" I don't feel like laughing. What next—he was born a girl? I've bent the truth, Kildare braids it.

The game show announcer in my head says, "But wait, there's more!" *K and I aren't legally married!* I'm *not* married to—an old man! I'm confused. I assumed, as most would, when you're walking down the aisle with a bouquet in your hands, the guy you're meeting at the altar is single.

That night, Kildare walks in and I'm waiting. "I spoke with Brenda today. Oh, we had a long chat. You lying *louse!* How *DARE* you do this to me? You . . . you old man! You old *married* man!"

His eyes blaze. "How dare *YOU* interfere with my relationship with Brenda! What is wrong with you? Are you so insecure that—" A ten-minute explosion of profanities, then silence for two weeks.

I cry and beg, "Pleeeze . . . talk to me. I'm sorry . . ."

When he finally speaks, his tone has a Sylvia chill, "I can never trust you again!"

My tone is baby-voice, "B-b-but . . . *you're* the one who—" I'm tumbling in the surf all over again, up is down.

Kildare decides I've begged long enough. He forgives me for "being a prying bitch." He missed the blow jobs.

March 1981. Life goes on, for most . . .

One night Kildare comes home tired. He pours some wine, lights a joint, chops the coke. I'm on the couch next to him, but he's a galaxy away.

He says softly, "It's the strangest thing. I have a new patient, David, and he's sick . . . cancer . . . none of his doctors know what to do. He doesn't have *an immune system*. Weird, huh?" Kildare snorts a line of coke and his mood is more positive. "I'm going to help him. I put David on megadoses of antioxidants and amino acids. He's coming in for adjustments three times a week. Medical doctors! They just throw chemicals at you and cut you up. They know nothing about prevention!"

David died. So would Rock Hudson, Liberace, Rudolph Nureyev, Arthur Ashe, and millions of others. Reverend Jerry Falwell's position is, "AIDS is God's judgment of a society that does not live by His rules." Pat Robertson's view, "Homosexuals want to come into churches, disrupt services, and throw blood all around and try to give people AIDS and spit in the face of ministers." And Ronald Reagan would go on to say, "Maybe the Lord brought down this plague because illicit sex is against the Ten Commandments." Whatever. Pop a 'lude and change the channel.

Quaaludes—
The Only Way to Do a Game Show

I'm on the couch watching "The Match Game."

I am the perfect contestant for this show. The object of the game is to match how celebrities will fill in a _____ . A no-brainer for me. Growing up in the *Asylum for the Inappropriate Reaction,* I learned to predict what Ma and Daddy would say and match my behavior to their moods.

I call CBS, force myself to the studio, and yank "fun girl" out from hiding. She does her act and I'm chosen to be a contestant.

Dropping a 'lude before the show relaxes me. What cameras? Money at stake? It's like being back home on the couch. I win *three* games, and go home with a few thousand dollars, a string of Majorca pearls, and a year's supply of Dr. Pepper.

I call my agent. "You didn't throw away my pictures, did you?" He hadn't.

"Good, send me in for something."

"You wanna be on *The Young and the Restless*?"

"Yes, I do."

"They need atmosphere."

"They do?" I'm thinking a smoke machine.

"Extras. Do you wanna be an extra?" No, never have, although I've played one all my life. But it pays and I'll qualify to get into the Screen Actors Guild. I do the show a few times. I play a nurse, a juror, a shopper and then— a drinker. It's a *bar* scene. I've rehearsed the role. They place me at a table with my male atmosphere counterpart. The props master and I had been flirting and instead of dumping the champagne and filling the bottle with sparkling cider, he uncorks the bottle and leaves it on my table. Good! I need it. Here I am in a major TV studio, on an actual set, and I'm playing wallpaper. Be quiet and look good; I've rehearsed that role too. I'm not appreciated for the great talent I know I am.

Cameras roll; I drink two glasses; they go well with the Quaalude I took in the bathroom. Then three glasses . . . then four. I fade, but not to black. I pretend dialogue with Mr. Extra in my naturally animated fashion when suddenly, a command from the control booth comes over the sound system, *"CUT!"* The director. "Will the woman flapping her arms like a big bird, please tone it down!"

I stop breathing and glue my arms to my sides until the scene is over. I grab my bag, and without stopping at wardrobe to return the silk dress they gave me for the scene, I drive off the lot. I'm never asked back.

If I can't be on TV, I'll watch it.

TV is the perfect drug . . . it's legal. (I only drive to the dealer *once*. And I can indulge all night without destroying my nose.) I've never OD'd or been arrested or gotten pregnant from TV. I keep it on all the time to drown out the screaming voice in my head, *"Do something! Go outside! Is a Nazi chasing you dat you should be afraid!"* Who said that? Late at night, with nothing left to watch, I look through the *TV Guide,* preparing for tomorrow, so at least I read.

Leaving the apartment by myself is *Mission: Impossible.* If Leroy didn't park in front of the apartment honking his horn, I'd never get to the gym.

The guilt produced from being nonproductive is so intense, I have to block it out with more television and snacks. My weight keeps going up. I'm becoming videobese.

I hide my empty Pringles cans under other kitchen trash. If there's not enough, I make fake garbage.

Kildare comes home. "Suzan, didn't you get the mail?" Why do they always ask that?

"No, I . . . was busy." How can I get the mail without running into some-one? They'll see me, and my thighs.

Who *they* are is not as important as what I *think* they're going to see.

What if they ask, "How are you?" I couldn't tell a shrink in fifty minutes, let alone a passerby in five seconds.

They say, "How are you?" I want to say, "How much time ya got?"

Adding to the dilemma, I'm expected to say, "How are you?" back. I just assume they're all doing better than me.

I'd say, "Good to see you!" but that's only true if I'm having a clear-skin day. I know "How are you" is meant to be polite, but I wish instead, people would offer a helpful-greeting hint. "Hi, don't park under that pine tree!" or "Hey—regular flossing promotes good dental hygiene." I need encouragement to floss.

I could respond to "How are you?" by saying, "Fine." But it's a lie. I hate to lie. I'm not good at it. When K asks what I've done all day, it's an effort to invent something. I may not *respect* him, but I don't want the bigamist to think badly of me.

Actually, when I tell him I'm too busy to get the mail, I'm not really lying. With all my worrying and drinking, I never find the right moment.

Circling the Drain

December 23, 1982, Kildare's big celeb patient throws a holiday bash . . .

Another Christmas party, *feh!* More parties I don't need, but he says we have to go. Parties—breeding ground for humiliation. Another night to experience lost potential and less-than-ism. God knows what someone will say to me, and what I'll *do* with what they say. And, of course, they're going to say, "How are you?" and I'll think, what have you heard? High-end TV people are the scariest of all people. They see me, I see a possible connection to an acting job. What follows isn't pretty.

I don't want to go to this horrible thing, but I can't let Kildare out alone at night. There's no telling—and I mean *no* telling, no matter how much I beg—where he'll *really* be, or who he'll be with. I pop a Quaalude to take the edge off getting ready.

Forty-five minutes later, the closet's empty, I'm still not dressed, and there's a mountain of clothes on the bed. What was I *thinking* in all of those dressing rooms? I panic. I have to look perfect to pass for normal. What if I catch my reflection in a mirror and discover my ass looks fat? My mind will be on my ass all night.

Maybe makeup first. I paint a lash at a time, two coats and, ah . . . ah . . . ACHOO! Oh hell! I'm a naked raccoon with a husband yelling, "*Let's go— we're late!*" Quick, a Q-tip and Noxema.

Mmmm . . . the smell of Noxema. The smell of Ma. She's tunneling through from childhood. I remember walking with her as she'd point out what really mattered. "*Gib a kik, a chazzer, a grobeh tuches, a meeskite—feh!*" (Take a look, a pig, a fat ass, so *ugly*—get it away from me!) Maybe criticizing others made Ma feel better about the state of *her own* ass, but I remember thinking if *this* is how people judge each other, I'm staying in my room.

◆ ◆ ◆

But I'm not in my room now. K's driving, I'm dreading. I don't even hear the car radio. My Sony Thinkman drowns it out, playing the same old standards: "Don't stammer. You're retaining water and your nose looks big in this dress."

I know some people enjoy getting together with others. They bond. But how can I carry on a conversation with somebody when I'm already deep in conversation with myself? Someone could say, "You're the prettiest woman in the room," and I'd think, "Sure, *this* room." Being with people isn't fun, it's *work*.

I should prepare something to talk about, but what? Nobody cares who Erica Kane married today. I can't talk about myself because I might come off as a self-involved egomaniac.

I'm at a loss. I'm exhausted. I've been through the *me* grinder.

What if some show business big shot asks, "Why are you here?" I could say, "My mother and father are Jews who got married in Poland during the Holocaust and they had me instead of an abortion. Why are *you* here?" Is that still about me?

So here we are, walking through the door. Intro, intro, smile, smile. I try to focus outside of myself. *Remember the name, associate it with something.* But what? Her face looks like a horse, let's see—Ed? It's not that I forget a name. I wasn't present for the introduction, so I never heard it to begin with. And what if Kildare comes over and wants to be introduced?

I'm being introduced to a woman and suddenly, I turn Tourette's. "I'm sorry, I didn't catch your name. I was distracted by your enormous breasts jutting out of your dress, giving me the impression that you're a slut and all the men here, including my husband, want to have sex with you. Did you *look* in the mirror before leaving the house? Forgive me, my mother was judgmental and it's a habit I've acquired. I'm trying to be a less critical person. Would you care to repeat your name?" It turns out that she's a casting director. Okay, so I never said it—but I *thought* it.

I gotta get out of here. Where's the bar?

Like a pig sniffs out truffles, I find booze. On the kitchen counter, next to sodas and Coffee-mate, is an unopened bottle of Smirnoff. I open it. That's the last thing I remember until I wake up in the Christmas tree.

I can't recall knocking the tree over, but I'm the only one *in* the tree. I sit, my dress up to my hips, with crushed ornaments and a plastic baby Jesus, hoping no one has noticed. I'm especially concerned because I haven't yet learned the value of panties. Who thinks of underwear? I have enough trouble putting on mascara.

I raise my head. Everyone is staring at me. The room is a still frame. The music's stopped. How do I get out of this gracefully? I focus on trying to put a broken angel ornament together, and mercifully slip back into my blackout.

When I come to, I'm in my carport trying to stop K from throwing his suits into the trunk of the Beamer.

We fight, he packs. We make up and he's left with a wrinkled wardrobe. His dry cleaning bills are ridiculous. You'd think, after all the times he's packed up to leave, he would have learned to grab the iron-free poly-blends first.

I drop to my knees and beg him to stay. He usually likes it when I get on my knees. He usually stops whatever he's doing. And begging is something I know from . . . *Pleeeze, Mummy . . . don't leave! I'm sorry, I'll never do it again, pleeeze, give me one more chance to make you like me again?*

He stays.

The next morning I wake up to the smell of coffee and a vague, "'Bye, see you later, don't forget to call her." By *her* he means the hostess of the party. I try to remember last night, and as I do, I try to forget. The great alcohol amnesia curtain lifts, bringing back another of last night's scenes—

I'm standing in front of an open oven, fanning my dress to dry it, and wondering how it got wet. I'm annoyed with the conversation taking place behind me. Spinning around, I address a lanky redhead, *"You* are *not* on *Falcon Crest* as you claim! I know this because *I'm* an actress! I watch *Falcon Crest!"* This I know. Why my dress is wet, I have no idea.

Now, in the light of day, I realize—OH GOD—she *is* on *Falcon Crest.* What an idiot I am! Cringe. The cringe that stole Christmas. I feel like I just swallowed a bad thing.

I dump what's left of the Tia Maria into the coffee, the coffee into me, and dial the hostess' number, preparing to pretend that last night's humiliation hasn't destroyed me.

I inquire about the condition of the Christmas tree, and assure my hostess that this sort of thing has *never* happened before.

She interrupts, "Suzan, are you aware that this was an Alcoholics Anonymous Christmas party and you were the only drunk person there?"

"No." I hadn't been aware of anything.

"After the party, we went to a meeting. It was really great."

I'll bet. I'd been the perfect Christmas gift for recovering alcoholics—"There but for the grace of God go *we*."

She continues, "I'd like to take you to a meeting. There are some women's groups." Oh, right! It's what you reformers live for, isn't it? Back off, you holier-than-thou, big-book-thumping recruiter. I ain't joining no clan of bitches!

But what I *actually* say is, "Thanks, but really, drinking's not a problem. I've decided to cut down to a couple glasses of wine with dinner." They'll be very *big* glasses.

I say goodbye and hang up the phone. Losers! And a little voice, a sad little voice, says quietly, "Even *those* losers won't like you."

Suicide Prevention Hangs Up on Me

Five days after my debut as the drunk Christmas tree-killing flasher—

SMASH!

Shit! Of all the things to slip out of my Bain du Soleil slathered arms, why did it have to be the bottle of *red* wine and not the *white*.

It's four p.m., I'm at the front door, keys in hand, watching the wine flow down the beige cement steps like a river of blood.

Quick—get the Clorox, a bucket of water, oh! the broken glass! Damn! Kildare can't see this, I'll look like an alcoholic! And he's still pissed at me for killing his client's Christmas tree. If I had a black beauty, I could clean this up in five minutes.

It turns out I have plenty of time. I could have grouted and retiled before he got home. Ten hours later and he hasn't even called. Obviously, he doesn't care about me. Who is she?

I pace, smoke, and lick anything we've ever done coke with. I find the communal straw from our last social occasion and slice it open. Hoping for a residue high, I lick the straw that's been up various crusty noses. Yes, I do that.

I open the freezer, pull out his Stoli and start chugging. Where's K? What's he doing? Who's he doing it to? I call 411.

"What city, please?"

"Brentwood." And not wanting to limit myself, "Or L.A."

"What listing, please?"

"Suicide Prevention." It comes out a little slurred.

"Hold for the number."

"Thanks for the warmth." The bar buddies in my head commiserate, "What'ja expect, kindness? On *this* planet?!"

I dial the number and start explaining my hopelessness to the man working the hotline. I tell him I don't *really* want to die. He's pissed. You'd think that would make him happy!

"Look, lady, it's Saturday night. I've got urgent calls." CLICK.

Now I *do* feel like killing myself. I'll show him who's urgent!

Then I get sidetracked rolling my exit joint. "Saturday night is primetime at Suicide Prevention? You'd think more people would want to kill themselves Monday morning."

Kildare's keys rattle at the door. Here he is with that goofy smile.

Decades of rage fly at him, I sound like the Ghostbusters' demon, *"Where the fuck were you?"*

He brushes me off, "If you weren't such a stinking drunk, I'd come home earlier." He's right. They're all right. It's my fault.

Once again, K's on his way down to the car, his Armani shirts bunched in his arms. I drop to my knees. "I'll go into recovery. Please . . . please don't leave me!" Does he see I've ripped open the seam of my pants flinging myself at his feet?

He looks down at my bloated face. He must be thinking, "Look at this— I screw around on her and she's begging to be forgiven!"

"You'll get into recovery?"

"Yes!" I say, figuring, sure, I'll go to one AA meeting and talk about it for months. Ma taught me how to stretch out a story. She turned a five-year war into a fifty-year trauma. *Trauma trying to resolve itself by reliving the trauma.*

Besides, there's no way I can cope without chemicals. And, New Year's Eve is three days away.

PART THREE

Where Have I Been All My Life?

There's an old joke—

A guy walks into a bar, there's a sign posted,
"All you can drink, one dollar."
He says to the bartender, "I'll have two dollars' worth."

Exactly.

I Hear My Pain Coming
From Their Mouths

December 28, 1982, I'm going to my first Alcoholics Anonymous meeting.

I need a drink.

I decide it's inappropriate. Hung over, shaking, but (thank God) tanned, I drive to the West Hollywood AA clubhouse, the one the big-book-thumping recruiter told me about. I'm wearing my *good* shorts, hoping I haven't over-dressed.

I walk in the room, praying no one notices me and afraid I'll be ignored.

If a room can be cheerful and depressing at the same time, this is it. Banquet tables and folding chairs are arranged in a circle. I panic. There's no way to sit in the back. It's like a King Arthur's round table of out-of-work actors.

Someone with a nose ring and a tattoo that says "Bite me" calls the meeting to order. A once-in-demand leading man in a baseball cap and sunglasses reads from a spiral notebook. I miss most of what he says because I'm busy coming up with lines for my turn to talk. I want people to know who I am before I'm not anymore.

Then, the ex-leading man reads something that catches my attention. "Please do not share unless you have twenty-four hours of continuous sobriety." How the hell do you do that?

Hands go up. The nose-ringed, tattooed leader points to a woman. She tells how, after a year of sobriety, she's regained custody of her kids. People cry. Next, a man says he's going broke and his girlfriend slept with his AA sponsor. People laugh. There's something demented about this group. I'm home. I finally fit in someplace. Now, like Ma and Daddy, I have my own group.

And the stories these survivors have—*oy!* It's ridiculous how these people are open about things normal people hide. The more humiliating the secret, the bigger the laugh; they're paralyzed with fear, they erupt with rage, and they've thrown up all over town. They have stuff I think nobody has but me. Me and Oedipus. Who knew that people who looked so good could find themselves disgusting and stupid. The more they hate themselves, the happier I am.

Other people feel this shitty? Yes! This is a program for people who feel shitty!

This group of lunatics is living and coping, chemically free, *One Day at a Time*—a dopey sitcom, but an exciting strategy. Keep my thoughts in the same time zone as my body? I never do *anything* one day at a time. I'm too busy feeling guilty about what was or worrying about what's coming—a Nazi here, a spider there. *Me* live without self-medicating? They don't understand—*I* have anxiety.

I spot a sign on the wall, "Terminal Uniqueness." I jot it down to think about later. There are colored signs pinned to every wall, "Lack of Power Is Our Dilemma." No fucking kidding. "Easy Does It." "Yesterday is history, tomorrow's a mystery, and today is a gift. That's why it's called the present." Cute. "If you start thinking you can have a drink, you have a thinking problem." I'm starting to like this.

And then—uh-oh. There's one that says, "Let Go, Let God." Let God? Let God do *what*? Did these people get their heads stuck up their butts from looking inward too much? They're *okay* with what God's done so far? They trust a God that allowed the Holocaust and the church's relocation policy for child-molesting priests?

Thanks, but I'll take my chances with coke and booze. You can *depend* on them. You know the trip. You choose. But . . . have I really been choosing? Why de-'lude myself? I know the way to hell, but I didn't get there by myself. *Help, I need somebody.* But how can I fall in with an army of cliché abusers? Is this a cult? I remember as a kid wanting to join a nice cult.

As the meeting members speak, I realize my whatever-it-is-I-thought-was-unique-to-me has a name. I'm something that other people are, too. I'm not a mistake. I'm—*an alcoholic!*

My hand has a mind to fling itself up in the air. I'll tell these people what's happened. I won't die without the world knowing how it's wronged me—Ma and Daddy and Sylvia, Dr. K, Miss Sawyer in third grade, the guy at the liquor store, Lana Liebman.

This AA group will understand why I drink. Especially, being the sensitive artist that I am, of course I drink. But I can't raise my hand. There's the twenty-four-hour rule. I haven't had twenty-four hours of sobriety in ten years, unless you count being passed out.

It doesn't occur to me to lie. Besides I can't lie, except about drugs or sex . . . and maybe a little shoplifting.

I'll come back tomorrow, raise my hand and say, "My name is Suzan and I'm an alcoholic." I'll share, then go home and drink.

Let's be real—I can't cope without medication. Who'll scrape me off the ceiling?

On the Couch with God

Right after sticking my toe in the AA pool

I bust into the apartment, eager to spread the gospel. Kildare is sitting on the couch, chopping coke on the glass-top coffee table. I freeze.

And then I remember, *breathe!* And in one big exhale my enthusiasm unleashes itself, "It was great and there were really nice sober people there and some haven't gotten high since the sixties and I'm going back and I'm an alcoholic and—"

"Got a gram from Danny."

A gram? Oh-oh. I've never turned down cocaine. Ever.

"C'mon, Little Honey, sit down." I sit.

Click, click, click. The sound of a razor—chopping through coke—hitting glass. The sound of music. The sound that's followed by a total loss of appetite, sleep, and self-respect. Hurry! Stop clicking, start snorting. I'm in a rush. To go back to hell. But I hate hell. Do I *have* to go? Wait a minute, *just say NO!*

Kildare configures the finely chopped cocaine into lines using the razor and then rolls up a hundred dollar bill to use as a straw.

The punks in my head start to rant. Hey, I *just say no* all the time:

Suzan, please stop taking drugs. "*No!*"

Suzan, please stop getting drunk. "*No!*"

Suzan, please put your bra back on. "*No!*"

No, I can't handle life without the relief that comes in bottles. No, I can't go to KMart without coke. No, I can't do aerobics without a pill. No, I can't get the mail without Smirnoff.

"No, Nancy." Nancy Reagan doing an anti-drug campaign is like having Alfalfa promoting Clairol. Angry, anxious kids are supposed to adopt this Pez dispenser in Chanel as a role model? Rigid, unempathetic bony-butt— you're no Betty Ford! But thanks for trying.

I need something to say *yes* to. But what? I'm not a *pray-er.* C'mon, how could God and the Holocaust coexist? Religion is about fear and finance. I'm not going to follow rules that were made up two thousand years ago by a bunch of old guys with control issues.

But just in case . . . looking up at the stucco I may snort later—I double-dare the Higher Power I wish existed. Okay, big boy, stop me from reaching for that straw. Well, this is ridiculous. I can't believe in a god that looks like the guy on the ceiling of the Sistine Chapel. If I'm going to pray, I need to find an image that I can believe in.

Star Wars! Would the committee agree to George Lucas' *force*? The AA people said your higher power could be a doorknob. Can I tap into something more powerful than my compulsion to get high? I'm dying to grab the straw from K and snort all these questions away. But I need my twenty-four hours of sobriety before I can share. It would be wrong to cheat in a program based on honesty. What a pickle! *God*, I wish I believed in you!

I sit tall, clutching the sofa pillow. My fingernails press into my palms.

And then, a *presence*. A warm heaviness spreads outward from my chest and fills my body. I hear a *voice*, clear and distinct. *"You don't have to do it. Go to bed. You'll be okay."*

Okay, where'd that come from? What's happening, am I mind melding with the universe? But it sounded so certain. Nancy, could this be a *yes*? As if by some invisible hand, I'm hoisted off the dangerous couch. If I can just get away from the snorting place, I'll have a better chance. Location, location, location.

"Kildare, I'm not getting high tonight. I'm going to bed." Who said that?

I'm almost safe in the bedroom when Kildare says, "But honey, coke's not your problem—*alcohol* is."

On booze, I'm loud and pissy, and I fall into trees. On coke, I'm his silent, skinny sex slave. I understand his drug of choice for me.

But I keep my focus: Wash face, take off clothes, get under blankets.

It's a night of firsts. K joins me. We wrap our bodies together. I flash on Ma in the forest. I, too, got through a whole day without dying.

Creating Honesty

The next day, I have my twenty-four hours of sobriety.

I walk into the Brentwood Methodist church at 12:25 p.m. The meeting starts at 12:30. I can't find the room, and the "you're late!" alarm is ringing. Not in the hall—in my head. I'm getting sweaty. This is a women's group, and I want them to know that I'm a *good* alcoholic.

I find the classroom just as the leader bangs a delicate gavel on the desk and take a seat in the back. To my relief, there is a *back*. There are three well-dressed ladies sitting next to the woman with the gavel. I look at the panelists, whispering to each other, munching snacks. There's a sparkle, an aliveness in their eyes. I think of the pictures I had taken for my portfolio. My eyes didn't sparkle.

I turn to the gal next to me and ask, "Excuse me, but what happens here?"

"Are you new?" New? I feel old, and used. She explains the meeting format: First, a panel chosen by the secretary speaks on a subject. Then, the meeting opens for sharing.

The leader's Mrs. Howell-like voice fills the room, and a dreadful feeling fills my gut. I knew this was an AA "women's" meeting, but I didn't realize it would be so full of *women*! Run, run, run! But these women don't look dangerous. They just look *rich*. Acrylic nails, Armani, jewelry, pantyhose. I thought all the Mercedes parked outside belonged to the clergy.

Again, as in kindergarten, I'm clearly in over my head. What if I'm not called on and don't get the chance to "share?"! I'll have stayed sober twenty-four hours for nothing! And what if I *am* called on! *Oooo*, it's the climb on a roller coaster.

The panel finishes speaking on something they call a tenth step, something about meditation. Or medication. Then there are "birthdays." The group sings "Happy Birthday" to women announcing various lengths of continuous sobriety. A hippie with long gray hair, wearing a flowing skirt, blows out twenty candles on a cake that's being held by a Doris Day. The room claps.

The happy hippie says, "Thanks to you and my sponsor, and my higher power, I haven't had to take a drink in twenty years!" That's a long time to go without vodka.

After the birthdays, the leader asks for a show of hands. "Due to the size of the meeting, those who shared last week are asked to not share this week." I *have* to share. I've got to let someone know who I am before I die. My plan is to share, go home, and let the alcohol kill me. I can't live without a buffer. But right now, I have an unbuffered twenty-four hours. I can legally share. I put up my hand. The leader points to me.

I know my line. "My name is Suzan, and I'm an alcoholic."

The room chants back, "Hi, Suzan!" Wow. I don't know what I said or how long I took saying it, but whatever it was, I said it with passion. The only thing I remember was expressing my astonishment over the hippie. "Twenty years of sobriety! I can't get twenty *minutes*." They laugh. What's with the glee? Don't they know they're *sober*? Do I have *sober* confused with *somber*?

A woman sitting in front of me turns around, pats my leg, and whispers, "Honey, we do it *one day at a time*." Hating yesterday and dreading tomorrow doesn't leave much time for today.

The meeting ends. Thanks for listening. I'm going home to drink now.

But I can't. A wall of women surrounds me. One after another, they ask for my phone number. They give me theirs, saying, "Call me." Call? As in— talk? On one hand, I feel I have a lot to say. On the other, I feel like no one wants to listen.

I gather up the pieces of paper, matchbook covers, and top left corners of deposit slips with the books and pamphlets that were given to me by "the literature secretary." I'm shoving as much as I can into my purse, wondering what to think, when one of the women looks in my eyes, and as if she *knows* my predicament, says, "Honey, let us love you until you can love yourself." That might take a long time.

"Thank you?" I don't know what to do with this. Someone is going to help me? Maybe we can negotiate. She can half-help me, and I can still drink a little. Driving home I think about Danny and the case of chablis in the cupboard . . . How can I get high now? I'll disappoint the women. AA has ruined my drinking.

The women said I'd never have to be alone again. They said more will be revealed, but will the "more" be tolerable? Will it be *too much* more? How can I trust? I have a history of trusting too fast. I must be careful.

Twenty-four hours of sobriety turns into forty-eight, seventy-two, then a week. They give out plastic chips, like medals, for periods of continuous abstinence. Thirty-day, sixty-day, six-month, and nine-month chips. I'm going for the gold. The 365-day birthday cake will be *mine*! I'm going to be the best newcomer ever!

I'm sober for a while, and women keep asking me, "Do you have a sponsor?" I get tired of hearing this because I have to say *no*. Then they give me this look of, *oh?* I get this feeling of *oh-oh*. In AA, you aren't assigned a sponsor. You have to go up to someone and ask, "Will you be my sponsor?" as in, "Will you be my Valentine?" There's the possibility of getting hit with a big, fat NO. Sick of no-sponsor guilt, I get brave one day and go up to a woman who's nursing her baby. How mean can she be?

"Will you sponsor me?"

She says, "Yes." She's very nice. Two years later, she wins a daytime Emmy for playing a bitch on a soap opera.

◆ ◆ ◆

Without anesthetizing life is a festival of feelings. Mostly bad. Every night I come home from meetings to the click, click, click on the coffee table. Kildare keeps it simple. Chop coke, carry wine. I watch him drink from a crystal glass. The stem is a frosted bird, the expanded wings cradle the glass. Pretty bubbles. How long can I go on resisting temptation? All I have to do to end my misery is pick up the straw . . . or the pretty crystal bird.

A Twelve-Step-Ford-Wife

I join Al-Anon, a support group for loved ones who've lost their alcholics to sobriety.

AA's sister twelve-step program was organized fifty years ago by Lois W., wife of Bill W., one of AA's co-founders. Bill got sober and Lois' job as vomit cleaner, excuse maker, and punishment architect ended. Bill's alcohol consumption no longer consumed her. But it's not like they started hanging out, going to movies and spas. Her husband's time and attention went to forming a little group of alcoholics who would try to keep each other sober. Having nothing better to do, Lois started a program.

A *good* Al-Anon member keeps her focus on her own life and off everyone else's. But I'm not a good Al-Anon. I am, according to the current trend of psychobabble, a full-blown *codependent*.

Now that Kildare knows he's being watched, he's become covert about his cocaine use. I scrutinize his substance intake. It's my new purpose. If I had been that focused in school, homework wouldn't have been a problem.

◆ ◆ ◆

K comes out of the bathroom one night with that dopey, buzzed-on-coke grin. As hall monitor, I stop him. With the authority of a Nazi calling for "papers!" I declare, "You're doing *coke*!"

He smiles like a demented sheep and puts his hand over his heart, "No! I swear, Little Honey, I'm not."

With spider sense and speed, I reach into the pocket of his robe, pull out a vial, and hold it triumphantly, "Then what's *this*?!"

Still grinning, Goofy swears, "On my mother's life, I don't know how it got there." Blasphemous! I make a mental note: will sacrifice loved ones— a character defect. I'm building my case to present to the AA and Al-Anon women. My hands on my hips—they're pretty much glued there lately—I demand, "You better call the paramedics to your mom's house right now, you, you . . . sociopath!"

On a drug sweep through the bathroom I spot, way up on the window ledge, a vial half-full of white powder. If I were still using, I'd see the vial as half-empty. With righteous zeal, I grab a dining room chair, snatch the vial from the window ledge and realize, I'm home alone . . . with a half-gram of coke in my hand. The coffee table is only a room away. Who'd know?

I'd know. A coke-come-down later, I'd want to jump out the window where I found the coke. My hands shake—my automatic response to the sight of a cocaine vial—I open the top, and before I change my mind, dump the we're-going-to-*fuck*-you-up stuff in the toilet. Later, I confront K. He tells me it must have been from the previous tenant. I actually wonder if he's telling the truth.

Will AA and *Donahue* be enough to keep me sober?

Anne Frank in Wonderland

Good things now come in AA meetings, not baggies.

I like AA. There are no dues or fees. You put a buck in the basket to pay for the coffee, cookies, and rental of the room. You laugh, cry, go "Oooo." You're empowered to get out and drench yourself in life rather than booze. There are no politics, no charismatic leaders, and no rules. Only suggestions. You may get rich while in AA, but no one gets rich off AA. If they're trying to be a cult, they're lousy at it.

These alcoholics are pretty smart for people stupid enough to let booze ruin their lives. I find the information I hear from the podium profound. I don't use any of it . . . but it's there if I choose to start. I might have stopped drinking earlier if I'd known there was something else to do.

During halftime, while pouring a little coffee on my sugar and Coffee-Mate, I overhear one guy whisper to another guy, "Speakers at meetings make up their stories." They do? But then I realize, he's me a week ago, determined not to be suckered in by these twelve-step Freudians.

I feel like I just woke up after a five-year snooze. Who am I? Processing . . . please wait . . .

Sobriety is changing my view of things. Is it my contact lenses? Certainly, my contact with everyone has been fuzzy.

As my vision improves, I see something is wrong . . . with Kildare. With *his hair*. What *is* it about his hair? I'm not putting blinders on this time. I've always managed to "not see things." I would bury baffling issues in a dark place where I wouldn't have to look at them. But I'm not going to overlook this.

I review our hair history. The first time we were "together," he said he didn't like having his hair touched. So instead of running my fingers through the hair, I ran them along his collar, his upper back, his neck. He stiffened if I got too far up the neck.

With my wet brain drying out, unsolved mysteries are capturing my attention. Without numbing agents, I become fully aware of each strangling thought. I can't turn them off.

I go to Leroy's. Perhaps he can shed light.

He takes a hit off a joint. "Yeah, it's interesting how Kildare's hair has been getting *thicker* since college." Yeah, especially because this is years before Rogaine.

Leroy hands me a book. "Here, see for yourself." It's a yearbook, I turn each page slowly, scared. And then I come across it. His name. His face. His scalp.

I've been living with an older bald married man for two years without knowing it. This can't be a typical AA problem. I'm sure.

Dear Abby: Have, unknowingly, married a man with dubious hair. Can't tell him I suspect baldness. Please advise. Signed, Hairy Issue.

What is the larger issue? That he was secretly bald, or that I didn't *know* he was bald? Right then, I swore to stay sober no matter what.

What adventures will I have here in Wonderland? Seeing through the looking glass is clearer than looking through the wineglass. Who knows what else I haven't noticed for five years?

So what the hell is that thing on his head? Telling him I know about his hair will make him madder than when I found out how old he was!

I don't say a thing. I obsess about it. I dream about it. I share about it at meetings. My sponsor tells me that if I mention Kildare's hair one more time, she'll *fire* me. So I switch sponsors.

There are many Susans in AA, and I become known as "the Suzan who talks about her husband's hair."

♦ ♦ ♦

One night, Kildare's sleeping. I'm awake and staring at his head. I must peek under the thing or I'll keep obsessing. He killed a bottle of wine with dinner so I figure he'll be unconscious till morning. I inch over to his pillow, careful not to shake the mattress. I reach my hand up and over to the *thing*. I touch it. So cautiously, I lift the furry mat and behold by moonlight, a smooth scalp. Only the front lifts, the sides and back are weaved into his real hair.

> *Every morning, K had locked the bathroom door. I'd find these pieces of blue cellophane floating in the toilet. Now I understand, they came from the double-stick tape. He **taped** the front of the hairpiece to his head to prevent it from flapping in the wind. The floating things always bugged me. They mocked me. Mystery solved.*

So I'm holding the thing, *hair-piecing* all this together, when I sense a shift in the room's energy. I look down. Kildare's eyes are wide and open. Some emergency alert system has awakened him. He says nothing!

I'm instantaneously consumed by guilt; you'd think I'd just *Bobbitt-ed* off his penis. We stare at each other. Then I realize I have (somebody's) hair in my hand. I lower the flap and back away. He turns and faces the wall.

I reach out gently. "It's . . . okay, it's . . . y'know . . . okay."

"Okay," he says.

Kildare's hair—it's his, he paid for it—is never mentioned again.

A Jewish Aerobics Instructor?
An Oxy-Moron?

"Are you finishing that?"

I stop doing cocaine, I start eating, and once I start, hold on to your matzo balls . . .

The only two things that get me to leave the house are the gym and twelve-step meetings. If I skip either, I could get myself in trouble. I combine the outings—I go from my aerobics class to my women's meeting.

I bring filtered water in a sports bottle; I'm prone to coughing, which is intrusive when someone's spilling her guts. This is 1983, pre-Evian, no one *buys* water. If you're thirsty at a meeting, you don't reach for the bottle in your bag; you walk down the hall to the fountain or you get coffee from the back of the room. So I have a new drinking problem, the women in the room look at the bottle suspiciously. Always anticipating the undeserved accusation, I take a sip and make sure I exhale on everyone around me.

A couple of the AA women suggest I become an aerobics instructor. Oh God, something new to think about that may lead to failure-to-act followed by self-disgust. Haven't the AA women been listening?! I'm the girl who cut gym class in high school because she sweated more than a sumo wrestler. I'm supposed to sweat for a living? With people watching? Besides, there are no Jewish aerobics instructors.

I think if you're going to exercise, you should get paid for it.

My two favorite instructors at the gym are Beverly—also the aerobics manager—and Beth. One day, after Beth's class, drunk with endorphins, I tell her about my background (dancing to Tom Jones in the basement) and that I want to teach class.

Her eyes roll slowly from my face to my feet and back. "Well, you'll have to lose at least twenty pounds."

Lesson: The price for dropping your vigilance? Searing pain.

I haul my fat ass home. Beth's voice joins the troupe in my head, singing a new verse, "At least twenty pounds." Not ten. *Twenty!* I eat two cans of Pringles. One per thigh. That's the best I can do.

A week later, a few pounds heavier, I make it to Beverly's class and tell her what Beth said. Beverly's disgusted.

"Put a routine together and I'll have you teach a class. If it goes okay, you can work here." Unfortunately for the neighbors below, I practice my high-impact aerobics routine at home. And when I can't put it off any longer, I call Bev.

I show up at the gym with albums. Leroy is there, his Jew-fro in a sweat-band, ready to hop along. Beverly sits on the floor in the back of the room.

I spend years hiding indoors for fear *they'd* see my thighs, and now my thighs are clad in tights, walking up to a microphone on a stage. My thighs will be flapping in front of a room full of people.

The only time I stand behind a microphone is when I speak at AA meetings, and before I can stop myself I say, "My name is Suzan, and I'm an . . . an aerobics instructor."

I start the music and begin shouting out orders. I jump, they jump. I wave, they wave. I shake, they shake. The best part of teaching aerobics? Yelling at people.

Suddenly, I feel a jab. Pain shoots through my leg. I've pulled my quadriceps muscle. I keep bouncing, smiling through the pain. I act as if I'm fine. No one suspects.

I'm hired, and I start losing weight.

Three months and fifteen pounds later, Beverly says they're going to lay me off. She keeps talking, but I have no idea what she's saying. Complaints or something . . . I fill in the blanks. *They hate me, they really hate me.*

I want to hide forever, but I need to come up with rent money to move out. There are other gyms. Other people to hate me. I muster up enough courage to go get rejected somewhere else. I call the Sports Connection, where Jamie Lee Curtis and John Travolta shot *Perfect*. Driving to the audition, the car keeps making U-turns. But AA's brainwashing is also at work. *Lace up and show up.* Oh brother, fucking clichés!

I show up, and am bouncing on the very stage Tony Curtis' daughter bounced on! Again, an aerobics manager sits at the back of the room taking notes. The review in her tiny office comes after. Luckily, I'm already drenched in sweat.

She's not warm. "Do you know that you had your eyebrows raised the whole hour?" Shock will do that. Bigger shock—I get the job.

Is It Too Much to Ask for My Husband to Stop Dating?

Now that I'm sober, I have different priorities. We're at Leroy's for another party.

Kildare says he has to leave for an hour, an emergency house call. A rich, thin, beautiful sitcom star is out of alignment, and he's going to adjust her. At her house. In Bel Air. I'm not fine with this. Sooo not. But who am I to complain? Not the important one in this relationship, that's for sure. I don't make the money.

Two and a half hours later, I'm watching my watch and the door, thinking—life just isn't that great! I might as well die drunk. My mind flashes scenes of wild, nude chiropractic frenzy. I think of the surprise party, when the surprise was finding Kildare in a closet getting a blow job.

I'm ninety days sober at a party with a philandering husband off "adjusting" a beautiful TV star. With all the drugs in the room, no one's feeling any pain except me. I'm feeling enough for everyone. I know if I just fling myself nostril first onto the cocaine-lined coffee table, the pain will subside. It's dangerous to wait here. AA says, "If you can't skate, stay off the ice." What am I doing at this *drug-a-paloosa*?

I find Leroy to say goodbye. But he insists I stay. "Let me introduce you to Jim, he produces commercials."

I tell Jim how I've been turned down by every commercial agent in town. "They say I'm too *exotic*, too *ethnic*, that I wouldn't be accepted in Iowa—a lifelong goal." Jane Pauley wouldn't have been persecuted in Poland.

Jim agrees with the agents. "I'd *never* use you in a commercial, *never*!" In other words, "Don't be handing me any pictures and résumés, girlie."

Under our dialogue, I hear the *atmosphere*—click, click, click, snort, guzzle. The extras are getting plastered. I'm *plutzing!* Can he hear the inner whimpering?

Then Jim says, "So, what are you doing about your career?"

"Nothing." I'm clearly peeved. "I'm recovering."

"Recovering? From what?"

"From alcoholism, *okay*?"

"You're a recovering alcoholic?!" (Rehab hasn't become trendy yet. Society's image of an alcoholic is a trench-coated, brown-bagging, grungy deadbeat—not a manicured aerobics instructor.)

With an air of . . . something, I answer, "Yes. I have three months of sobriety and if I don't get out of here right now, I could be snorting stucco by morning."

Jim says, "Listen, it's *Sue*, right? I'm directing a commercial for *New Beginnings*. Have you heard of it? They have substance abuse centers all over the country, so the spot will run nationally. We have to cast actors who are *real* alcoholics, or else we have to use the disclaimer 'This is a dramatization.' and I want to avoid that. Would you consider coming in for an audition?" (Like it would be tough finding actors in Hollywood who are real alcoholics.)

I guess *never* isn't as long as it used to be. Luck is when opportunity meets preparation. As far as playing a drunk, I'm prepared!

The manipulating doctor is no longer my main focus. I spend the next hour telling Jim about AA, how it works, all the slogans, and the humor. And then I go home and call my sponsor.

My first national commercial—

The screen is dark, Pachelbel's *Canon in D* plays quietly. There is the sound of a match being struck and then a close-up of a face—my face—illuminated by the candle I'm holding.

"My name is Suzan and I'm an alcoholic." The camera pans right as I light the candle of the person next to me. He says his name and that he's an alcoholic. He lights the candle of the person next to him, who does the same. Then the camera pulls back to reveal fifty of us holding candles. We're in black, all you see are glowing faces. (My friends from AA. They were happy to show that alcoholics look like normal upstanding citizens.) The voice-over: "At New Beginnings, we help one person at a time, one day at a time."

> *The commercial ran for six years. After I left the lying-dog-of-a-chiropractor, the residuals helped pay the rent. Also, my close-up was used in the New Beginnings print campaign, and I kept seeing myself in newspapers with the candle. But my role with New Beginnings didn't end there . . . .*

I come home from meetings to the click, click, click . . .

K makes lines of cocaine on the coffee table. They draw my attention. They *are* power lines. *Danger, Will Robinson!*

I feel desperate enough to call one of the women from the Brentwood meeting. Alice R., she looks like Harriet Nelson. The first time I heard her share, she talked about the car mechanic who ripped her off. She called him a motherfucker! I love the woman.

"Alice, I'm losing my mind!"

"Just hang on."

"How do I hang on?"

"By letting go." The woman's a Zen master.

I have to let go of trying to get *him* sober. I live with an alcoholic, and that's the way it will be until I do something about it.

She says, "Suzan, honey, it's easier to ride a horse in the direction it's going." She doesn't know what a strong rider I am. I'll turn the beast around by feeding him doses of twelve-stepology at meals and on weekends. I couldn't cure Ma and Daddy, but I was a kid. I'm smarter now.

To Leave or Not to Leave

I'm three months sober—

There are two half-packed valises on the bed. I call my sponsor and between gulps, "I'm leaving Kildare . . . really . . . I am! *I DON'T WANNNA GOOO!*"

My sponsor says, with a compassion so foreign to me, that my sobbing stops, "Oh, honey, when the time is right, you'll leave. You'll know. You'll just know. And you won't second-guess it."

How does she know this shit? Perhaps the woman overestimates me. Is she one more person telling me I can do things I can't?

I unpack.

I'm five months sober—

If I have to live on my own, I'll need furniture, clothes, groceries—so I get on another game show. *Child's Play* is hosted by Bill Cullen. This time I don't have Quaaludes to kill the stage fright.

I stand in front of the cameras, shaking, about to go for the big money bonus. Bill, who is physically handicapped, whispers in my ear, "If you win, please don't jump on me. I fall over easily." I can relate to that.

So when I win the $7,300, I jump straight up in the air. Had I been loaded, he'd have gone down.

I get home, I'm in the tub, and I hear "click"! But it's not the razor on the coffee table. It's the thought: Move out or die drunk.

When the check comes in the mail, I run out and get a brand new car. I drive to the newsstand and scan the classifieds for rent-control apartments in Santa Monica. There is one! I zoom over as fast as my new six cylinders will go, only to find a dozen people already there. Gulp. It's a large one-bedroom, second floor, nineteen blocks from the ocean: $325 a month! With the determination grandmothers use to lift trucks off babies, I approach the small bald man handing out forms—he owns the building. The line of tenants looks greedy and eager. This game show is called *Fuck the Other Contestants*. In times of desperation, we're often given a feeling of entitlement we don't normally have. It's called—survival. Or—living with Dr. Strangelove will one day kill me.

Suddenly, I realize, I'm *a woman*. A human with breasts! I pull Mr. Landlord aside. "Excuse me, may I have a minute of your time?"

"Yes," his eyes say, "take my time. Please!"

Hooking my arm under his, I guide him to the street and doing a full-blown Vanna White, present my just-washed, bright orange, bird-shit-free car. The Fiat glistens as I speak wistfully, "Remember Snow White at the dwarfs' house? *I* don't like to see a mess, either." It's true, I don't like to see a mess, that's why I keep it dark in my house. This man doesn't need to know how, as I'm putting one thing away, my focus is already on the next thing, so things get left all over the place. Do you have any idea how much I get done between putting on each shoe? Yes, I'm messy. But I'm sober now, I can change.

Two hours later the landlord calls. I have the apartment.

I call Ma again, and like when I left Lewis, Ma's paying full fare for a ticket to L.A. to help me move out. I'm packing when Kildare comes home. "My mother's flying in from Montreal tomorrow. She's going to help me move."

We talk about what I'll be taking. "The bed, it was mine, and that lamp."

"Uh-uh," he says, "I paid for that lamp."

"But K, there's no overhead lighting in the apartment."

"Too bad."

"Look, Kildare, in a divorce I could get *half*, I'm only asking for the lamp—"

He's snickering, "No, Little Honey, you can't get anything. I had the marriage nullified when we got back from Vegas."

I try to make sense out of what he's saying. "But how can you do that without my knowing?"

He smiles, pouring wine into a crystal glass. That's how I found he could forge my signature. So the real story is—he's old and bald, already married, and a felon.

The next day Ma comes and she makes sure we leave *with* the lamp. A few guys from AA help me move my bed, wicker chair, easel, couch, and my twenty-one-inch TV.

It's late, Ma is asleep in the bedroom—

I'm lying on the floor of my new living room, on a bed made of blankets, with boxes all around, and my lamp, the only light in the room. I'm feeling sorry for myself. How did Ma do it in the forest with branches and Nazis? As I fall asleep, a warming thought comes, "Hey, I got into recovery so Kildare wouldn't leave, and then I end up leaving him."

> *I have a dream—I'm on stage in a dimly lit, smoky theater ready for rehearsal. My costar makes his entrance. I know it's my turn to speak and I can't remember my line. I look down at the script, but the dialogue is in hieroglyphics. So I improvise and run across the stage, jump on the actor, arms around his neck and legs around his waist, kiss him and say, "Hi, honey, how was your day?" He hisses, "That's not your line." The director and the others from the audience echo, "That's not your line." I slither off the actor, looking to the audience for prompting, for direction. None comes. I plead, "I don't know what else to say . . . " If living for others is not my purpose, what the hell is? I see my sponsor in the audience. She's holding a bag of groceries. How nurturing. I go to her. She presents me with a baby, "Here." I'm confused. As I cradle the infant, it shrinks into . . . a tiny, paper doll, so delicate. To my horror, as I stroke the doll, the arms come off. Then the legs. I'm crying, "I can't take care of her! Please! She's falling apart. Please somebody take her!"*

During the day my mind is busy figuring out if I should go left or right, so my subconscious faxes me at night.

I left the man I thought I'd spend the rest of my life detoxing with. Who will take care of me now?

From the woods (Brentwood) to the 'hoods (South Santa Monica).

It's morning, I'm making coffee and looking out the window. I'm surprised to see how *dark* it is. When I first came to see the apartment, I hadn't noticed there were no white people. I live in the 'hood. I plan to go out on the balcony with the Coppertone and get dark as quickly as possible. I'm still trying to blend in.

Ma and I walk to Eddie's liquor store on the corner to get some milk. Looking around, she says, "*Shvartzehs!* Nuting but *shvartzehs* everyvhere!"

"Ma! Shh!"

"Vhat? Dey understand Yiddish?"

Good point.

◆ ◆ ◆

Later, we take a rest from unpacking. I turn on the TV. Calgon, take me away. Thank God the previous tenant had been pirating cable and the connection is still hot. And thanks to Radio Shack, I have coaxial cable.

Ma wants to watch the news, so I turn on KNBC.

This just in: Kelly Lange—a good news anchor, her hair would stay put in a tornado—sounds serious, "Two whales are stuck!" We cut to a live video of two whales trapped by encroaching glaciers. They're swimming around in circles, like at SeaWorld, only they're in Alaska. Apparently, if the whales don't break free of the ice and get to open sea, they'll die. Ships dispatched from nations around the globe steam to their rescue. I flip stations. This is the *lead* story on every news show.

Ma and I sit and watch, munching on cheese danishes she brought from Montreal. Me, I'm more interested in the danish. My obsession has switched from Kildare to carbohydrates.

I flip back to a somber-sounding Kelly. "Will the multinational task force be in time to cut through the frozen sea, or will the glacial cage close in and seal the fate of the mammoth couple, entombing them as the world looks on helplessly?"

At least they're in a relationship.

"Oy," Ma shakes her head. "Hanala, look at dis! To save two vales, da whole vorld comes. But to save *six million Jews*, nobody came."

I put down my danish. "Sure Ma. The world *likes* whales."

> The second night I have another dream—my tropical fish are floating out of their tank! I'm running around the apartment, trying to catch them and get them back into water. If I don't, they won't survive. I'm the fish out of water. I knew how to do a relationship. I don't know how to do **alone.** I call Kildare.

Ma's back in Montreal, Kildare and I are still living apart, but dating.

I want to see him four nights a week, he's arguing for three. On the nights alone, I think I'm going to shrivel from the lack of him.

Friday night is date night. We're at his place necking, kisses so good, I'm twinkling.

He says, "Oh, Herb called. Arnold's insurance company decided to settle the case." (Remember, after the car accident, my lawyer Herb sent me to Dr. Kildare.)

"Thank God, I'm not gonna have to go to court. Did Herb say how much he got? I should call him."

K says, "Oh, you don't have to Little Honey, he told me. $12,000. He's sending you a check for $9,000, and me a check for $3,000."

"Huh?"

"For chiropractic services."

"Oh, ha-ha."

"Hey, I took the time to treat you, you owe for the appointments. But I want to be fair, so I'm giving you a 30 percent discount."

You know in cartoons, how a light bulb appears over someone's head? The Vegas Strip flashes above me, "HE'S PUTTING ROSEWOOD IN THE CONTROL PANEL OF HIS CESSNA, YOU'RE STRUGGLING TO PAY FOR SOCKS, AND HE WANTS YOU TO GIVE HIM $3,000! Wake up, girl—he doesn't care about you! And that's *not* okay!"

He's batting those long lashes. "If you don't sign this agreement, the case will just have to go to court."

I put my clothes back on. "Fine, I'll sign. But, you know the last kiss we had? That's the last kiss we're ever going to have. We're over." He smiles. Bat-bat. I leave.

Kildare keeps calling, I shake, but I hang up.

"Hi, honey, you didn't really mean . . . " CLICK.

"Oh, Little Honey, c'mon let's get together tonight . . . " CLICK.

"I bought you a bracelet . . ." (pause) CLICK.

It's much better being the one who does the clicking.

When you're going through hell—don't stop!

It's been three weeks off K, but I'm still obsessed. Can't think unless thinking is about him. How convenient it would be if he'd die. If he were dead, I could live. I imagine him crashing his plane and his face embedded with splinters from the new wood paneling. I don't really want him dead—limping maybe—I want my *thoughts* about him to die. But they don't.

I must make my hell a drive-through, not an all-you-can-eat buffet. For this I need help. AA works because we're not all terrified on the same day. I load up on meetings. A woman shares what she calls an obsession antidote. It becomes my mantra. When I catch my mind drifting back to him, I repeat, "God, keep Kildare out of my heart and out of my mind; keep me centered and active in my own life." I shift my focus off him and where his cheatin' lips might be, and onto my career, my workout, my Fritos.

Thoughts of Kildare come in fast, hundreds a day, like Spam. Pop, pop, delete, delete. I get faster at catching obsessive thoughts. They come less.

What's going to happen now that my significant other is becoming insignificant? Thinking less about *him* is giving me more time to think about *me* and my new role in the world.

One night, I'm falling asleep and suddenly jerk into a sitting position. Wow! I went a *whole day* without thinking about him!

A Typical Day (Okay, So Not in Idaho)

Eight months sober—

My neighbor Heather is a supermodel. I like her anyway. She's the only other white person living within a mile. And, boy, is she white. Her heavy blond hair swings in slow motion. It wouldn't dare split, frizz, or cowlick. It doesn't get attacked by heavy metal, like curling irons. Heather's hair is smooth and straight without being gooped, rolled up, or otherwise persecuted. My hair recoils from my scalp in all directions and can pick up the BBC.

She has that just-thrown-together look by just throwing something together. Her jeans are comfortable. For twenty years I've looked for comfortable. Whether they're designer or from K-Mart, blue jeans give me a wedgie. If they fit at the waist, they're tight at the crotch, and they're so tight on my thighs, I can't bend my knees. The denim's always too coarse, and I chafe. I don't know how farmers do it.

Heather rolls up her baggy off-brand jeans and her legs still look longer than my whole body. When we talk, I'm fascinated by her face and how she moves it. She pouts. Not that she's pouting, it's just her default position. And the cheekbones, the ones I've wanted since my first Barbie, stay still, she doesn't move them at all.

One morning we're in my kitchen. I'm pouring coffee—without Kahlua—when Heather says, "I need your total attention."

I put down my coffee cup.

She places her hands in front of her ears and slowly . . . dramatically . . . pulls the skin back and looks at me, her eyes wide with expectation.

"Heather, I don't know what you're doing."

"*LOOK!*" she says. I'm looking.

"Look! My jowls, the smile lines . . . GONE!"

Jowls? "Heather, nothing's, uh . . . different."

"Grrr!" Again she pulls the skin, "SEE!!! *See* how much better I look?!" Apparently, she's given this a lot of thought, and is committed to this point of view.

"Heather, I'm sorry, but your face is perfect."

Boy, is she pissed. *Not* needing a face-lift is a problem? But I understand. She's mad because I've been dismissive—or at least nonsupportive—of something that's of great importance to her. She wants me to bless a face-lift. Then she can feel less guilty about having one. I know this because I'm studying psychology, and I know everything now. I've diagnosed Heather with body dysmorphic disorder. The BDD causes her to see herself differently than we do. Not that there isn't basis for her concerns; now that Heather's older—twenty-four—she's facing older age and has been downgraded from practically supermodel to hand model. She must be totally freaked, even though her agent has no trouble getting her hand jobs. She wears dainty white gloves when tanning by the pool to avoid freckling her moneymakers.

Her childlike voice is tin-thin. "Okay, Sue, never mind. I've got this doctor's appointment in Beverly Hills . . ." Then, in a whisper, "A plastic surgeon—"

"Oh?"

Still whispering, "And, I've taken some Vicodin."

"Ohhh?" *Some?*

Ingratiatingly, baby-beggingly, she's all snuggly. "I probably shouldn't drive. Can you take me?" This beautiful, rich, thin, tall and blonde woman—who's stoned on drugs *I'd* like to be on—is asking me to drive her to the plastic surgeon, when *I* have *multiple* defective parts I can't afford to fix?

So I agree.

When her name is called in the waiting room, she turns to me and clutches my arm. "Come in with me, you've got to meet Melvin."

Dr. Melvin Shapiro of Beverly Hills peeks in the exam room and tells Heather he'll only be a moment. He's a fatherly sort, gray hair, big crooked nose, crooked little smile. He looks at me, and not knowing what to think, closes the door. Heather whispers her confession, "I'm in love with him."

I have no response. I try to organize all of this. What's in it for him I understand: she's twenty-four, five-foot-ten in stocking feet, and a *shiksa*—gold to aging Jewish men. He's fifty and five-foot-three; what is she, on a frequent-fucking program? Three blow jobs and two screws later, she'll qualify for a butt lift? I'm weighing the mutual benefits as Heather introduces me to her married, aging, scalpel-wielding midget, Dr. Shapiro.

He scrutinizes my face and says, "You have a beautiful face, your nose does nothing for it." He thinks I need his professional opinion? I've been studying my profile in mirrors since my nose grew a nose. I turn sideways to the mirror, use two fingers, and block the bump. I want to kill the bump.

I burst out crying. They can hear me in the waiting room of the doctor down the hall. "I can't afford it. I hate my nose but"—huge sob—"I don't have money!" I go to auditions, trying to hold in my nose. Doesn't he know that?

He waves his hands in front of me. He's saying something. What is it? I try to focus. I have to come back from outer space.

He's frantic, "Stop crying, it's okay! I'll give you a free nose job."

A free nose job? But no blow job? I'm afraid to ask.

Where do I sign up? One month later, I'm on the table experiencing *twilight sleep*. I want to make sure he gives me the right nose, so I coach him, without moving my lips. "Doc, I do *not* want the nose of Morgan Fairchild. Don't touch the nostrils. I like my nostrils. Did you do Michael Jackson?"

I decide this operation has gone on too long. I'm bored. I need more Demerol. Or a phone. "Listen, I got some calls I gotta make." I figure it's a good time to find an agent.

"Grace, how many milligrams of Demerol did you give Suzan?" She tells him. He's surprised I can still talk.

"Doc," I say, looking directly into his eyes, "I used to go to the mall on more than this! And I'd come home with fabulous shopping choices."

Three weeks later, the swelling subsides and I have the nose I always wanted. Heather and I are back in the kitchen admiring me, when she says, "I need your total attention."

I turn to her.

"Look. No really, look!" She pushes out her chest.

I'm looking.

She whips out her shoulder pads, sticks them in her bra, stands tall, and says, "Don't you think I need bigger boobs?"

I'm Free to Date Again!
. . . and I Should Be Happy About This?

Obsession-free me—

Sometimes, when I see a man, I think back, but I can't be sure if we've ever had sex. Not just because I spent so many nights in alcoholic blackouts, but because—even sober—I've gone on dates without being *on* them. My body went, but my mind was elsewhere.

I see guys in meetings, but you know how a dog doesn't poop where he eats? It's a bad idea to date men where you go to recover. After the character-bashing ends, you keep bumping into the dogs at meetings.

As a practicing agoraphobic, my options are limited. The pizza boy? FedEx? Also, there's a problem with my standards. I'm looking for Tom Cruise with Alan Alda's personality.

Which presents another problem—who am I good enough for? The answer depends on who I've been talking to. Ma, Sylvia, or my support group. I can't trust my support group. Their job is to support me, no matter how disgusting I am.

And it depends on the time of the month. Once a month, my self-approval rating sinks lower than when I try on bikinis. Men may get moody, but nothing comes close to the creativity of PMS. When I turn into one big ovary, I wanna move to Wyoming—where the average woman is a size sixteen—and work on a cattle ranch. Standing next to a cow I look skinny.

I can feel skinny, and an hour later, I'm fat. I'm split in two.

"You're too yucky to find a man."

"Shut up, leave her alone."

"But look at the back of her arms."

"Somebody will love her."

Maybe somebody will—but first I have to get out the door to find him.

◆ ◆ ◆

I join a video dating service. The guys out there, *oy*. The best of the bunch is a guy who drives a Rolls-Royce. He snarls all the way to dinner, "Why do people always have to fucking stare at me?"

"Buy a Honda," I tell him. "Nobody will look."

He was very hard of hearing . . .

Harry Putzman, M.D., and I meet at AA one evening, pouring Coffee-Mate into our decafs. He's a not-as-attractive, not-as-tall Danny DeVito. I'm starved for a connection. I forgive his shortcomings.

Harry is an anesthesiologist. He jokes, "One pill for the patient, one pill for me. One pill for the patient, two pills for me." We leave at halftime for Pancakes A'Plenty and he tells me, "Funny, ha-ha, all those surgeries, and no one knew I was as buzzed as the person I was operating on!"

A voice in my head says, oh, I couldn't have heard right. I'm just hoping he's a good guy who could become a friend.

On to my place. On to my couch. At 2:00 a.m., after hours of just saying *NO*, I say, oh, all right! (It seems easier. After all, he bought dinner. And I want him to like me. And I have temporary brain damage from years of not knowing I have the right to say *NO*.)

As far as birth control, I tell him I'm not on the pill. He doesn't have condoms.

He assures me, "I'll pull out just before I—"

"Harry, do you know what they call people who use the *pull-out* technique? *Parents*."

"Don't worry," he tells me. "I'm a doctor."

It's painful, a sloppy mess. I plead with my newly found higher power for an out-of-body experience. If this is what *sober sex* is like, maybe I *will* wait till I'm married. Having sex loaded was never like this! Having sex on a Quaalude, I felt . . . like a guy. I could jump out of bed, stand naked underneath fluorescent lighting, and not give a shit about cellulite. But it's different now. I grab a blanket and put my thighs under wrap before I walk to the bathroom.

And then, a funny thing—I'm at the bathroom sink, I look at myself in the mirror and say, "I'm pregnant." I'd never said that before. But I know. Like I knew about Host, the game show, and coming to L.A. I knew.

The morning after . . .

I'm pooped from punching myself in the inner-child all night. I want to sleep until it's the morning after the morning after.

But I drag myself to my women's AA meeting, head hung in shame. How could I let myself be used like that? Why didn't I just say, "Get the hell out!"? Why was pleasing him so important that I'd do something I found disgusting? And where are the doughnuts? Normally there are doughnuts! I'm pathetic. I'll do anything to avoid being angered at.

AA states: You're as sick as your secrets. To stay sober, I've got to share honestly. But what will they think of me, this group of housewives and career women? I need them—like a child needs a mother. But mothers can turn sour faster than milk left in the sun. I can't let the women know how low I had sunk. Yeah, I've been lonely, but that's no excuse for having sex with someone I wouldn't have *pizza* with. I'm a sober slut. I'm determined to go to the grave with the secret. So, naturally, as the meeting begins, the leader calls on me first.

I blurt out the events of last night. When my five minutes are up, sharer's remorse sets in. I regret revealing the humiliating details of my debauched night with the slimy sex salesman. Will these acrylic-nailed, face-lifted women now think less of me? If they do, I will too. But it's too late to take it back. I sit in my chair—making myself as thin as possible—wishing I were in Quebec.

And then, Rose W.—fiftyish, June Cleaver hair, pearls, and a sweater set—shares that she'd been raped as a teenager and it took her decades to recover. She's happy to report now, when having sex with her husband, she bites her pillow to avoid disturbing neighbors with her screams of delight. Then Beverly B. tells us when her guy grabs her after the gym, she feels scuzzy and pushes him away; when he grabs her after her shower, she tells him to forget it, she's too clean. The meeting turns into a confessional of oral sex, gay sex, and even gerbil-related sex. It's nice to know I'm not alone.

◆ ◆ ◆

Oh . . . the pregnant thing? Yup. The first test turned blue, the second had a line through it, the third test formed a dot. I wanted the opinion of three manufacturers.

I call Dr. Pull-out. "Hi Harry, I'm pregnant."

"Who's this?" Oh, right, I hadn't said. I'd been distracted. Hormones were playing tennis in my frontal lobes.

"It's Suzan. From the AA meeting." Then from the bed, remember?

"You're pregnant? Well, it can't be mine. What kind of a game are you playing?" I feel like I do when I see a swastika.

He goes on, "So what do you want, money? Why don't you try getting it out of some other guy." Click.

The next day. I'm at Abortions Are Us. I must remove the collection of cells before it forms fingers.

The procedure is over, I'm in bed in a recovery room the size of a Costco and in pain. Did they take out a yard of intestines, too? I'm cramping and nauseous from the anesthesia. And from the anesthesiologist who's half the reason I'm here.

Women of many colors lie in beds, screaming and crying. Mothers, husbands, and friends are consoling them. I'm trying to console myself, but I feel too guilty. I wanted to ask one of the women from my AA meeting to come with me today, but I was sure she had better things to do with her time. I hadn't shared about the pregnancy.

I never questioned "should I have it, should I not." Only *real* people have babies.

My Blind Date

Next victim—

Mia, my best AA friend, introduces me to Justin, the psychoanalyst. He's in the program, but lives in the Valley so if we date, and then split up, we'll never see each other again.

A couple of weeks into the relationship, we have our first fight. We're arguing, analyzing, annihilating, when all of a sudden, he calls me a *narcissist*.

I fire back, "I can't be a narcissist, you idiot! I *hate* myself!"

"A narcissist, you dingbat, is someone who's so self-involved, she's oblivious to the feelings of others!"

"Huh?"

He explains, "If a child's needs aren't met, they can grow up to become an adult who's self-centered and only thinks of him, or *herself*. He or *she* has an organizing system that says, 'You're not going to think about me, so I have to. All the time.'"

Oh. I thought being a narcissist meant you thought *highly* of yourself, not *only* of yourself. So what's his point? I'm Ma? And what do I do with this? I break up with him. I can't be with someone who knows me that well.

But as I tell him it's over, his eyes tear up and he says, "I'm sorry. I know I hurt you, and I'm so sorry." Words I've waited a lifetime for. I give him sex.

The following Saturday we're standing in the 7-Eleven choosing candy to go along with our video rental. I notice him leaning into the candy shelves. His head is in the M&M's rack. He's squinting.

I giggle, "Whadaya blind?!" He straightens up.

He tells the Gummi Bears, "Yes, technically."

Finally, he looks at me. Well *toward* me. "I don't know how to tell you . . . I, uh, I started going blind when I was twenty-six. It's gotten worse."

I'm thinking *asshole*! Why, pray tell, are you driving with *ME* in the fucking car if you're BLIND?! My goodness, I *am* a narcissist.

I try to appear not too *it's-all-about-me*. "That's awful! And, by the by, can you . . . see well enough to drive? I mean, have you had any, uh, accidents?"

"I hit a man."

"Oh, my God! What happened?"

"He died." Died. Just like that, he says, "died." Details, please. Give me the six o'clock sound bite, the *USA Today* rapid report.

"It was dark, the man was eighty. He was wearing black and he walked out from an alley." Okay, so it's not first degree. Okay, so Justin's almost blind. I can accept that. It's not all bad—now I can walk around the house without makeup.

But a few months later, Justin tells me he's decided to move to Morro Bay where you don't have to see. It's a small town. And it's always foggy.

He moves. I'm devastated, but also relieved. I was tired of holding my stomach in.

A Zit So Big, It Makes Its Own Weather

I'm breaking out in new places . . .

The skin on my face isn't milky white, it's the Milky Way. I'm talking the Big Dipper, the Seven Sisters, on a bad day—Mars. I know it's not good to squeeze, but I'm Mr. Whipple. I've made *more* zits, and created scars. And there's no twelve-step program for compulsive zit squeezers.

Leaving the gym, I catch my reflection in the rear-view mirror. A bump is blossoming between my eye and my nose. No way will I mess with that! Heather knew a girl who squeezed a pimple there and died three weeks later. It infected her brain.

But I can't let the thing live as if to announce to the world that I'm defective. *Refu-geek* pushing through. I sterilize a safety pin by stabbing it in a bar of Dove soap, which is 44 percent cold cream. I'll operate and moisturize at the same time. I zero in on the magnifying mirror—which I look in whenever I'm feeling too good about myself—and jab it. Ow. Press, press. Nothing comes out. Oh God, it's going inside! Killer pus is making its way to my brain!

No, worse. The bump swells into a blueberry. And there it stays, casting a shadow for a whole year. It obstructs my vision. It was hard to leave the house *before* the blueberry. I want to just die. I'd see a dermatologist, but that costs money. I try Clearasiling it, so now I have a dry and flaky bump.

Then one day, the thing starts growing. South. Face cancer. I know it. This is the price I pay for the years of Bain du Soleiling.

I'm back at UCLA Medical Center. The doctors in the ER *have* to see me. Doogie Howser cuts into my face and removes a chunk. He stitches me up and I'm sent home.

I wait for the results of the biopsy. Nothing on TV can stop my funeral fantasies. I want to drink. No news for ten days. Then the call, "Negative." I'll live; I'll be Scarface, but I'll be alive.

At the window of the aerobics room, I'm waiting for the class before mine to end—

In a moment my benign cyst will be up on that stage with lights shining on it.

A man in shorts speaks. "I love your class."

"Oh! Thank you."

"Listen, I don't want to make you feel uncomfortable but—" Oh no. Please, anything but a *but*! Please be kind. How can he know how fragile I am when my goal in life is to act tough and secure? I hunker down, grabbing the ground with my toes so I don't shoot off the planet.

"I'm a dermatologist and I can help you."

For someone big and strong, I feel small and weak. "Well, thank you, but my money goes into aerobic music and sweatbands."

He pulls a card from his gym bag. "Oh, no—I mean, I just want to see a beautiful girl like you look her best. No charge."

I take his card. I'm afraid to speak. What if he changes his mind?

As I'm teaching the class, jumping and screaming "eight more" over and over, no one sees the tears through the sweat.

I become a regular at his office and like magic, my Dr. Welby smooths out the scars.

My agent calls—

"You know the guys who produced *Airplane!*?"

"You mean David and Jerry Zucker and Jim Abrahams?" You'd think given my love of TV shows and movies I'd have a knowledge of who creates them, but I've remained oblivious of the behind-the-scenes people. There are exceptions. I know Carl Reiner, the creator of *The Dick Van Dyke Show,* because he played Alan Brady; and Alfred Hitchcock, who appeared in everything he did. It's as if I didn't *want* to know production people existed. My TV life is real to me, not created.

However, I've seen *Airplane!* a dozen times. A traumatized pilot gives up on life and flying, and then rises above debilitating fear to become the hero.

My agent says, "You'll be auditioning for the producers. They're doing a movie called *Ruthless People.* Big budget. Bette Midler, Danny DeVito." *Oy.* This could mean free SAG health insurance!

Something happens to me as I walk into the conference room and I see the men who made *Airplane!* sitting behind the table. Suddenly, I start performing my favorite scenes. I'm Leslie Nielson, Julie Hagerty, I'm the gay guy who made a pterodactyl out of a piece of paper. I ask, "Whose idea was the double sunglasses?" and I mime Robert Stack whipping off a pair of glasses.

Here's the difference between this audition and every other one I've ever been on: I'm not trying to tuck in my thighs—I'm having an honest-to-good time. Jim, Jerry, David and I spend twenty minutes doing improv.

I get home, there's a message on my machine, "You got the part."

I play a TV aerobics instructor. It's a stretch. I wrote my own lines, "Squeeze your buns! If *you* don't, no one else will!" "Lift those pepperoni thighs!" "Breathe!" Okay, the last line I stole.

The night of the premiere, I'm sitting in the dark, waiting for me to come on the screen. Breathe? I can't. And then, there I am, a happy-looking thing, bouncing around and yelling. That's when I hear a shout from the back of the theater, *"Hey—that's my aerobics instructor!"*

And I thought I'd die without anyone knowing who I was.

Resentment—Taking Poison
and Waiting for the Other Person to Die

A call from Montreal, and a mystery solved.

Ma and Chochu have been in a two-year feud. Once more, I ask Ma what happened.

"From dis you don't need to know, all vhat I'm saying is, da Chochu is a *groisseh falsha*."

"A fake? What do you mean?"

"Nuting, I'm saying nuting. Better you don't know what she is."

If reverse psychology was ever necessary—"Fine Ma, don't tell me, I don't care, and you're probably just overreacting."

"Oh, yeah?! Okay, I'll tell you, and you tell me if I'm overreacting! Everybody tinks da Chochu is such an angel, a *haimisha balabusta*. Vell, she's not vhat she pretends!"

Finally, the rest of the story—

Rewind to Poland, 1940 (could be '42, '44), Ma and Chochu have found each other in the forest. Chochu is pregnant and has been hiding with her family.

One night, Chochu's group invites Ma's group to their camp for dinner. Ma, Daddy, Gedala and their friends are eating when Chochu's brawny brothers come up from behind, pounce, and grab their guns. The group tries reasoning with the brothers. Ma pleads, "Please give us back our guns, how will we survive?" The brothers laugh and tell them to leave.

One of them polishes what *was* Ma's pistol. "Go away, little woman." The other brothers join in, mocking Ma.

Ma turns to Chochu, who's stirring a pot over the fire. "Freidel, how can *you* do this? You are my cousin! Tell your brothers—for God's sake—to give us back our guns!"

Chochu won't look at Ma. She keeps stirring. Her brothers grab Ma by the arms. They're dragging her into the woods when Ma calls back, "You think our guns will save you? They won't. We will survive without them!" They release her, and she returns to her camp.

The following night Daddy sneaks off to the mayor's house. He goes for food and weapons, he comes back with news. "The mayor asked me, 'Fishel, did you hear what happened?' No, I told him. Then he told me, the brothers were looking for food near the village, and they were cornered by soldiers. They were all killed.'" They were dead—but *armed!*

Something rustles in the woods. Chochu appears, timid, husband Berel at her side. She's in labor. With the help of the women in *da group*, she gives birth. A boy. One of the men takes the baby, covers its crying mouth with a cloth, and disappears into the trees. He comes back alone. The group doesn't talk about this again. The baby or the guns. Is *this* Chochu's fifty-year headache?

◆ ◆ ◆

So now I understand. Holocaust leftovers. The gun thing had gotten stuck in a far corner of Ma's mind, like leftovers hidden behind cartons of milk in the fridge. Like smelly green mold, the stench of Ma's resentment was seeping out. She'd hidden the pain of Chochu's betrayal behind her need to stay connected to her cousin. Chochu is proof that Ma once had a family. But thirty years later, memories of Chochu's brother polishing Ma's gun pop into her conscious mind. She can't ignore them. *Resentment: reliving old hurts.*

The confrontation takes place in Chochu's kitchen—

The two women are alone. Ma asks Chochu how she could have just stood by while her brothers stole the guns.

Chochu says it was Ma's group's own fault. They'd been in the village the night before stealing food and calling each other by *Chochu's brother's names* as a trick so Chochu's family would be blamed.

Ma says Chochu is "making up a big lie!" The screaming is nonstop. And then they say nothing. For two years.

I play Kissinger again, I work on ending the cold war. Finally, a peace settlement. They're talking again. Maybe they figure they'll be dead soon anyway.

Chochu has a stroke . . .

Machines keep her alive. Weeks later, she's released from the hospital on the condition she stay at home. Chochu left her house seven times in twenty years. Now she can stay home without guilt. I wonder if she *wants* to get out.

One year later—

Berel comes home from synagogue and finds Chochu on the kitchen floor. They rush to the hospital, but there's been internal bleeding.

Ma calls me. "Da Chochu is dead. *Eighty years old* she vas, and *not one wrinkle* she had!" Important information.

"*OY!*" Ma says. "On da stairs, leaving da hospital, da Daddy yelled, and he shook da finger at me, '*YOU DID DIS!* Your *groisseh pisk* is vhat killed Freidel!' "

"Ma, how did *your mouth* kill her?"

"Da *y'idiot* says, 'Vhy you had to bring up da stories from da forest after so many years?' " Again, not really a question.

Ma says, "*Da y'idiot! I* killed da Chochu? I didn't kill da Chochu!" Was she asking, "I didn't kill Chochu, *did I?*" Ma despised Chochu, but they were best friends. Sure, best friends can bring on the worst pain.

Ma says, "Stay in L.A., don't come to da funeral, come for someting happy." I don't cry over Chochu dying. Strange, I cry over AT&T commercials. I cry at the end of *Scrooge,* every version, every time. My first-grade teacher read *Charlotte's Web,* I cried when Charlotte died—and I *hate* spiders. I must be carrying a resentment, too.

My sadness is for Berel and my cousins Molly and Jackie. And for Michael, Molly's son who called Chochu *Bubbe.*

Chochu's internal bleeding has stopped. Or would it keep spilling into my-cousin-Molly forever? And the guilt goes on, and the guilt goes on . . . drums keep pounding rhythm to my *chaynick.*

The Ninth Step

With my successful drinking career now over, I make amends to those I've harmed.

I owe CBS an apology for stealing from *The Young and the Restless*. The last time I did the show, I got drunk and walked off with the dress that wardrobe had given me. Karmic justice: This was the dress that slid up when I slid down the Christmas tree.

I can't get the dress back to *Y&R* because I gave it to a girl I sponsor in AA who's disappeared. I have two *babies*—as they are called by their sponsors—and neither has stayed sober; I call them my pair of slippers.

So, I make amends to *Y&R* by watching the show. I become addicted.

My habit comes to an end when one of the characters inadvertently gets engaged to her brother. I'm appalled. Not because a brother and sister are marrying—it happens, watch *Jerry Springer*—but because they just ran this plot a couple of years ago! It's like they're saying, "Y&R means: *You're all Retarded*." No way are they going to call me stupid. As far as I'm concerned, they owe *me* amends.

How can I make amends to Host's wife? What would I say? "Mrs. H, I apologize for humping your husband while you were in Florida doing the telethon for crippled children. Although I do think of your bed fondly, as it was the first place I ever saw myself in a ceiling mirror while engaged in a sexual act?" The ninth step says to make amends to those we've harmed *unless* to do so would injure them or others. Perhaps this one is best left alone.

Ma! Enthusiasm bubbles up inside as I think of clearing the air. Our relationship will no longer stink.

She picks up the phone. "Ma, hi. Ma, I have something to tell you. I'm an alcoholic."

She says, "Dere are no Jewish alcoholics, you must be someting else."

"Ma, what I want to say is, I'm sorry for the times I lied, and yelled—"

"Yeah, dis I heard a'ready, same story, you're alvays *sorry*." What comes out my mouth next creates more to make amends for later.

❖ ❖ ❖

Then—there's the amends I need to make to Arnold. I had flown Kildare and me to Vegas on Arnold's MasterCard: $400. Trashy Lingerie: $500. Imagining Arnold's face when he opened the bill: priceless. I feel justified, he jilted me and threw me out without a penny. But I'm working this stupid program so I call him.

Arnold's now living with his parents. Ida answers the phone sounding like one of the raspy, weathered women working multiple slots at the Desert Inn. "Suzan!" She can still make my name sound like a buzz saw cutting through steel in New Jersey.

"You wanna speak to Ah-nold? Hold on, Aaah-NOLD, PICK UP THE TELEPHONE. It's Suzan! OLD Suzan . . . Whaaat? . . ."

And then to me, "Hold on a second, dahling. He's on the toilet."

A second later, Arnold's on the phone. Only a slight slur to his voice. "How are you?"

"Fine. So here's the thing, Arnold. I'm in AA and there are these twelve steps, and one is to make amends to anyone I injured when I was drinking. I think it's about getting honest with anyone you've hurt, so you don't have to run if you see them coming up the street. And, it was wrong of me to charge my honeymoon on your MasterCard after you left me for Mona."

Man! That was hard to say! I mean the part about paying him back.

His tone is meek, not nasty. "I . . . I don't want you to pay me. I need . . . uh . . . can you . . . help me get sober?"

I hear Ida gasp. She must have taken her hand off the mouthpiece of the extension and slapped it over her mouth in shock.

Risking a freeway panic attack, I hop on the 405. Arnold's lost his car. He parked it, got drunk, blacked out, and never saw it again.

Ida pulls me into the kitchen with her curled, red nails. A cigarette dangling from her thin outlined lips, she croaks, "I don't know how to thank you. A *mitzvah*, you're doing me a *mitzvah*, I'm telling you. Help him, he's crazy, he's been in prison! Just imagine! We don't know what to do!"

Puff, puff.

I think Arnold might have a better shot at sobriety living in Santa Monica, so I move him in. We commit to meetings, we study the steps, we even pray, but as soon as I leave the house, Arnold takes the bus to Danny the dealer. I come home, he's comatose on the couch with the TV on and sunflower seeds in his beard. Perhaps I went one AA cliché too far.

I call the cops on Dealer Dan, they don't seem interested. There should be a program for snitches. Oh, yeah—Al-Anon.

I'll get Arnold spiritual, goddamn it.

One morning we're arguing the points of *The Serenity Prayer* when he shoves me against the wall and squeezes my hand so hard my ring cuts into my finger. (I still have the scar.) I'd like to tell you I stopped arguing with him, but I still have a few things to say. One is, "Arnold, it's time you left."

We cry at the door, then I watch him go down the street holding grocery bags filled with his stuff. I rehearse in my head the future phone call telling me of his death.

◆ ◆ ◆

A month later I get the phone call. From Arnold. "Hey, Floozen, you know the rehab you did the commercial for? I checked in last week."

New Beginnings ran a print campaign with the commercial. Behind the nurses station, they hung the ad of me holding the candle. When Arnold was admitted loaded and drooling, he pointed to my picture on the wall and slurred, "I used to be engaged to that girl."

Tilly, the nurse, said, "Yes, dear, I'm sure you were."

I come to visit. Arnold has an idea. He says, "The activities counselor here is a flake. You should try to get that job."

Me work in Century City? That's where the grown-ups go. Arnold keeps pushing, and I make an appointment to meet the program director. He tells me they've already replaced the flake. I'm not as much disappointed as relieved.

But Arnold won't shut up. "This new guy *needs* a counselor, he shouldn't *be* one. Call the director again."

More rejection? I'm just recovering from the first interview. AA says, "Take positive action whether you feel like it or not." Sometimes AA is really annoying. There's another saying: "FEAR is False Evidence Appearing Real." Or, what I like better, "Fuck Everything And Run."

I call. The program director gets on the phone and before I can say, "You don't want to hire me, *do* you?" he says, "Welcome aboard!" *Oy*. Now I have to show up and pretend I know what I'm doing.

I run group therapy, I run the patients around the park and I invent a new game show, *Wheel of Misfortune*. "Name six rock stars who overdosed before 1980." They love the challenge and never notice my subtle education style. Some patients want to continue therapy with me after being discharged. I join the National Association of Alcoholism and Drug Abuse Counselors, and start a private practice out of my house.

After leaving New Beginnings, Arnold manages to stay sober for three months. After his fourth *slip*, I strongly suggest he make amends to the people he harmed while using, like ex-partners Pete and Gary.

Pete and Arnold show up at my door—

Pete lives in an executive bachelor apartment. He rents his furniture. He even rents his pots and pans. He'd just done an intervention on himself. He drove to a hotel in the desert *near* the Betty Ford Center, and survived a self-imposed detox program. He yelled at himself for two days about how Quaaludes and coke ruined his life. Then he sat by the pool drinking water and sweating. The lounges were bolted to the ground so Pete had to keep switching chaises to follow the sun. He was determined to come back to L.A. sober and evenly tanned.

Marijuana was another thing. He asked Arnold if AA could help him stay off pot.

Re Pete

Arnold, Pete, and I go to an AA meeting—

The two of them are trashing the speaker. It's Ma all over again, only it isn't about the speaker's fat ass; it's about Pete and Arnold's fat egos.

Pete drops Arnold off, then drives me home. We're sitting in his Toyota and I don't know if it's his sarcastic humor, or that he looks like Captain Kirk, but all I can think is, "I wonder what it would be like to kiss him."

I say, "Kiss me." He's shocked, but willing. He leans in. It's a timid kiss. Damn. I want him to be confident, cave-manly. But he is sweet. And like with Kirk, you know he'll save the day. If there's one thing about Pete—he's dependable.

We become an *us*.

Arnold stops joining us for meetings. He stops calling. Mutual friends say they've also lost contact. (Years later, I search the Internet and come up with nothing. But I still think about him—how he'd smile, shake his head, and doing Jimmy Durante, say, "Come here, Floozen. Uncurl your toes. Let go of the planet . . . " Floozen.)

Three months later, Pete and I move in together . . .

AA says alcoholics don't take lovers, we take hostages. I take Pete, and he takes me to Palm Springs and Hawaii. I finally have a cruise director—someone to help me leave the house. And he makes me laugh.

I tell Pete I keep hearing odd noises in the house, and he says, "We have ghosts."

"We have goats?"

"Yeah—we have goats."

A week later, middle of the night, there's a loud *thunk*. I wake Pete.

"Pete, did you hear that? What is it?

"Poltergoats."

✦ ✦ ✦

A U.S. Supreme Court ruling declares alcoholism is not a disease. Insurance companies stop covering rehab. New Beginnings closes.

I fantasize about becoming a trophy wife—I'd have more time to work out and burn the calories from the bon-bons I eat while watching *Donahue*. But I don't feel like a trophy, I feel scared. With the hospital job gone, I can only go two places: AA meetings and the gym. I have *specific roles* to play there. Alcoholic aerobics instructor.

I get a laptop computer. It's fourteen pounds. Maybe I'll write a book. Maybe I'll watch TV and eat.

Pete becomes my primary job.

Weather Vain

I'm half-watching TV—

Kelly Lange looks concerned. Uh-oh. Terrorist attack? Breast implant meltdown? More whales stuck? Then I see the caption under Kelly's face, "STORM WATCH!"

Kelly says, "Fritz, is that . . . *RAIN*?" They cut to a close-up of water drops on a window.

"Yes, Kelly!" Fritz replies. "I'm afraid it is. Back to you." I flip channels. Killer drizzle is the lead story on every news show. You'd think Malibu was sliding into the Pacific. Nothing has slid anywhere, but just in case it does, we don't want to miss it.

Having grown up in Montreal—where January would *kill* a Southern Californian—I'm yelling at the TV, "It's *raining!* Oh, God, no. And, it's 57 degrees! Who'd be crazy enough to go out in that?? Attention, California shoppers, it's called *a coat.* They sell them at malls. Umbrellas too. The wands on the windshield aren't just for holding down parking tickets." Grrr. Okay, okay. It's not like they don't know about rain gear, it's just that living in L.A., who wants to *wear* it? We don't put up with smog, earthquakes, ridiculous rent, and bumper-to-bumper traffic to wear galoshes. If there's going to be *weather* here, might as well move someplace where kids can play outdoors without getting shot.

In Montreal, we pack a shovel in the car, not a magnum. *That's* weather.

Pete's devotion to weathermen is mystifying to me. They predict so wrong so often, I've developed trust issues. When I see Pete flipping channels to catch every five-day weather report, I'm astounded. He scans in search of highs and lows, pausing on the Discovery Channel to watch a zebra get its butt bitten by a tiger; then, feeling optimistic about his placement on the food chain, he's off to find more weather.

Sometimes Pete's out late and calls home, "Tape the weather." Uh, there *is* no weather. If the TV predicts 72 degrees and sunny, rather than 78 degrees and sunny, is Pete going to wear his *thicker* Gap T-shirt? If rain is forecast, will he get up early to compensate for highway Sigalerts?

Practicality is not the driving issue for Pete. He *must* catch the weather every night. It's his way of organizing his confusing, out-of-control universe. Weathermen are an ongoing certainty in uncertain times. Pete can tune them in like Batman—same time, same channel—every night. They're *there*, unlike so much of his life that isn't.

When I was a kid, there were winter mornings when I'd turn on the radio to hear if I had to get out of a warm fluffy bed and stand in a blizzard waiting for a bus to take me to a school full of icy classmates. My happiest childhood memories were the frozen mornings that school was canceled. I'd bury myself in the down comforter for another few hours and dream of one day living in Los Angeles, where the threat of rain makes the news.

This is the way I do weather: If it's dark in the middle of the day, I take an umbrella. It's not an exact science. I'm not saying I *never* tune in to watch Dallas Raines—real name—do the weather. He has *good daddy* qualities. He cares about what kind of day Pete and I will have. He tells us what to expect, and we'll know what to do. Or at least how to dress. And Dallas is rather good to look at just before bed. Although I question his choice of makeup. I'd lighten up the base, pull back on the orange hue, incorporate pink, and powder, powder, powder . . .

Must the Show Go On?

I answer an ad in Variety—Wanted: foreign actresses.

I call the number. Well, Canada *isn't* in the United States.

It's for a public access show. The producer is desperate and I'm invited on. After the shoot, she tells me I should do my own show.

Yeah, right! What am I gonna talk about? Drugs? Aerobics? The Holocaust? Well, why not? It's never been done. But produce? I don't even know what a producer does. Where do they go? Do they make money? Forget it.

Months later, this access show idea isn't going away. I have this important recovery message I want to deliver to the world. And I'll get a good table at Spago. I'll tip big. I'll do it for all women and dispel the rumor that we're terrible tippers. And with designer clothes I'll look better on the yacht.

Famous, rich people will open doors for me. Smart people will admire my big brains. And, of course, everyone will speak of how humble I am. "She's *so* down to earth!"

I want fans. Millions of them. If I'm on TV, it'll make me real. On stage, I'm not *alone* anymore. The audience is with me; their attention is on me; they are enjoying me. Like when Ma used to.

I call Century Cable. "How do I get a show?" A two-day workshop later, I become a producer. Money's not a problem. Anyone with thirty-five dollars can produce a show. And anyone does.

The name will be *Shape Up L.A.* The city needs a pep talk. My format will be inspirational and uplifting: Fitness for mind and body. (A fairly new concept at the time.)

I use my laptop to create a disk for the teleprompter. It takes me a month to write each show. Most of the time is spent yelling at the computer. I take a few lessons on the aspects of DOS, and it becomes long, late nights of me, the computer, and a manual written by a woman hater.

People are turning me on and I'm excited—

I tape exercise bits on the beach, at parks, in gyms and get buff guys to workout behind me. It's *Wayne's World* in tights. I learn how to edit and splice fitness bits into the monologue. I tape all over town—the hairdresser, restaurants, even a public bathroom.

"One word," I say, standing next to a toilet with my foot on the handle. "PRE-FLUSH. You don't know what may splash up and say 'hello.'"

I distribute tapes to stations throughout Los Angeles, find places to hold workshops, and promote them on my show. I'm building a client base.

I'm amazed anyone watches the chanting-with-crystals, past-life, porno Channel 3, yet they do. People keep saying, "You're Suzan Stadner. What's the name of your show?" So *Shape Up L.A.* becomes *The Suzan Stadner Show*.

At the studio . . .

As the camera rolls, I try to "have fun" with the delivery. But as I'm reading off the teleprompter, a teeny teleprompter in my head is running a different script, one Ma helped write years ago. "This show is stupid. Who cares about this? My delivery sucks. And I look fat. Well, I *blew* that line! I wasn't concentrating. Okay, I'll concentrate now. Oh shit, I was concentrating on concentrating, and blew another line. Stop the show! No, there's no time for a do-over. I'm starting to sweat. Why am I wearing beige?" This isn't about "fun," but about me trying to wow the audience and become famous so I can hang out with famous people and then the *real* fun will start.

I teach others not to postpone joy, while Saran Wrapping mine. I need to learn what I'm teaching. Later. It'll keep.

Being at the studio/battleground is about trying to corral a crew. It's about fixing jammed equipment and fighting for the right to use the good microphone.

And the lighting? Bela Lugosi. I'm at Camp Fresh Acres with a flashlight under my face telling ghost stories. "Tune in next veek vhen the topic vill be drrrinking bloood!" No wonder people say I look better in person.

Doorbells ring in the middle of shooting. Phones ring. Pizza delivery guys saunter across the set. The studio—a room with three cameras and one camera operator—is barren except for a small stage, two orange chairs, a metal coffee table and a plastic plant. Plastic. I have two hours to set up and shoot. If time runs out—regardless of technical difficulties—I leave with an unfinished show. And I have to wait a month to use the studio again.

During the taping of a show about Ma's Holocaust experience, I bend sideways to check out the reaction of the new cameraman. "Wasn't that a good story?" I ask. He stares blankly.

Then I joke, "You *do* speak English?"

"No, is not. I come last six veeks from Germany." So he didn't get the reference to Mayberry. I apologize for the Nazi comments.

English is a second language for much of the crew, and I become accustomed to not getting any audience response. When a teleprompter guy laughed in the middle of a segment on the significance of thigh-acceptance, I stopped the show. I thought something was wrong.

Camera operators consistently cut off the top of my head or bottom of my chin despite my detailed diagrams. "You need to include the neck and eyebrows or I'll look like a big head in a box." Head in a box is what I get.

The best is the shoot where the director forgets to turn on the microphone and afterward suggests I loop the twenty-eight minutes in post-production.

I stay up till 2:00 a.m. finishing the script called "Stress Less, Enjoy the Mess."

Between my four hours of hair, makeup, and wardrobe changes, I'm running late. All I need to do is save the script to a floppy for the teleprompter and—the computer betrays me.

A box with red writing pops up on the screen. This can't be good. "You have performed an illegal operation and will be shut down!" It's hard not to take that personally.

"Uh-uh!" I yell back. "I did not! You can't shut me down, you Nazi!" Do the people at *60 Minutes* know about this?

I click and mouse around feverishly and another box appears: "You do not have the rights to do this."

"Yes I do!" I scream. "I bought the software. I wrote the damn document. I can do with it whatever I want!" My computer has entitlement issues. What kind of anal-retentive, techno-terrorist came up with this passive-aggressive phraseology? It's not polite. Are these the same people who came up with the gentle *floppy*? The boxes could just as easily say, "Try again, honey; I know you're in a hurry, but you made a boo-boo."

I remember a secret a computer guy once told me. "When I get a broken unit in the shop, I turn it on and off a few times, and it usually starts working fine." That's what I do. It works.

By the time I grab the floppy copy, I have five minutes to get to the studio. They'll cancel the show if I'm more than fifteen minutes late! You can't get anywhere in L.A. in fifteen minutes between 4:00 and 6:00 p.m.! The stress from producing the "coping with stress" show almost kills me.

I make it to the studio a little late. All in all, I think the shoot goes well until the following day. At the edit bay, I discover that, throughout the shoot, two long hairs were sticking straight up out of my head, catching the light. I'm *My Favorite Martian*. No one thought to mention it. In any language.

❖ ❖ ❖

At home, I watch my shows air on one single breath. "Here's where I flub the joke." "Here's where the cameraman cut off my lips." The first year of programs suck so bad, I can watch them only while running on the treadmill. The endorphins numb the pain. The show I did on self-acceptance was so awful I hated myself for a week.

Pete watches and, wanting to help, says, "Just relax when you're doing it." Does he think I'm *trying* to be tense? It's amazing I let him live.

But the more shows I do the more confident I get, which makes my delivery better and watching myself easier.

❖ ❖ ❖

My show has a strong gay-man following. I become a star in West Hollywood. So when the going gets tough, I get to the Beverly Center in West Hollywood. I walk to the Estee Lauder counter at Bloomingdale's, and a tidy, well-dressed man rushes over in a flurry. "Oh, my God! My partner and I *love* your show! I have the perfect blusher for you! You helped me sooo much. Tell me those aren't colored contacts?!"

CelebrityLite

1990—A call comes in on the business line.

It's a man saying he's Marlon Brando. I tell him it's a great impersonation.
He says, "What can I do to prove it's really me?"
"Yell '*Stella.*' "
He laughs, and then invites me up to his Mulholland home. "Drive up to the bushes, speak into the rock, and the hedge will open." And people say he's strange.

I pass through the hedge, and yes, it is Marlon Brando, actually a Brando-and-a-half. He gives me a tour of the house. He shows me the room where his treadmill is. It's also the room where his son shot and killed his daughter's boyfriend. *Yes, I had heard of the case. You can't turn on the TV or open the newspaper without hearing about it.* He points to the bloodstain, explaining, "The police won't let me change the carpet until the criminal investigation is done, so I can't use the treadmill." There's always an excuse.

We sip iced tea sitting on the couch in his bedroom. Marlon Brando says to me, "I'm your biggest fan." Pound for pound, it might be true. He says the show makes him feel better. He says it's mesmerizing. I find it difficult to call him *Marlon.* To me, it sounds like I'm addressing a fish; so I ask him what his friends call him. To my dismay, he says, "Marlon."

Doing what seems to be a great impression of The Godfather, he asks questions about the show. "You go off on extraordinary tangents, but you always make it back to your original point. How do you remember what you were talking about?"

"Because I'm reading. It takes three weeks and a thesaurus to come up with the spontaneous things I say."

He leans back on the sofa, hands folded on his stomach. "You're reading a teleprompter? I couldn't tell. You're a good actor." He confesses he hasn't memorized lines since *Last Tango in Paris;* he uses an earprompter.

I say, " I can act when I write the lines, but what if someone else writes the lines?"

He says, "Fuck the lines. I shit on the lines."

And I say, "No wonder no one can understand what you're saying."

We talk a few more hours and he says, "You should write a book. It's hard, I know. I got an advance from a publisher, and I never wrote it. I'm going to have to give the money back. But if you write your book, I'll write the foreword." I float home on that.

Ma comes to visit for a month.

As happens every trip, we're having too much fun and I keep changing her reservation.

"You have to pay every time you change da flight, no?"

"Ma, it's only fifty bucks."

"*Only?!*"

"I save that in food. Instead of going out, I eat your pea soup and chicken."

"Oh, den it's okay."

We go to the gym; I drive. Ma rewinds the tapes I use to teach my aerobics class. "You vant dis one, 'Bad Boy You'?"

"Yes, rewind it to the beginning, please." Ma follows orders.

At the gym, she stands in the hallway watching me teach my class through the window. Every once in a while, I see her talking to someone. She says something, the person's eyebrows go up, the person smiles and looks at me. She's proud. For that moment, she's five feet tall—up from four-eleven.

One night after class I check my answering machine. Marlon likes to leave long, rambling messages, usually after he's watched one of my shows.

I say, "Ma, c'mere. Listen to this message. It's from one of the *biggest* actors in the world."

Ma listens intently. When he finally hangs up, she says, "He's an actor? He can't even speak! He mumbles, 'mffn, vffn, bimble, shmimble,' Such *mishugas!* Hanala, *you* should be a big star, you speak so clear. I don't know vhy you never can get a big TV show like Oprah."

"Because when I go on meetings at the studios, I leave my personality in the car. My body goes up the elevator, but my talent is in the parking lot. I'm up in the TV executive's office trying not to fall off the chair. I think about how to cross my legs so that my thighs don't look fat. Nobody's going to give me a network show."

"*Oy! Dat's* vhat happens? Den, no vonder."

I'm better at auditions when I already have the job—

After seeing my show, producers of informercials hire me. I've done nine. The Air-Bra. How to aerobicize your face. SlimVision (For $149, you get a disposable camera. You take a picture of yourself and send it back. SlimVision puts it through a software program that makes you look skinny and sends you a photo to put on your fridge.) Magnet jewelry. Exercise balls. Anti-aging shmears. Motivational tapes, one on personal growth, one on relationships. And weight-management candy (ephredra-laced junior mints).

Some of them offered me a percentage of the profits, but I took the cash up front. I remember *Ishtar*.

I bring Ma to one of the shoots. I co-host with Meredith MacRae, from *Petticoat Junction*. The script? "Thank you, back to you, Meredith." "Why thank *you*, Suzan . . . and back to you." At one point, in the middle of me explaining to America why folks should dial that 800 number, the director yells "CUT! Suzan, drop the New York *Jew*. We're selling to Nebraska."

Ma, sitting behind the cameras, has now stopped kvelling. "*Oy!*" she says, "A Hitler! A complete Hitler."

The director says, "Take ten," and we break. Ma is using Yiddish I never heard before. She's mumbling and tells me he's a *gepaygeteh fayert*.

"What's that, Ma?"

"From dis, you don't need to know. Ach, I hate him."

Yeah, I hate him, too.

After three months, I finally let Ma go back home to Daddy. I cry so hard at the airport she yells, "Hanala, I'm not dying! I'm going to Canada!" We laugh.

When I get home, there's a message from Playboy.

They want me to appear in a workout video for lovers. No clothes. I explain that being over thirty and Jewish, I don't even appear in the nude at home. I agree to choreograph and co-write. It's the only time Pete's ever wanted to come to work with me.

It's like playing with Porno Barbie and erectile-dysfunction Ken. I'm tempted to make them do jumping jacks.

I turn down the next exercise video they call me for. It stars an ex-football player. O.J. somebody. I hear a blip about him on the news a while later.

At an AIDS benefit . . .

I'm stuck in the paparazzi bottleneck. The stars (and I) are trying to get to the Universal Amphitheater, where Barbra Streisand is to sing. Flashes exploding, people shouting names of celebrities, my brain is buzzing. I'm nine feet away from Valerie Bertinelli and Eddie Van Halen.

Valerie grabs Eddie's arm. "It's her, Eddie!" I whip around thinking Barbra is behind me. Valerie and Eddie push their way over to me, and Valerie says, "Suzan, we love your show! You make so much sense, like your segment in the public bathroom. I always pre-flush now."

I stand in awe. I can't think of what to say.

Then Eddie says, "Suzan, you're fucking incredible!"

I find the words, "Fuck, thanks Eddie."

Later, John Ritter comes up to me and says, "I related to your show about having to entertain the valet guy. I do that too, like if I make him laugh he'll forgive me for driving a really expensive car, and park it closer." Nice man.

At the next benefit—

I'm all dolled up, looking hot. The photographers come running up to me. I'm flattered until one says to the group, "Oh, she's nobody." Have they talked to Sylvia? I'm preparing to wallow, when the handsomest man I've ever seen in person walks up to me. Even his entourage is attractive.

He says, "I'm a fan, your show is great."

"Oh, thank you." He's so cute that I'm having a hard time thinking.

He says, "You're beautiful." I don't do well with compliments. (Or without them.)

I respond, "Well, it takes a lot of money. And lighting's everything." Doesn't he see the wrinkles? And with that, he and his party of five breeze off. I grab one who's trailing behind.

"Hey, who *is* that man?"

"Are you kidding?! He's Kevin Sorbo. You know, *Hercules*, the TV show? My TV obsession must be subsiding. I missed that one.

◆ ◆ ◆

The adulation is confusing. Surreal. I try to sort me out. *Playboy* wants me? Brando says I can act? I've been asked to speak at MENSA. (Yes, they're brainy but, I swear, they can't dress.)

I'm ready, God, take me now. I am completely realized and fulfilled. It doesn't matter if I never do another thing for the rest of my life. This buzz lasts exactly two minutes. I go back to assuring myself that I'm not doing enough, that my life is about lost potential.

My agent calls . . .

He says, "You're in the breakdowns! A major studio is looking for a *Suzan Stadner type.*" The breakdowns is a list of acting roles distributed to agents by casting directors. Breakdowns is also what I have after auditions, knowing I screwed up.

I go to the Suzan Stadner audition. I don't get the part.

Between writing, shooting, editing and distributing the show, I'm *doing* TV as much as I am watching it. And that's not counting the hours I spend physically preparing. My maintenance is worse than a Fiat's. I have to spend time trying to look good, I'm on TV. TV age is like dog years. You make staying young a second career so you can keep doing your first one. At least, that's what I tell myself to justify my obsessions.

I shoot poison in my face to prevent wrinkles. I drop acid to remove sun damage. Not the acid I dropped in the seventies. There's liposuction, laser, nails, teeth, hair and a nose job. (Nose job, like blow job, should really be one word by now, and not highlighted by Microsoft's spell check, which should also be one word. Bill Gates should consider this. Surely he's gotten blow jobs and knows they exist.) I aerobicize, camouflage, moisturize, blend, tone, line, and realign. I watch segments on *Minimizing Visible Signs of Aging,* and I have a collection of articles on the latest miracle procedures and creams. Some are from the previous millennium but, as I try to toss them, I'm distracted by titles such as, "Sexual Positions That Burn the Most Calories." It's depressing to think how much time it takes to be me.

The year blow jobs are nicknamed Lewinskys—

I'm at the NATPE convention (the National Association of Television Producers and Executives). I'm here to be ignored by people who buy and sell TV shows around the world. I have a brochure of my show, and I'm hoping to make connections.

And then, holy fazer! It's a late model Captain Kirk promoting his new TV show. As if drawn by the tractor beam that pulls the Enterprise toward doomed planets, I move toward William Shatner. Dead fan walking . . .

Face to face, all I can say is, "I'm Jewish, too. We bought our first color TV from the same store in Montreal where you bought yours, the salesman told me . . . my mother. . . that you bought a TV for your mother." He's ready to call security. I should kiss him. At least that will force my mouth shut. I want to cling-on, but I back away slowly, making no sudden moves.

If my brain hadn't lost its power, I'd have told him, "*Star Trek* was my great escape. Kirk was a strong, funny, gentle man—a new concept. A man could be like this? Kirk never gave up fighting for life, I decided, 'neither will I.'" I'd have thanked him for helping me survive some bad nights. I'd have told him how, in sixth grade, I lay in bed holding my pillow, kissing the back of my hand—"Oh, Captain Kirk, I am the most beautiful woman in the universe? And the best kisser? You'd know!" I'd have told him all this . . . but I'm a quark in progress.

When the Going Gets Tough, the Tough Get Carbohydrates

Food and I are still embroiled in a clandestine relationship.

After teaching an aerobics class, I am approached by a woman who says, "You've really lost weight! I used to wonder how you could teach with such a big butt!"

Give me a TV and some food—fast. Fast, food. When I'm down, food brings me up. My weight goes up, too. I have three sets of clothes. Small. Medium. And Lardo. I get serious about losing weight when I can't get into my biggest pants. Even Lycra has an *outer limit*.

I can adhere to the recommended 2,000 calories a day. The 8,000 at night is the problem. Yes, I exercise, but calorically, two hours of hopping around can be wiped out by two minutes of concentrated eating.

At night, empty from a day of dieting, my stomach grumbles and I begin to fantasize: a drive-through burger, a big juicy hot dog, a rib-eye. I want some hot, tasty meat in my mouth. But I'm a supposed health nut. So the meat and I rendezvous at an out-of-the-way place—like my car, or a dark room with a TV. My eyes roll back. I follow the fat with sugar. And a diet Coke. It's a catered affair.

I hate when the yum ends. If it comes in a carton, like ice cream, I use my tongue to lap the lid. I lick bowls, which we all do, but I do it in restaurants. French bread speaks to me. "'Ey, *Suzanne,* you know you want to eat me. *Oui, oui,* just one piece. Or two. You don' look so fat, I won't 'urt you, 'ey?" Funny, how it always sounds like French *Canadian* bread. And if I've taken one piece, I may as well eat the whole basket.

When someone asks how much I want, I say, "The whole thing." Whatever it is, I'm sure I'm not getting enough. I like *a lot.* The idea of *a little* makes me nervous. A little means we'll run out soon and may never get any more. I stock up. Plenty of whatever makes me feel secure.

When it comes to servings I figure if one is good, six is better. Eat it now, the Nazis may be coming. Besides, you can't trust food manufacturers on the right serving sizes of their processed, packaged foods. Have you seen what they consider to be *one* serving? One serving for who, a shipwrecked anorexic?

When the fat-free-food phenomenon hit the market, I got excited. At first, one ice cream sandwich was a delicacy, a privilege, a temptation finally indulged in after years of resistance. I brought the box home from the market and savored that ice cream sandwich as if Wolfgang Puck had made it himself. After a while, *one* didn't do it for me anymore. *Hey, it's calorie-reduced, I can have two. I'll just eat less tomorrow.* Soon, my prescription increased to three sandwiches, three times a week.

I'm a math moron, but put *calorie* after a number, and I become Pythagoras—"If Suzie eats nine ice cream sandwiches a week, and each sandwich is 150 calories, how much will Suzie weigh at the end of the millennium?" The answer: "Suzie will weigh ten pounds more than Oprah did in 1987."

◆ ◆ ◆

I join Overeaters Anonymous, another twelve-step program. Counting AA and Al-Anon, that makes thirty-six. The food steps are the hardest to climb. With drinking, you just don't; out of mouth, out of mind—sometimes literally—but you *have* to eat. Unless you're a woman on a sitcom.

Where do you draw the checkout line?

Pete and I are at the market, at the register, when I see he had the nerve to place a jar of Skippy in the cart. So I accuse him of not loving me. "You *know* I can't have peanut butter in the house! It's fattening!"

He says, "Just don't eat it. Or just eat a little."

"Oh yeah, the *just-say-no* plan! Like how Nancy Reagan ended drug use in America. It didn't work for the country, it's not gonna work for my thighs. If I *can't* eat the peanut butter in the cupboard, guess what I'm going to obsess over? If I could eat *just a little*, I wouldn't be in therapy three times a week. I wouldn't be in Overeaters Anonymous, listening to women complain about the selfish men who bring home peanut butter! Maybe you want to put a padlock on the pantry like my father did."

At this point, the man in line behind us says, "I watch your TV show. You're not a raving bitch on it."

Sure, on my show I'm acting normal. Here, I'm acting out.

Pete in a Nutshell

Pete kvetches, I kvetch about his kvetching.

In his right mind, Pete is smart, witty, kind and adorable. But he's often not in his right mind. He's cranky, like he's got a scratchy label permanently sewn into his underwear. And by the way he acts, *I* sewed it there.

Pete, the first born son, started supporting his family when he was a kid by handing out fliers in parking lots. At sixteen he bought his parents a car. The flier business grew into the poster business. I watched as his office expanded from a two room marijuana-smoke filled, casual environment, to a coast-to-coast, warehouse-filled, high-stress commercial enterprise. Pete—or as his nephew calls him, *Uncle Moneybags*—instituted an extended-family-welfare program. He bought all their fish, which left them with no reason to learn *how* to fish.

His family keeps calling the house—"Pete, pay my rent." "Pete, fix my pool." "Pete, make my bail." You know it's bad when the heroin addict is the *good* sister. If the phone rings and Caller ID says, "PRISON"—and itreally does say that—I know it's Pete's family calling. Pete to the rescue. He's a martyr. He can't help himself. Meant both ways.

He wants to fix them, I want to fix him. We are Al-Anon.

Pete doesn't admit it to himself, but he's a *kvetchaholic*. He has down syndrome. He gets down on people, on life, but mostly, on himself. Something is always bothering him. Any minute now, the business is going under, and he's too short. His mantra, "My back is killing me!" Like it has a plot. His parts have been sprained, strained, pulled, enlarged, shrunken and removed. And teeth? Don't ask; the enamel keeps disappearing. His teeth must hate his mouth at the rate they fall out.

Just thinking about all this makes me tired. *Sooooo tired.* Oy.

Pete and I sound like two old Jews, "You think *that's* bad . . . ?" The phrase *irritable bowel syndrome* has worked its way into our dinner conversation. We whine and dine.

When one of Pete's problems subsides another pops in, like spam on AOL. When life gets good for a minute, he calls on his old reliable obsession—his hair.

Unlike Kildare, Pete's openly balding. Since his twenties, he's been victim to the Unfair Law of Hair. It falls off his head and comes back where it's not wanted. As if to mock him, no matter how much he shaves, plucks, and electrocutes it, it resurfaces—out of his ears, his nose, his shoulders. He's become *ChiaPete.* The only place his hair says goodbye forever, is the top of his head—where he would kill for it to come back. He combs it from where it is, over to where it used to be. He's considered transplants. He saw a plastic surgeon, who, until a year ago, was a proctologist.

Pete is cute enough to pull off baldness, but he doesn't think so. He battles with himself. "Do I buy hair or a Porsche? Is wearing a hat—cheating? Will therapy help me accept myself? Will I have money for therapy if I get transplants?"

At least he's surrendered Dorothy. He's been seeing her, twice a week, since he was twenty-one. Dorothy, a bead-and-mumu-wearing woman, rubs a potion into Pete's scalp. Not Rogaine. This comes from a caldron of a coven of housewives trying to make enough money to pay for Liposuction. The week he gave up Dorothy, he spoke of Dr. Keivorkian. I looked down at my thighs. I understood.

◆ ◆ ◆

But the worst of all *kvetches:* He wants me self-supporting through my own contributions. Because my TV show doesn't generate much income, Pete doesn't consider it *working.* I'm just another dependent worthless, blood-sucker. He *hates* that I'm not helping pay bills. I hate feeling hated.

Shrink This

A typical Friday night fight—

Me: "Stop talking to me in that tone of voice."

Pete: "I don't have a tone."

Me: "Yes you do! You said, 'I don't *think* so!' "

Pete: "I didn't say it with that tone!"

Me: "Oooo—I wish I had a tape recorder!"

Pete: "Yeah, me too, then you'd hear that I had no tone."

Me: "But, *everybody* has a fucking tone of one kind of or another!"

Pete: "Well, I didn't have one."

Me: "You . . . you . . . you are tone-deaf!"

Pete (*with an air of aristocracy*): "I simply said, 'I don't think so.'"
Suddenly he's Rex Harrison.

Me: "YOU DID *NOT* SAY IT LIKE *THAT*. YOU SAID IT *ANGRY*!"

Pete: "You just *heard* angry. *You* have a hearing problem. Your history makes you hear anger . . . but I'm *NOT* ANGRY!"

Here's where I go nuts. "*Y'idiot*" flies out of my mouth like spit on a sneeze. "Pete, you don't *LISTEN*! You know the leaf blower José uses? You've got one between your ears."

It's familiar. It's a revival meeting. *Ma, Daddy . . . listen to me!*

Pete says, "Look at everything I do for you. You should be grateful! Instead you always want more. You're selfish!" Ma in Pete's clothing.

AA is not enough.

The twelve steps don't go to my basement where the secrets are buried.

I start seeing Kati, a five-foot-ten, blond, blue-eyed psychoanalyst. I go to sessions filled with self-hate, and leave fifty minutes later with self-understanding.

There's too much shame on me. Kati is a shame exterminator.

I tell her all the things I've been ashamed of . . . I had a list.

I tell her how Pete and I have turned into Ma and Daddy. I explain Ma and Daddy and brisket, Sylvia, the Holocaust, but mostly, Pete—and how he's wrecking our relationship.

Kati says, "When Pete snaps at you, rather than interpret it, and react to it, and get stuck on proving to him he's wrong about you, if you could ask him what his comments mean, you might be able to break the pattern that your parents never could."

It's easier to yell. I resort to the F word—fight, flight, freeze. Or fall asleep—sometimes, I almost pass out. But usually, I fight back.

Hugging the porcupine.

I know, intellectually, that when Pete's being prickly, he needs more love, but how do you hug a porcupine?

"NO!" is usually the first word out of Pete's mouth. Even when he means yes. He's just contrary. With growling.

For example, I find the *perfect* house for us and Pete says, "*No!* No way!

Do you know how much the mortgage would be? Who's going to pay it, *you?* " For twenty minutes he drones on, sounding like a contemptuous computerized voice mail— *The resentment box you are trying to reach is full and cannot receive any new resentments at this time. Please try again later.* Can't he erase some?

But an hour later Pete says, "We can go look at it."

A week later, we're in escrow. Okay, it may not be the *perfect* house.

When it rains outside, it rains inside. The foundation is crooked; drop a marble, it'll roll from the kitchen to the garage. We spend two-and-a-half gray-hair-owing years battling contractors. And each other. Other than that, *perfect*.

So now, I have a beautiful new home—who am I to complain? But I *do* complain.

4:00 a.m., after another fight with Pete. It's a nightmare—

Poland, 1939—I'm me, but back then. I know what's coming . . . I'm the only one who knows. Well, me and maybe Hitler. I'm in a house filled with family. Whose, I'm not sure. I am sure of one thing—these people, these children, are about to die, because they happen to be Jewish. I have no way of stopping it. I'd try to warn them, but they'll think I'm crazy. The horror mushrooms through me. Six million Jews will die. They'll be gassed, burned, used in lab experiments, turned into lampshades, and I can't do a thing to stop it! I feel my brain cells burst trying to figure this out. Six MILLION? The Nazis worked very hard. They had only a few years to kill all those families. If people were grains of sand, the Nazis would have killed a small beach. How can this be? I fold in half. I must escape. Perhaps I can tell America, and they'll come and help me prevent the annihilation. My best shot is the forest. Pete's waiting. But, which knapsack do I take? There are three. What if I take the wrong one and Pete gets angry or annoyed? Hurry. They're coming . . . boots marching . . . and everyone in the house, laughing, oblivious! I can't choose the wrong bag. What do I do?

I wake up. Drenched. The Nazis are coming and I'm afraid of getting Pete angry? What's *that* about? Pete may not be the man of my dreams, but he's not a nightmare. Is he? I'm confused. I know that I'm petrified of getting his *annoyed* look. Why? Can a look kill me? It's Ma's *feh* look. Pete's disgusted with me. Unbearable. His sarcastic jabs are like an annihilation. The good ME doesn't exist in his head. Once, after a fight, I looked up *sarcasm* in the dictionary. It comes from the Latin: "to tear flesh."

I need Pete to appreciate me and cherish me—not criticize me. Why isn't he nicer?

Why? A good question, but it's said in a child's voice. I'm going around the Decarie Circle again, Daddy's booming, Ma's screaming—*we'll never get home.*

The *then* is screwing up my *now.*

It *never* got better with Ma and Daddy. They *never* stopped fighting. They *never* saw what their behavior did to me. *Never.* It's on my permanent record.

And now when Pete's yelling at me, I believe it'll never get better with him.

When I was little, Ma and Daddy were the only game in town—I had no choice but to play it. I'm an adult now, I can leave . . . but I don't wanna.

Pete might change, to the *good* Pete. I don't want to miss that. So I wait for the change, not like I did with Ma by hiding behind the couch, now I hit him over the head with the couch. Well, I'd like to. But is he really so bad? So, the man cannot shut a door. Mosquitoes fly in, car batteries run down and how many times do I have to say, *"Pete! The refrigerator is not a nightlight."*

Nobody's perfect. But, like Ma, once I get a good resentment going, it's hard to let go. Pete detects coldness and says, "What's wrong?"

I say (sing along if you know the song), *"Nothing."* A week later he complains about the laundry and I go Charlton Heston on him. I blast him for what he did a week—or a year ago. The relationship counselor asks why I want to break up, I say, "Laundry." Brisket.

My unexpressed anger also shows up as overeating, sarcasm (my particular favorite), and remote-control hogging.

Then again . . .

One night I'm sitting in front of the TV with a pound of grapes, reviewing my resentments (just to make sure I'm right), Pete walks in the room holding up the Sharper Image catalog and says, "Here—buy everything on this page." You can't beat Pete for sweet. I love him as much as hate him. Can I make this relationship work, or will I run out of therapy money first?

But If I Stop Criticizing Him, How Will He Grow?

So I'm thinking . . .

I'll never be a *Stepford Wife* (e.g., "Bondage tonight? Why certainly, dear"), but would it be so wrong to think of Pete as my hero? Wouldn't a hero want to make me happy? What's a jerk gonna do but make me miserable? And, if I keep expecting Pete to do something stupid, it could make me see stupid when stupid's not there. And, don't we all have the right to be morons in the privacy of our own homes?

So, here's the problem. If Pete's having a moron moment, how do I contain my urge to comment? Don't we *have* to show our loved ones what idiots they're being so they stop? I must point out Pete's flaws—so they'll go away. Right?

Then again, "You're an idiot" is not a statement meant for closeness.

One night on the Discovery Channel, I'm watching a scientist put bugs under a microscope, and it hits me: I've magnified Pete's flaws and now they're all I see.

Sunday morning, I'm in the kitchen . . .

Pete yells from the bedroom, *"The game's starting and the fucking cable's out again. SUZAAAN! Call your stupid cable company!"*

My cable company? Because I have a show on Channel 3? Pete's an intelligent man, but put a TV remote in his hand, he turns into Gilligan. And

I'm the professor. I flashback on the million times I've explained the remote to him. I get an adrenaline rush. Pressure builds and the storage cabinet in my head pops open. Out flies the file, *"He Doesn't Listen, I Must Be Unimportant."* He must be punished.

But wait . . . is there cheese at the end of this corridor? I unclench my jaw, breathe into my belly, and ask myself, "So, would it *kill* you to be nice?" I'm not sure. I decide to try a new and improved approach.

Sweet. But not artificially sweetened. I take a moment to empathize with Pete's plight. And then, I call out with compassion rather than with impatience, "Did you press the TV/VCR button . . . *honey*?" (Okay, I lost a bit of the compassion on *honey*.)

It gets quiet. A minute later, the inevitable communiqué comes from the bedroom, "Never mind, the, uh, cable came back on."

Oooo! I want to strut into that room, hand on hip, smug look on face, and convey to him that I *know* the cable didn't *magically* come back on. But, if I serve him my special side of snide, I know it'll come back to bite me.

So what if Pete can't figure out how to work a remote control? This is grounds for divorce? Tech support you can always pay for. Where can I find another man who walks into the living room naked, with his underpants on his head, saying, "How do I look as a chef?" There's no dot-com for that. I accept if there's snow on the TV, I get handed the remote. I stay present in the moment so I don't react in an automatic way. I don't roll my eyes and sigh.

I just push the right button and the snow goes away. When I love Pete for who he is today, and not who I hope he'll be tomorrow, I remember why I took him hostage in the first place.

Hitler Spoils You for Regular Suffering

Pete's somewhere in Africa—

Pete and Gary aren't only business partners, they're also travel buddies. Every December business slows for the season, and they *traipse* to places where you need shots and can't drink the water.

Their typical dialogue goes like this:

Pete: "Wanna drive six-thousand miles to see that mountain?"

Gary: "Okay." And they're off, filling the back seat of their rental with candy wrappers and potato chip bags.

Meanwhile here in L.A., I'm ready to approach strangers on the street: "Excuse me, can you spare a dialogue?" But that would mean being out in the streets—and with my penchant to stay home on the couch—that doesn't happen.

I buy Ma a plane ticket so she can come babysit me.

We're at baggage claim. The flight was nice. She liked the meal. "Da sen-a-vich vas so *tasty*, a meat, I don't know vhat kind it vas." I don't tell her I suspect the mystery meat was ham. Ma likes ham, she just doesn't like to know she's eating it.

Then, Ma's resent face appears. She says she's mad at Sylvia; they've been fighting. I find that refreshing. I've never known Ma to have a problem with Sylvia!

I'm *shlepping* the crate of smoked meat off the carousel and Ma says, "Oy, who vould tink Sylvia could open such a mouth to me? She vas screaming on da phone like a *meshugeneh*!" The rope slips from my hand. If not for the miles of twine around the box, salamis would be circling with the Samsonites.

· Sylvia *never* raises her voice to Ma, she'll call and tell *me* how disgusted she is, but to Ma's face, she's the devoted daughter that I "should be more like!"

I bring Ma to my Spanish hacienda wedged between the Tudor mansion and the Colonial manor. I show her my office. "Here's where I see clients who I get from my TV show."

I show her to her room. "Here's the new orthopedic bed. I had cable installed so it works on this TV, too, and we fixed the Jacuzzi so you can soak if your arthritis gets bad."

Ma shakes her head. "I alvays tought dat *Sylvia* vas da good one. Now I see it's da odder vay around." This is a compliment.

The emergency broadcast system siren sounds. In my head. Deer in headlights. Ma has confirmed what I always thought she thought. Good! We all need our viewpoints validated. I *wasn't* just imagining it—I *was* the designated *bad* one.

We're unpacking, and I see an opportunity to put a wedge in Ma's narcissism. "Ma, Sylvia's remembering some bad stuff that happened to her as a child—"

"Vhat could be so bad. *I* had it bad! Vhat did Sylvia have to complain about! Dat she had torn undervear? Dat should be my biggest problem. I had *no* undervear! I had *no shoes!*" Once more the Holocaust wins. How can it not?

I stack Ma's big, white cotton underpants in the drawer.

"Ma, nothing could compare to what you and Daddy went through, but sometimes something hurts us when we're little and we either suffer from it or we try to get over it. You don't have to have a bullet in you to feel pain. One child may whine, try to get more attention; another learns they can't be hurt if they stop feeling. When they grow up, they're cold."

"Vhy is it Sylvia has a heart like a stone, and you, you have a heart so big, it's from your head to your feet?"

I don't think that's really a question, but I answer it anyway.

"Ma, Sylvia looks like a snob. It's her way of keeping people at a distance. She acts tough to cover up her fear of being hurt. But, it's an act, an act that everyone believes."

"Yeah! Dat's true, *ketzele. A doctor*, I'm telling you! A doctor you should be!"

That's encouraging. I continue. "Sometimes, a parent doesn't realize their child is in pain. The mother figures the child has no reason to feel bad, or she has guilt for not being a good parent, or she doesn't know how to fix the problem so she ignores her child's emotional distress. When the child gets mad at the mother, the mother gets mad at the child for getting mad. She tells the child how bad life is for *her*, and the child should shut up and be grateful. So the child gets even madder, but she keeps it inside. For years."

Ma treks between the ancient blue vinyl suitcase and the closet, placing her floral polyester dresses (with oversized shoulder pads) on hangers and squeezing them in between the ski stuff. She seems pretty much unaffected by my dissertation. I search for an example that won't get her defensive. Something she might relate to. Death! Ma understands death!

"Ma, remember when Sylvia was little, she went up north for the summer with that woman, and the woman *died?* That must have been terrible for Sylvia!"

"No, it vasn't terrible," Ma says, closing the closet door. "It vas a nice hotel!"

If a Nazi Isn't Chasing You—
It's a Good Day

"The Holocaust was worse" continues—

I take a break from explaining my theories and ask Ma to cook salami and eggs. She's happy again; I've given her a task she does well. I compliment her on the meal and I'm her angel again. With Ma, you're only as good as your last conversation. I decide to tell her that I'm going to therapy three times a week.

She reacts like I set her mink on fire. "VHAT? Are you crazy!"

Well . . . wasn't that the point? I want her to know that just because I'm not drooling doesn't mean I'm okay.

But all she sees is a money emergency. "Tell me, *who* goes to terapy tree times a veek?! It's impossible!"

"Some people do."

"Vell, maybe in America, but *dis*—ve don't have in Canada!"

"You've gone door to door?"

"Okay, leave me alone. It's not normal vhat you do. I can't speak good to explain." She gets the message through just fine.

Ma's determined to stop this therapy business. "Going to a terapist is stupid, you vaste so much money."

"But, Ma, therapy is how I *make* money."

"Dat's different. You are a smart girl, and so you don't need help from nobody."

"What if I don't *feel* smart?"

"So you pay a tousand dollars so she can tell you you're smart?"

"Do you think I *want* to spend money on a shrink? Don't you think I'd rather buy shoes? Ma, just because I stopped doing drugs doesn't mean I'm okay now. Most of the time I'm trying to act *normal*, like if someone saw the real me, they'd run."

"You shouldn't feel dat vay."

"Yes, I agree. *That's* why I see Kati. Whether you accept it or not, there are things from my past I need to deal with."

"You should leave the past alone."

"Like *you* did? Ma—how can you leave something alone when it won't leave you alone? I can't be successful if I feel this insecure."

"You shouldn't be insecure. You are beautiful and talented—"

My hands clench as if around her throat. "Ma, you used to tell me I wasn't normal, so I grew up thinking I was crazy. You used to call me stupid. So now I feel stupid, not smart and talented."

"You're making tings up! I never told you dat you vere stupid! That's stupid!"

"You criticized what I did. You said I shouldn't feel what I was feeling, or want what I wanted. It mixed me up. You said I should do things the *right* way, *your* way. You didn't try to understand, you just called me *meshugeh*, don't you remember?"

"No, dis isn't true. Let's talk about someting else."

"Ma, how old was I when I started talking?"

"Talking . . . I don't remember."

"Do you remember when I failed arithmetic and Daddy hit me with the belt?"

"No, dis I don't remember."

"Do you remember how I picked you up at the bakery at eleven-thirty, and sometimes we sat in the TV room eating cheese danishes?"

"Dis, I don't remember." It's like cross-examining Reagan.

But I remember. It started when I turned sixteen. I'd be falling asleep, on a school night, the phone would ring. "But Ma, I'm already in bed . . ."

And her words would cut into my gut. "OY! I vork like a dog for you to have everyting, and dis is da tanks I get? You don't vant to come pick me up in da car? You vant I should take a bus? You should be happy to give me a lift home!"

Happy is not what I felt. I had to leave my cozy comforter for the freezing front seat, wait while the defroster cleared enough of the windshield to drive, and then wait outside the bakery for Ma to wind up her chit chatting with co-workers. And, I couldn't even complain about it. How dare I? So I stopped daring. For . . . ever.

Back to the cross-examination. "Ma, why didn't we ever eat dinner together?"

"I vorked six nights at da bakery! I had time to sit for dinner? Vhy are you asking me all dese qvestions?"

"Well . . . I saw a commercial on TV that said, 'Remember what mom told you—if it sounds too good to be true, it probably is.' It made me think about what *you* taught me, what words of wisdom you gave me. Other than 'don't touch the iron,' I couldn't come up with anything."

"So you touched da iron anyvay, and I had to put your hand under cold vater. *Oy,* you burned off all da skin, it made me sick."

"You were so angry, you kept yelling. I know it scared you, but I was hurt. I needed comfort. I was a little girl."

"You vere stubborn! You didn't listen. You vere alvays like dat!"

"Like what?"

"You didn't vant to listen!"

"Maybe I would have learned *how* to listen, if I were ever listened *to*. You never listened, Ma. Maybe that's why I pay someone to listen to me today."

"*Oy,* you tink I had time to listen to Sylvia? Sylvia had da same childhood, she's not in terapy."

"No, Ma. Everyone *around* her is." Ma gives me the *feh* look.

"Ma, I wish you'd respect how I feel. What's important to me has value, even if you don't understand why. Can you imagine how I feel when you tell me that I shouldn't care about something I care a lot about?"

"You alvays cared too much; you should be more like Sylvia. Sylvia's okay."

I breathe and keep my tone low. "If Sylvia's so okay, then why does she push David away when he tries to hug or kiss her? Why is she mad at him all the time? One time when I was on the phone with her, we were saying goodbye and Sylvia said, 'Bye, I love you.' I almost dropped the receiver. Then I realized, that's how she gets off the phone with the kids, it's automatic. The 'I love you' slipped out accidentally. Ma, Sylvia never said 'I love you' to me."

"You should know she loves you, she's your sister."

"I don't want to have to *know* it, I want to *feel* it. And I can only feel it if she treats me with love. She thinks I don't want to visit her in Akron because I'm holding a grudge from childhood, but that's not it. I don't feel good about myself when I'm with her, she's critical. It's exhausting being near her. Kati's helping me understand why Sylvia affects me so much. And there's something else, Ma, Sylvia's boring. She's *dead* inside, and it's contagious."

"Oh. I didn't know dis."

Ma thinks for a minute and comes to a conclusion. "She shouldn't be like dat."

"Sure. I shouldn't be depressed and Sylvia shouldn't be cold. But we *are*."

"I don't know vhy she's cold."

"Maybe she tries to tell you. Maybe she needs therapy, too."

Ma reaches for her purse—always close by—and starts leafing through old sales receipts. "*Oy*, vhat a crazy vorld. In *da Old Country*, nobody was in terapy. A person should know vhat to do, and *do* it. Terapy, shmerapy . . ."

Words of wisdom coming from a woman who stayed married to a man for sixty years because he was a snappy dresser and had a bike.

Poor Ma! Her biggest source of pride is her two daughters, and we'd both like to beat the shit out of her.

That night I have another dream—I'm at a formal party for the U.N. I sense a horrible presence. Then I see them. Gray demons, translucent manta rays hover overhead. No one else in the room sees this? No—they ignore my frenzied warnings. The mantas drift, then dive between the delegates. "C'mon, people, get the wagons in a circle! There's danger. Please, pay attention!" Damn! They don't take me seriously! They're not listening. Perhaps it has to do with the way I'm dressed. They're in white tie, I'm in workout clothes. The room starts to shake. I'm freaked. Really freaked—yet satisfied. Yes, I'm glad. The fancy people are panicking. NOW they'll all know I was right and they should have listened. I'm redeemed, but, oh-oh, the building is coming down. Shit! Can I get out? And then, from across the room, I see Ma's face. She's staring into my eyes. Beaming. The woman is in full-kvell. Suddenly I'm Supergirl. The mantas rays can't get me, and I can escape the building—I'm safe.

The next day—

I decide to show Ma the video I did on how parents' traumas can affect children. I figure, when people see a story on TV, they tend to give it more credibility.

I put the tape in the VCR. The title comes up: *The Holocaust: The Gift That Keeps on Giving.*

I start with back story: "Fifty years ago, my parents were happy little Polish villagers, farming the land, plucking chickens, then the Nazis marched in and killed everyone they loved. As a result, we lived in a state of emergency."

After describing highlights from their history, I go into mine. I explain how the invalidation and dismissal of my subjective reality, and the whippings with the belt and the screaming and coldness affected my psychological development. I speak of Ma's and Daddy's abuse of each other, and what it taught me about relationships. I go into my drug-a-logue, agoraphobia, and anorexia and my struggle with depression and loneliness. I end with an uplifting transition back to health. (The cameraman was in tears—and he hardly spoke English.)

Ma watches the tape without expression or a word. When it's over, she shakes her head. Her lips are angrily pursed together. That's the expression I grew up with—*the look that shook.*

"What, Ma? Did the show disturb you?"

"Yeah!"

"What in specific, tell me."

She's indignant. "I *never* plucked chickens!" She says nothing else.

My eyes are spinning, as they'd been since I was a baby neurotic. Once more, I can't organize what Ma's putting in my head. I switch to sort-it-out mode. Aha, I get it! *Peasants* pluck chickens. Ma's afraid of being thought of as a low-life chicken plucker, Poland's version of guests on *Jerry Springer.*

"Ma, I just said the chicken-plucking thing for dramatic purpose. I don't think anyone will really believe that. What about the *rest* of the show?"

She clicks back into relief. "It vas good."

Ma's concrete. It vas a nice hotel. You're da good one. I never plucked chickens.

The Sperm Dealer

The next day Ma's out soaking in the Jacuzzi—

The phone rings—it's Sylvia. "I just called Daddy; I swear he's getting senile."

"How can you tell?"

"Yeah, he's always been crazy . . . how's Ma?"

"Wanna ask her?"

"No. I don't want to have anything to do with that woman. She is so stupid. Why can't she just *listen* and take responsibility for what she did to me when I was a kid? All she does is talk about how hard it was for *her*!"

"Uh, yeah . . . she does that. It's infuriating. You know, Syl, when I was little, it hurt when you made fun of me and called me obnoxious."

"Suzan, you *were* obnoxious. You'd throw yourself on the floor and have a tantrum if you didn't get what you wanted. Nobody knew what to do with you; you were so spoiled."

"I wasn't spoiled, I just smelled that way. Something was rotten inside. And instead of helping me, you hurt me more. I worshiped you and I meant nothing to you. You even named your dog Suzie, and when I got upset, you said it didn't cross your mind that it was my name. When we talk sometimes you say '*my mother.*' She's *our* mother. You blame your issues on her and Daddy, but you have no empathy for me. I had the same parents. I also had *you.*"

"Suzan, I never asked you to worship me. I was just a kid myself. Ma would stick me with you. I had friends of my own."

"Syl, even *you* can't just listen and say, 'I'm sorry I hurt you.' How do you expect *Ma* to do it?"

Silence. Then, "Point well taken."

Call waiting bleeps in. It's a friend I met in AA, Marsha Applebaum. She's stressing. I tell Sylvia I'll call her back. Marsha's been trying to get pregnant through artificial insemination. She and Marvin Applebaum moved to Irvine, a fifty-minute drive from Los Angeles. Ovulating in Irvine that afternoon, she realized she wouldn't get to the sperm bank in West L.A. before it closed. Can I pick up her next installment before 5:00 p.m.?

I explain the situation to Ma. She understands the urgency. Slipping on her Reeboks, she says, "Let's go!" She's up to the task!

We're driving to the clinic and Ma's rethinking our earlier conversation.

"If I knew you ver doing drugs, I never vould send you money. You vere like a bag mit a hole, I put money in and it falls out da bottom."

We drive in silence. What I want to hear is, "My poor baby, you must have been in so much pain to do drugs." I have to say something or explode. I search for just the right words.

"Ma! Don't you ever fucking *think* that what you say *hurts me*?! Just *reflect!* Maybe you're *insensitive!*"

"Vhat, I'm a mirror I should reflect?!" I'm learning more about what doesn't work.

Calm down, breathe.

"Ma, Sylvia and I want you to *know* what we've experienced. You told us what you went through. We want you to know *our* story."

"*You* have a story?"

"We're not *blaming* you for everything. We just want you to say things like, 'I'm sorry you were sad,' or 'I wish I spent more time with you. You deserved more.'" Ma listens. What's she gonna do, leap from the moving vehicle? She's seventy-eight.

Looking out the window at Olympic and Bundy, she says, "*Oy*, vhat a big satellite dish on dat building!"

"Maaa!"

"Okay, okay, dat vas good vhat you said. Can you pretend I said it? I can't say it so good. You're like a doctor. I don't know how you got so smart."

"My mother's smart. She's one in a million."

Ma sighs, "Tank God for dat."

"Ma . . . you're talented. You know how to program a VCR . . . I got so much good stuff from you, you don't even know."

"Oh, yeah? Not just da bad stuff?"

"Ma, if you like the person I am today, you have to take some responsibility for that."

"Okay."

Ma will forget this conversation. CSD (convenient senility disorder) lets her remember only what supports her beliefs. But, even if only for a moment, I was heard.

I park at the first sperm bank I've ever been to.

This is no Wells Fargo. Usually I'm cautious leaving a bank, afraid of being mugged. Now I'm cautious *entering* the bank, afraid of being recognized.

I come out with what looks like a scuba tank. Opening the passenger door, I place the steel container on the floor between Ma's feet and we drive off. The car phone rings. It's Marsha. She wants to know if I got to the clinic on time.

I say, "It's a big tank for such little critters. Oh, and the lab guy said it has to remain vertical, so my mother's holding onto it."

Ma calls out proudly, "Dat's right, Marsha, I got da sperm betveen my legs!"

If this were *The $25,000 Pyramid*, the category would be under, *"Things you NEVER imagine your mother saying."*

The next day Ma and I drive to the Cineplex . . .

When I was a kid, Ma never had time to play with me—but she's mine now! I can shlep her everywhere.

I buy tickets for *The Jungle Book*. Good family fun. Finally, Ma and I are going to see that cartoon.

Ma says, "It's a movie about da jungle?"

"Yeah."

"Da jungle I had enough of. Can ve see anader movie?" She tells me she's been dreaming about Nazis again. "Vhy am I still dreaming about da var? Da Nazis I'm finished mit already. It's good dey didn't finish me."

How can I explain this? "Ma, when something terrible happens, the mind stores it. It's called trauma. No matter how long ago it happened, or how many times you've talked about it, it's like you're telling it for the first time. Your head is like my computer. It doesn't matter if I wrote a show ten years ago, I can find it as quickly as a show I wrote yesterday."

Ma says, "So dere's popcorn?"

"Yes. But, do you see what I'm saying? When it comes to emotions, time means nothing. A terrible event can stay fresh in your mind, like it's stored in plastic." *Plastic*—a concept Ma gets.

"Yeah, you're right! I can remember like it vas yesterday, mine niece mit da bullet holes in da arm, and da farmer . . ."

So I exchange the tickets for *Disclosure*, starring Demi Moore and Michael Douglas. I'm sitting in the dark theater next to Ma, watching Demi's head bob up and down in Michael's lap. She's pulling his fly down with her teeth. He's ripping off her underwear. The F word rebounds through the theater—in Dolby, digital, Lucas-film sound.

The audience is listening.

I'm not. I've shrunk into the seat, my head in the popcorn, wishing I'd read the reviews. They really should include *NAP* in the rating system: "Not to be Accompanied by a Parent." (I'm just lucky Ben Stiller isn't on the screen, and I'm not having to explain what's hanging from his ear.)

Ma and I never talked about sex, and now we're watching people having it! Nobody admitted to breathing hard or licking each other in Montreal when I was a child. Daddy slept in the bedroom; Ma slept in the TV room. Daddy snored; Ma liked TV.

My head is positioned straight ahead. I'm hoping to hear snoring coming from Ma's seat. She fell asleep when I took her to see *The Terminator*. Later I asked how she could sleep with all the explosions.

She rolled her eyes, "Hanala, I slept in da forest, I can sleep in a Shvartzanegger movie." The Holocaust—the great leveler.

Ma's motto: "If you're not being chased by Germans, you might as well take a nap." But Ma does *not* sleep through the sex scenes in *Disclosure*.

The movie *finally* ends and we shuffle up the aisle, and gaining back some semblance of my personhood (I had regressed three decades), I ask, "So, Ma, whatj'a think?"

"*Oy!*" she says, eyes wide, with a satisfied thumbs up. "Now *DIS* vas a *MOVIE!*"

That night, I dream of Nazis—big gray ones with sharp teeth.

I'm treading in dark, choppy, ocean water, miles from land or boat, but it's okay because I'm safe inside the shark cage. Shark cage? I focus outside the bars and see man-eaters circling. Is the cage strong enough to keep them out?

The water is getting choppier and my arms are growing tired. I'm trying to keep my head above water. Annoying little waves splash up my nose, making me cough and choke. It's only a matter of time.

What's that dark shadow under the water just to my left? Oh-oh!

Whew, it's just Ma and Daddy. Ma and Daddy?! They're floating a few feet below the surface as if they're calmly relaxing on La-z-boys.

"How strange," I think. "Why aren't they drowning?" I look closer. Aha! They're wearing scuba gear! Nobody gave me any. And so I'm drowning. So sad. I can see Ma's and Daddy's faces clearly through their scuba masks. Their eyes are blank and lifeless. They don't see me. They don't see a problem. They just stare straight ahead.

I wake up. I'm struck by the realization that I hadn't even *thought* to ask Ma and Daddy for a hit off their oxygen. It never entered my mind. I take for granted that they don't help. It's not what they do.

Pete's scheduled to come back from his globe trot with Gary in a few days . . .

I put Ma on the plane. "Thanks for babysitting!"

I get home from the airport and the phone rings. It's Gary calling from Africa. "There's been an accident. Pete's head hit the windshield. He's . . . *okay*. He's coming home."

He comes home. But okay—he isn't.

Gone With the Windshield

Africa—earlier that morning . . .

Gary drives through a stop sign and hits a car full of African Africans. Pete, not wearing his seat belt, is propelled through the windshield. The glass shatters and scalps him. From forehead to crown, a long patch of skin—containing hair follicles—is sliced off, almost exposing skull. The emergency room doctor tells him the skin will rejuvenate, but not the follicles. Pete is now officially bald. A skinned head.

Hair today, gone to Maui.

I pick him up at the airport. He comes off the plane in a turban of gauze looking like he's joined the Taliban—the depressed and hopeless branch. He's in mourning. Years of watching his hair fall out slowly have been stolen from him.

His *kvetches* sound sadder than normal. "I can't go back to work like this. Gary said we should go someplace, he'd take care of the business. Why did this have to happen!"

"Well, Pete, what you focus on can become real, and you should have been wearing your seat belt," is what I'm thinking, but, for fear of my life, don't say.

We fly to Hawaii, where we can hide under hats. And underwater. Pete's African bandages have been removed, and I'm going mental looking at his forlorn face. We need a distraction. "Hey, Pete, let's become certified divers!"

So at 5:00 a.m., weighed down by scuba equipment, we step into an uncovered, arthritic putt-putt. It's pouring, I'm seasick and freezing, and Pete keeps throwing me dirty this-is-your-fault looks. The rain is slapping me as if to say, "Stupid, stupid, stupid!" To make myself feel better, I'm counting the calories being burned: actual dive—200 calories; shivering and barfing—400 calories; my anger at Pete's shitty attitude—a box of Krispy Kremes.

This goes on for three days. I lose eight pounds.

Our last day of certification—

We fall backward off the boat. On purpose. It's a good way to get in the water with a sixty-pound tank on your back. I begin my descent. I look around—no Pete. I look up. Pete is suspended in the water, about ten feet below surface.

So I shrug, with palms facing up. (The underwater signal for *what the fuck?*) No response. Again I shrug. Still no response. Our group is already at the bottom, following fish. I motion for the dive master to come back up. We're involved in an emergency, but what kind? How bad? Pete looks dopey, blank—like Ma and Daddy in the scuba dream. I'm concerned. And annoyed. I want the fun to start. I want to look at fish. Pete I could look at, at home.

The dive master and I take Pete to the surface. Our heads pop up out of the water and that's when I see it. Holy blow fish! Pete's eyeballs are bulging out of their sockets like the characters in *Mission to Mars* when air-pressure sucked their eyes out! The divemaster tries to pull Pete's mask off, but it's stuck to his face—like another movie with a sucking killer squid.

POP! Off it comes and Pete's eyes are sucked back into his head. Suddenly, every corpuscle in and around his eyes bursts and he looks like a demonic racoon.

"What happened!" I ask him, frightened (and, I'm embarrassed to say . . . annoyed. Will this man *ever* learn to take care of himself?!).

"I don't know . . . everything went black . . ." *Oy!*

Okay, Pete's eyeballs are back in his head, and he decides to continue the dive.

We're descending and somehow the air regulator gets knocked out of his mouth. I'm already down so I don't see this happening. He's holding his breath, struggling to find his mouthpiece. Giving up hope he prepares to die. In his relaxed state of acceptance, waiting for the white tunnel, his hand hits the mouthpiece and he gets air.

You'd think he'd have hung up his flippers, but no. The costliest dive is yet to come.

From head to toe.

Pete, the dive master, and I waddle from the Sheraton's scuba shack down to the water balancing our oxygen tanks. Picture Daffy Duck, with a Harley strapped to his back.

AND SUDDENLY—
HER THIGHS DIDN'T MATTER

The ocean is rough. The waves come in waves. Waves. No waves. Our job is to run into the sea during *no* waves. I think of Malibu and my Poseidon adventure. My heart pounds as my webbed feet smack into the surf. The cold water makes me gasp, even in the wet suit, which is aptly named, considering you are not *dry* wearing one in water. I'm nervous, but I want to see the creatures that come out at night. Like octopus. For a fish, an octopus is very smart. Not a genius, though. (Kildare and I had an octopus in our aquarium. It was smart enough to figure out how to climb out of the tank, but not smart enough to think the plan through. I found him walking to the closet.)

Pete's treading water and spitting into his mask. He *is* angry at the mask, but that's not why he's spitting in it. Saliva clears away fog.

Every mask he's ever tried fogs up or leaks. He thinks he's cursed with a leaky face. I suggest the fog is caused by little *puffs* of air that he lets escape from his nostrils. He disagrees. With intensity.

I tell him, "And, you grimace. That lets water in."

This brings out the Gladys Kravitz in him. "Not everyone is that *lucky!*" I interpret this as: "Lucky, like you, you selfish bitch, wearing a mask I paid for!" Meaning: "I pay and struggle while everyone *else* has a good time."

It's true, I have a face that fits all. And I was a bad daughter . . . selfish . . . I do a lot of interpreting.

His mask in place, we voyage to the bottom of the sea, which, luckily, is only twelve feet down. Dive master shines his flashlight on an octopus! I look at Pete for a shared moment.

The moment he's having isn't one I care to share. He's drifting horizontally, his arms tightly folded across his chest, his eyes shooting daggers at me. This is the underwater equivalent of yelling. I expect the water to begin boiling around him.

"WHAAAT?" I signal him the *shrug-with-palms-up-I-did-nothing-wrong* sign (not scuba-speak, it's universal).

He points two fingers toward his eyes, like Moe from the Three Stooges, then points the fingers emphatically at me. I get it! This accusatory finger dance is indicating that I haven't been watching him buddy-style. *I'm a bad girl.*

At this point, I don't care if his head does explode. Let his eyeballs shoot across to Honolulu!

With a few deep breaths, trying to regulate my air, I calm myself. *This is more about him than you . . .* okay. I pantomime that I will, from now on, turn toward him and do a buddy check often. And this is when I notice the bottom third of his mask is filled with water. The leaky-face curse. Boy, you can dress him up, but you can't take him underwater. Lloyd Bridges, he's not.

Back at the scuba shack, Pete unstraps the steel tank and places it behind him on a shelf. But . . . not fully on the shelf. He turns around as it tips and falls, spigot first, onto his big toe. Blood spurts like Old Faithful. Pete goes down. I start laughing. Not because it's funny, it's because I'm trying *not* to laugh. The madder he gets, the harder I laugh.

He gets up. To come kill me? Hopping on one leg, holding his injured foot with his hand, in a wet suit with a snorkel dangling from his head, he's chasing me around the shack. I'm laughing so hard, I'm crying. One more time, Pete's in trouble, and it's my fault.

I drop my voice, trying to show my sincerity. "We have . . . to . . . hee-hee . . . rush you . . . (deep breath), to the doctor." Okay, I'm under control.

The dive master says, "Yeah, man, that looks bad. You better go see Dr. Estin at the Westin." I'm hysterical again.

Turns out, not only is the cut down to the bone, but the bone is fractured in three places. Dr. Estin's orders: Don't go into the ocean for the rest of the trip.

Pete's contempt knows no bounds. Diving was my idea. *Oy.*

What are we going to do now, sit by the pool? Pete's not going to sit by the pool, listening to "Marco!" "Polo!" "Marco!" "Polo!" We kill a day driving the famous road to Hana. I can't allow myself to enjoy the ride, not I, the criminal who did in Pete's toe. When his toe broke, so did my spirit. Even my fractured spirit is my own fault. I should have boundaries!

The next day we go for a walk. I walk, Pete limps, mumbling, "night dive, mumble, mumble, toe, mumble . . . "And suddenly, I get a sign!

A big yellow sign: Condos for sale. A week later, we're proud parents of an oceanfront studio. Good investment, I think. Actually, a blatant co-dependently driven desire to turn lemons into lemonade. A month later,

Saddam Hussein (damn him) invades Kuwait and the Gulf War puts an end to tourism in Maui. We can't rent the thing out. Then, the Japanese market crashes, and we lose the Asian vacationers. Hawaii's hit by disaster! Only this time, it's because the Japanese *aren't* coming. Pete ends up selling the condo at a loss of $40,000. And we never even stayed in it. In times like these, you look for someone to blame . . . Gary's driving, Pete's defiance of the seat belt, my get-Pete-happy-so-I-can-be-happy agenda, Saddam Hussein. . . .

In the years to come, Pete calls from the bathroom, "SUZAAAN, come here, and bring your tweezers." I dig slivers of the African windshield out of Pete's scalp as they surface. I distract myself with thoughts of, "$40,000 . . . how many pairs of shoes is that?" If I don't think about something else while pulling glass out of his head, I might throw up and he'll get mad.

Asspen

Pete and I meet Sylvia and David in Aspen for some ski-ing and passive/aggressive behavior.

We're riding the four-seat chairlift up the mountain. It's the kind of day that makes you wish you'd learned to ski as a kid. Big, white puff clouds reflect in lakes, the breeze is gentle. The quiet is broken by the occasional bird call. It's spring.

We've been riding up silently for a few glorious minutes. Sylvia pulls a piece of paper out of her pocket. "David, what is this? What do you want me to do with it?"

David's rage jumps out of the thin air. "Why don't you shove it up your *fucking* ass!" Pete and I burst out laughing—I grab him so he doesn't fall out of the chair.

Sylvia turns to us and shrugs. "You see what I put up with?" She has no clue that ten minutes back—when she bit off David's head for something—that her bite would come back to bite her in the ass.

❖ ❖ ❖

Sylvia is an expert skier. I've been on skis nine times, hated each time. Skiing is my idea of when you can't feel bad enough at home, get on a cold mountain with clunky boots.

We're at the top of the mountain, and I use mantras to get me through the fear. On steep runs I'm traversing, repeating under my breath, "Turn ski tips *up* the mountain, turn ski tips *up* the mountain." Either that or, "Those dirty bastards, those dirty bastards." Then it comes, the mother of all runs. I freeze despite my toe warmers. But Sylvia does not abandon me, nor does she roll her eyes. Gently supporting, guiding, and encouraging, she stays by my side. A blatant display of caring. Could my sister love me after all? I ease down the run, whooshing back and forth, carried by her care. It's heaven. It's a whoosh fulfilled.

Fast forward six months, Pete and I are in our kitchen.

I find a receipt on the counter. "Pete, what is this? What do you want me to do with it?"

He whips his head around. "Why don't you shove it up your *fucking* ass!" We're on the floor, laughing to tears.

A Blast From the Past

Pete and I are racking up frequent flyer miles.

We're in beautiful British Columbia, and just for a lark, I look up old pal Linda's name in the phone book. I heard she'd moved to Vancouver. There it is! I call.

A familiar voice answers the phone, "Hello."

"Linda, is this Linda Resnick?"

"Uh, yes it is. Who's this?"

"Linda, it's me—Suzan. Suzan Stadner."

"*Hi!*"

"Hi."

"*Hi!*"

"Hi. I'm here, in Canada, Vancouver. Now. I just . . . . how are you?"

"Oh, I hate my life."

"Oh. Do you want to get together?"

"Sure."

"How about, at the Botanical Gardens, the restaurant. I heard it's good."

"Yes, okay."

"Tomorrow, lunch, at, say, noon?"

"Okay."

"Okay!"

"I'll bring my husband. And my two sons."

"Oh! You're married! I didn't know, your name's the same."

"I hate him."

Nothing's changed.

Linda's an hour late.

I see a woman limping through the gardens, heading toward the restaurant. She's followed by two young boys and a man who looks like he's having allergy problems. Limping? The coma. Paralyzed. By the time she regained the use of her leg, the muscles had atrophied. She's in a skirt, one leg looks normal, the other like a stick.

Hug. Uncomfortable.

"I'm sorry I'm late. It took forever to get out of the house." I can see why. Linda is still wearing the never-for-daytime foundation. And the spider-leg lashes are coated heavily. Her hair is bouffy. It must have taken all morning to get her hair and makeup back to the seventies. I meet her boys and husband. She rolls her eyes when he says something about power tools.

We talk as if nothing ever happened—like she didn't try to commit suicide with my pills because of the pain and shame of her unrequited love for me. We eat and take a ferry ride to Victoria. We talk for seven hours. And never run out of things to say. We hug goodbye. This is the last time I see Linda, the girl who saved my life in seventh grade.

Dragging My Mother
Around the Lake

We pick Ma up in Montreal—

"Ma, Pete and I are going to drive through New England to see the fall colors. We're taking you."

"Oh yeah? Okay."

We're in Vermont. She goes to pay for something at an outlet store with Canadian dollars.

"Ma, you have to use American."

"I didn't bring da American mit me."

"How come?"

"You said dat ve vere going to New England, dat's Canada, no?"

Turns out, they *do* take Canadian dollars; just many more of them. Ma and Daddy saved every cent they ever made, and currently, with the Canadian economy, it's worth half.

We drag Ma on a boat to tour one of the lakes. She's at the back of the boat being blown by the wind. She puts her sweater over her head. The sweater has shoulder pads. She looks like Minnie Mouse.

"Ma, are you okay?"

"Yeah." She's smiling. I keep looking back at her. She's still smiling.

After a couple of hours, we get off the boat. Ma puts her foot on the dock and says, "Tank God dat hell is over!" I love this woman.

A New Pair of Contacts

Ma and Daddy come to L.A. to see the new, new house—

I show Ma the canyon from my bedroom balcony. Miles of forest going down to ocean. "Look, Ma. It's national parklands, so nobody can build on it and ruin the view."

Ma looks. "Dere's a lot of places to hide. Da Germans vould never find me here."

Gulp. Poor Mummy. Fifty-five years later . . . the Holocaust—it keeps going and going and going . . . .

"Vhy are you crying, Hanala?"

"I love you, Ma."

"I know dat."

With Ma and Daddy visiting, I schedule extra therapy sessions.

"Kati, for some reason, I've been thinking about when we moved to Cote Saint Luc, when I ran home all excited to tell my mother that Margo wanted to make up and be friends again, and how my mother was disgusted. She practically spit on me, she goes, 'What's da matter mit you? Don't you have any pride?'"

"Your mother didn't say that she knew how lonely you'd been, and that she was happy you and Margo were friends again?"

"No, that's what happened to the Beaver. Besides, Ma was right, I was lame, jumping up and down just because Margo wanted to be my friend."

"Your mother's reaction lacked any empathy."

"But what she said was true."

"That's what was so confusing—there may have been a smidgen of truth to whatever your mother said, but she'd miss the main point, the whole picture. She seemed to make sense, but it was also non-sense. In this case, you were a little girl in a new school; you needed Margo. Of course you were ecstatic. That's normal."

"Maybe my mother was embarrassed. Maybe she was trying to get me to be like Sylvia, more secure. Ha—I got more insecure."

"When your mother repeatedly told you that your feelings were wrong, she confused your idea of who you were. And Sylvia, in her judgmental, superior style, confirmed your wrongness. You didn't stand a chance."

I think back to The World of Suzie Wrong. "This is creepy. It's like . . . I was infected by a computer virus."

"One that made the system unstable; and you believed even that was your own fault."

"I've always defaulted to—it's my fault! Now wonder I crashed."

I'm feeling a strange awe, like the colors in the room are brightening, edges seem crisper. "Kati . . . I made a million decisions based on a belief that I was bad . . . My whole life I've been asking, is it normal to feel this, am I nuts?"

"If anyone had a psychological disorder, it was your mother, but there's no way you could have known that then. She acted tough, but really, she could get derailed by the slightest push. All she needed was someone to challenge the way she looked at something, and she'd attack to defend her*self*."

"Does my mother have some kind of disorder like paranoid schizophrenia or something?"

"No. I have a patient who has a paranoid schizophrenic mother; she believes all her dentists are injecting poison into her gums."

"My mother believes they're all overcharging." Kati and I laugh a lot.

She says, "*Borderline* personality disorder might be a better description. I'm not big on labels—a person can have symptoms of a disorder one minute but not the next. And, of course, I can't diagnose your mother without meeting her."

"Wanna? Can I bring my parents in for a session?"

"Sure. But, what is it you want from that?"

"Seeing is believing. They're actually really cute. So what exactly *is* borderline personality disorder?"

"Borderlines split a person or a thing into good or bad. Someone who's *good* one day can be *bad* the next. They can't hold a complex view of others in their minds. It's like emotional amnesia. A person is only as good as the last interaction. They're completely in one mood and don't remember what it was like to be in another. And they tend to react intensely to stress."

"Yeah, like the other day when Ma panicked, '*OY! I don't have da keys!*' We were *inside* the house."

"Right. They peak higher emotionally on less provocation and take longer coming down. They can stay mad a long time. Normally, they were raised in environments in which their beliefs about themselves and their experiences were continually devalued and invalidated. These factors combine to create adults who are uncertain of the truth of their own feelings."

"Oh, so me, too."

Next time I go to Kati's, I bring Ma and Daddy.

Ma sits tall on the couch, a lady wearing pearls and a cautious attitude. Daddy looks confused but relaxed.

"Daddy, why don't you tell Kati what I was like as a child."

"A child? You . . . vere . . . I don't remember. I vorked all da time."

"But, Daddy, you must remember *something*."

"No . . . I don't remember."

Oww. Does he realize how this might disturb me? Nope. Like in my drowning dream—his eyes through the scuba mask—blankness. I shoot Kati a frustrated *"do something!"*

Kati says, "Mr. Stadwoner, did you ever have to care for Suzie?"

Daddy's face gets dark, "I had no choice! Mania vent to vork and left me mit her!" Gulp. Might this be connected to the dream where I stand helpless as a baby is being thrown across a ravine? Kati tosses me a sympathetic look, a rope to hang on to.

She turns back to Daddy. "Was there anything special, something that she did that you can remember?"

Daddy comes up with something. "I can tell you one ting, Suzie vas verrry smart." My ears, which had sunk down to my shoulders, perk up.

"Oh yeah, Daddy? How was I smart?"

"Vhen you vanted someting from a high shelf, you vould take da broom, and you vould knock it down and you vould get it. Since a baby, you alvays knew how to do everyting by yourself!" Yes, I learned to be self-reliant.

"And when I was *bad*, do you remember taking off your belt?"

"No, I don't remember."

"Ma, what did I do to make Daddy give me the strap?"

"Daddy never gave you da strap. I vouldn't let him do someting like dat." Thanks to Oprah she now believes whipping children might be harmful to their mental health.

"Ma, of course Daddy used the strap on me!" She looks like she's just been told something ridiculous.

I turn to Daddy. "Daddy, think! You'd take off your belt—"

"Maybe I vas going to scare you mit da belt, but *hit* you? No."

I turn to Kati. I'm the fly with the human head, stuck in the web as the giant spider closes in. "Hel-l-lp me-e-e-e." Kati smiles as if to say, "I'm sorry your parents are so fucked."

Did I just imagine getting hit with the belt? Now I'm not sure.

Kati once said, "When you are raised in a fear-based, critical family your sense of reality becomes impaired." (I'd have reached this conclusion myself, but my sense of reality was impaired.)

If Daddy only threatened me with the belt then why do I remember the marks on my legs, the burning, the fear of next time? *Da strap,* they named it. "You're going to get da strap again if you don't shurrup!"

Ma's still sitting all ladylike, hands folded on her lap. Like she's watching *Dr. Phil.*

"Ma, normally, you were fighting with Daddy, but you also fought with me, and—"

Ma says, "*Oy!* Da Daddy and I didn't fight. Who had time to fight? I vas vorking all da time! Time to fight I had?"

Maybe Ma took for granted that this was life, what's to remember? You don't remember you had arms as a child, you just took them for granted.

A week later I drop Ma and Daddy off at the airport.

Ma's kissing me. "Goodbye. Tank you for a nice time. *Oy*, you look just like my sister Hanala." Hana, the one I'm named after.

Ma has tears in her eyes. "Hanala vas so full of life, nobody had such pep! And she vas so beautiful! She had all her teeth. And dey vere very white. And so smart she vas, people came from all around da village to talk mit her." My heart—it's reaching out to hers. Must not cry.

"Okay, bye, Ma. Eat the *dark green* lettuce, iceberg lettuce has no nutritional value. And take the vitamins I got you. And walk Ma, go on walks with Daddy. Bye, Daddy, be nice to Ma."

"I'm alvays nice to da Mummy."

I don't know how to describe my feelings. Hollow. Dread. Abandoned. I need a drink. I need to share. It's hours until an AA meeting. Get me to the gym. There's one thing I can always count on—most AA people would say God, but for me it's the gym. After an hour of musically driven heart-pounding, lung-wringing, panting, sweating on the treadmill, I go from "Oh God, what am I gonna do?" to "Oh God, I'm so grateful to be alive." I wonder how many more people would stay sober if they knew there was a way to alter their brain chemistry without drugs or alcohol. Endorphins have kept me sober.

So here I am running on the treadmill and I'm having a problem. My diamond ring keeps hitting the grip bar. It's what AA calls a problem of abundance. Suddenly my sweat turns cold. *Hanala.* As I jog along in the fancyshmancy Sports Club L.A., in my $135 Nikes, bopping to my Sony Walkman, trying to keep my diamond from bashing the treadmill, I compare my life to Hanala's—the woman who stripped, walked into a gas chamber, saw gas come out of the shower heads, coughed, choked and suffocated.

I decide I will honor her life. Hanala's bigger-than-life life. Her pre-Hitler life. I'm changing my name back to Hanala. And besides, *Suzan's* too common, Hanala's cooler.

I tell Pete about my diamond/gas chamber moment.

He says, "Yeah, this world is fucked. Kids starve, the air's polluted, global warming is killing the planet, idiots and assholes are in power . . . " Okay, Pete is making good points, they're just *not* the ones I was addressing. Do I feel unseen? Yes. Do I hate that? Yup. Did I get what I wanted? No. But I know what he's trying to do. Make my boo-boo better. He feels bad when I feel bad.

What did I want from him? What all women want—their man to say the three magic words, "Tell me more." Simple. But if I say that to Pete right now, he'll just defend himself, and I'll seethe through another dinner. I'll tell him the three magic words later, maybe right after sex. He's more responsive and less defensive then.

Instead, I say, "Pete, I want to be called Hanala. I know it'll be hard to remember, but I'd like it if you tried." Does he hate that? Yup. He's scared. What will I do next? Nonetheless, my name is Hanala. That's my name. *Wear it out.*

Dora Biber Dropped Dead— and You're Still Not Married?

Ma calls from Montreal with Daddy bulletins. This just in:

"*Oy*, so listen to vhat *d'y'idiot* did now! I'm in da TV room, I'm having someting wrong mit my heart. I tink it's attacking me. I feel like to fall down, so I yell, 'Fishel, I'm sick, call da 911!' He calls back, 'Vait a minute, I'm putting in numbers to cook in da microvave.' Can you imagine such a *y'idiot*? So I yell again—and who had da strength, tell me—'Fishel, I'm having a heart attack, I *can't* vait!' So now he runs in and starts yelling dat I vatch too much TV! 'Qvick, I tell him, call 911!' And he says, 'Vhat's da number?' A person could *plutz!* So I pull da cord of da telephone, and I call dem myself. *Oy*, dey vere here fast, and so cute dey vere. Nice boys, I tink one vas Jewish!"

I'm on brain freeze. "Ma, are you telling me you had *a heart attack?*"

"No."

"Oh, thank God."

"It vas a stroke."

All I can think is, *fix it*. "Ma, you *have* to cut out the cream cheese and eat more fruits and vegetables and *walk* Ma, you need to—"

"It vas only a mild stroke. But listen, dis person, you don't know dem, she dropped dead, just like dat. Da neighbor down da street dropped dead. Dora Biber dropped dead—and you're still not married?" She disapproves of Pete and me co-habitating.

"What are you saying?? I should hurry up and get married before you die?"

She says, "Vhat's so wrong mit dat?"

I need to change the channel. "Ma, do you believe in an afterlife?"

"I don't believe in *dis* life, I'm going to vorry about after?"

"But do you believe in heaven?"

"Heaven, *ach a bubbe-myseh*—vhen you're dead, you're dead, dat's it. Dey put you in da ground, end of story." I don't like that story, tell me another one, Mummy.

Ma's on this marriage thing, like a pissed-off pitbull on a postman. "Tell me, Hanala, *how* can you be happy if you're not married?"

"Ma, you've been married for fifty years. Has it *ever* made you happy?"

"Dat's different. Pete's not a *y'idiot* like da Daddy."

"Okay, maybe *y'idiot-lite*. He does dumb things too. He doesn't believe in expiration dates. I looked at his Pepto Bismol. It expired June 1997. I tell him, 'That bottle is from the last century, it's too old to work!' He says, 'It's fine. They just *put* those dates on the bottles.' Ma, he has Tylenol from the eighties; they could be laced with strychnine. You think he cares? He'd take the vitamin C Christopher Columbus used on the *Pinta* to avoid scurvy. Is he trying to save money, this man, who picks up every check on a restaurant table, whether he eats or not? Isn't that idiotic?"

"Okay, so let him pay for da vedding."

Pete comes home, and I tell him about the stroke and Dora-Biber's-dead-and-you're-still-not-married conversation. For the next few years, when he sees I'm on the phone with Ma, he says, "So, is Dora Biber still dead?"

❖ ❖ ❖

But Ma's nagging is not going to make me marry Pete. Nope. I'm a big girl now!

The Vedding

November 4, 1995, Yitzhak Rabin, the prime minister of Israel, is assassinated.

Malibu. The *chupah* stands at the end of the garden where Pete and the rabbi are waiting. Behind them the sun is setting into the sea. Guests are seated on white wooden chairs. Jackson Browne's brother plays "You've Got a Friend" on acoustic guitar, as Daddy escorts me—and the princess dress—from the mansion to the lawn.

I step on the white runner and the heel of my shoe sinks into the grass. I start to tip. Guests gasp.

"Daddy! Hold me up!" But Daddy, now drunk, starts to fall. *Daddy can't support me. I must support him or else we both go down. And what else is new?* I use my ten-pound bouquet of roses to regain my balance, grab Daddy, pull him straight, and say, "Never mind, Daddy, I'll hold *you* up!" Guests laugh.

I finally make it up to the *chupah*. Are those tears in Pete's eyes? During the ceremony, I keep turning my head to sneak peeks at everybody. Sylvia's smiling. The whole family flew in from Akron. AA women are glowing. Guys from my aerobics class drove from West Hollywood. I make little waves.

The rabbi says, "Go ahead, turn around, take a good look." I do. And now I'm ready to concentrate. As the rabbi goes into the "Do you . . . " I turn back, once more, to check Ma's expression; I expect big *kvelling*. Instead, I see space. She's out in it. I have to pull her back. She can't miss the moment she's been guilting me about for thirty years. Really, though, *telling* her friends I'm married is what she'll most enjoy.

"Ma!" I say, just loud enough to wake her. "Pay attention!"

"*OY!*" she's startled. "Yeah. Tank you." She'd regret missing the whole thing. Then again, she can always catch it later on video. She likes to watch TV. It makes things *real-er*.

The ceremony is over. Pete and I are now Mr. and Mrs. Pete. We sit at the head table enjoying the wedding feast—chicken or fish (one tofu) on tables decked in white embroidery, baby's breath, and candles. The videographer is going from guest to guest taping private messages for the bride and groom. It's Daddy's turn. He's handed the microphone. He's not aware of the camera, he thinks he's been asked to make a speech. He rises, smooths the fresh-from-the-cedar-closet tux, and stands grandly with puffed-out chest and held-in stomach. Holding the mic like a master of ceremonies, Daddy looks ready to address the nation.

With the demeanor of Wolf Blitzer, smack in the middle of the chicken or fish (or tofu), Daddy starts, "In 1939, Hitler marched in and took away my family to da gas chambers . . . "

A chill spreads like the wave through a sports arena. The mingling, laughter-filled atmosphere is replaced by silence. The only one still whooping it up is Alex, my new brother-in-law, who is clearly coming onto his acid.

Daddy's emphatic, like Captain Kirk: Captain Stadwoner, Stardate 1995, the wedding party crew is transported to 1940. There IS—no way out. We're—TRAPPED in a time/mind warp being held prisoner by a Polish narcissistic, power-hungry, sad man!

"I vas da head of *da group*. I had *many* friends in da government . . . and dey told me, 'Mr. Stadwoner,' " he pauses for dramatic effect, "here is a gun, and you should hide over here—NOT—over dere. So, I made a plan . . ."

Beam me outta here, Scotty, and don't give me any of the "I don't have the power" shit. Pete puts his hand on mine.

Daddy gives highlights from WWII, an insider's view. Forest, starving, hiding from Nazis . . . People put down their forks—at $50 a plate. Interestingly, there's no mention of Ma. He continues giving a face to the great horror of the twentieth century.

"And now, after all dees years," ah, he's winding down, after what feels longer than the twentieth century itself, "I don't believe . . . how I should survive, you know dat I'm a Holocaust survivor, dat I should live so long, to be so proud of my beautiful grandchildren." *Grandchildren*? What are Pete and I, chopped liver (which no one is eating)?

"Mine sisters and brodders wouldn't see grandchildren . . . " He takes a long breath, nods his head, and with a suddenly cheery tone, adds, "but now is not the time to speak of such tings! Okay, dat's all." He hands back the mic and sits down. And that's where my jaw is, down in disbelief. Okay, never mind . . . move along.

If I move quickly, I can get away from the bad feeling. Oh POOP! The bad is catching up. Here comes the unpleasant tingle that starts in my head and flows to my stomach, and now—ADP. Absent Daddy Pang, "I'm over here, Daddy! Daddy?!" I had not been given a guest spot in his head tonight.

The murmuring in the room resumes, with new words like, "Senile."

Aprés dinner, we convene for *the dancing*. After a couple glasses of wine (and a 5mg Valium), Pete is able to leave behind his *don't-look-at-me* phobia and we have a lovely, romantic dance. The next dance is the father of the bride's. Daddy's expected to take the floor with his girl.

I'm thinking where's the daddy/daughter teary-eyed meeting, when she's grateful and he bursts with pride? Daddy's eyes have the *vilda* look. He's drunk. He's dramatic. He performs theatrical sweeping gestures. Suddenly, he's Rudolph Valentino. Daddy grabs my hand as if it's a tool provided for his performance, and begins to tango! A tango he's doing? Melodramatic facial expression, arm stiff out in front, he whisks me across the room in the spirit of the dance. He glides toward the crowd, pulls me, and I bump into the piano.

By the end of the night, Daddy's sobered. He's sitting quietly in the corner of the couch. Ma's in the kitchen counting the silverware. I go over and give her a kiss.

The caterer says, "Mrs. Stadwoner, you have a beautiful daughter."

Ma says, "You tink she's beautiful *now?* You should have seen her ten years ago!"

I go back to the living room and sit next to Daddy. "So, Daddy, did you enjoy today?" I want a special moment . . .

But his face darkens, going from oblivious to hateful. "Vhat's da matter mit you?! How can I enjoy today—da day dey shot Rabin?!"

Logjam in frontal lobe. Thoughts can't flow. Cells stuck in spin mode. I sift through the day, scanning. What did he mean? I'd heard a blurb about a shooting, Israel's prime minister, but with it being my wedding and all, I'd had a lot on my mind. (Oh, and all week the meteorologists—including Dallas Raines—had predicted the storm of the year was moving in from the north. There was no indoor facility available at my original location. So at the last minute, I found this place and had sixty people to contact and tell about the switch. It never rained.) So, a little tired and busy, I put assassinations on my post-wedding to-do list. And this conversation would have to be put on that list, too; I have my wedding day to finish.

I'm saying goodbye to guests when a skirmish breaks out. It's not the Germans coming in, it's just Alex being tackled to the floor by other guests. He was trying to sneak out with a two-hundred-year-old bottle of wine he stole from the cellar.

All in all, for me, November the fourth will always be my lovely wedding day, a day of celebration, when Pete looked at me in the white dress with love and tears in his eyes. For Daddy, it'll be "the day they shot Rabin." Separate realities. It's all subjective.

❖ ❖ ❖

Honeymooning in Spain, I tell Pete about "Rabin."

He says, "You were a feral child."

"A what?"

"You don't *know* what a feral child is?"

"No, I'm an idiot, why don't you tell me, oh superior one." He's flaunting his vocabulary.

Sometimes he corrects my English to make himself look smart, as if he's trying to make up for being bald. I still have resentments.

He says quietly, "A feral child is a wild thing, like a kid who's been abandoned and raised by wolves." Now he's flaunting the Discovery Channel.

Then he says, "Only, wolves would have raised you better."

Huh? I *did* have to raise myself, but I thought that was . . . "normal."

I start to cry.

He understands.

A Fishel

Ma calls from Montreal—

"*Oy*! Listen vhat da *y'idiot* did now!" I listen. It's what I do.

"I'm showing da Daddy da video vhere he made da speech. and he says, 'I never said dis!'

"'*Y'idiot!*, you *see* dat you're saying dis!' So, he tells me, 'Suzie can take from one place in a movie and to put in anader movie!' '*Y'idiot!*' I tell him, 'You *see* you're vearing da same clothes. And vhere vould Suzie get a movie mit you saying dis?!' He says to me, 'Sharrup!' and valks out from da room. So vhat do you tink?!"

Think? I think I *like* this story; I didn't know that Daddy knew I could edit!

"Ma, he was probably embarrassed and couldn't explain his behavior, so he denied it." In Poland, his *y'idiot*-syncracies weren't captured on videotape.

"Oh, okay. Dis person, you don't know her, dropped dead. Da neighbor next door dropped dead. Dora Biber dropped dead—and you still don't have children?"

To me "having a baby" is synonymous with: If a child of mine dies, my life will end as well, and I'll never get a proper shot at happiness. There's so much out there to hurt a child. Dying in childbirth is unlikely, but dying in child death is certain.

"Ma, it's too risky! What if something happens to my child? And I don't know if I'd be a good mother. Besides, only *real* people can be mothers."

"Vhat, are you crazy! Who ever heard a ting like dat! Have da baby, and vorry about dis later."

"And you say you never called me stupid!"

"I didn't say dat. But sometimes you say crazy tings. If you don't have children, who's going take care of you?"

"Ma, *parents* take care of *children*. Listen I've gotta go."

"So, are you going to have a baby?"

"No. I'm going to the gym. Bye."

I jog along not being able to get Daddy out of my mind. *Is he crazy?* His doctor once asked me if I thought Daddy was becoming senile. "No," I said, "that's Daddy."

Then he asked, "When did your father first show signs of confusion or forgetfulness?"

I said, "Well . . . like Ronald Reagan, we may disagree as to exactly *when* mindlessness began. Ma said he was crazy in Poland. Since I was little, I remember him raging, ranting, and interrupting—Reagan could act smart better, he had writers. Daddy had Hitler."

The doctor said Daddy has senile dementia: Short-term memory loss and decreased cognitive function. It's not Alzheimer's. He knows who everyone is, he just doesn't know when he's seen them last.

But Daddy can also be adorable. Like at my niece Shelley's wedding, when he walked into the room wearing a beret, I said, "You look quite European in that hat, Daddy."

His eyes twinkled, and with a boyish exuberance said, "Vell—I'm not from *Asia!*"

And . . . when I saw a pair of slippers I wanted to buy him for his birthday, I called Montreal. "Daddy what size shoes do you wear?"

"Vy do you vant to know dis?"

"I saw slippers I thought you'd like."

"I don't need you to buy me nuting! I can buy my own slippers. Nobody has to buy dem for me!"

"But, Daddy . . . I . . . you . . . they're on sale."

"Okay. So buy dem."

"What size shoe do you wear?"

He says, "I ver a nine. Sometimes a half-past nine."

"So, Daddy, what are you going to do today?"

"Today? Today, I do almost nuting."

"Still walking to the mall?"

"I don't valk fast like before."

"Slowing down a little, huh?"

"Vell, I'm no springing chick'n!"

Ma butts in, "Don't listen! He valks so fast, nobody can catch him."

"How old are you now Daddy, eighty?"

Daddy laughs, "Eighty?! I'm already eighty-two!"

Ma's annoyed, "*Oy!* You hear dis? Eighty-two? You're eighty-two?! He's eighty-one!"

Daddy says, "Eighty-one, I finished in May."

"Daddy, you're in your eighty-second year of life, but we still say you're eighty-one, not eighty-two."

"Suzie, now I'm alive eighty-two years!"

"*Oy!* Dat's vhat he says no matter how many people tell him he's a *y'idiot.*"

I've tried correcting these people since I was five. You'd think I'd know better, but I continue trying. "Okay, Daddy, *how many birthdays* have you had?"

Daddy says, "Birtdays? I had *one.*"

He was starting to make sense, so I dropped the subject.

Next December Pete's in China with Gary, hopefully wearing a seat belt.

Ma and Daddy are in L.A., we're watching TV. There's a commercial. I mute the television. It's quiet. Too quiet.

Ma seizes the opportunity, "So now he thinks he's *eighty-tree!*"

Daddy starts laying out the numbers again. "Eighty-two, I'm no more!"

I say, "Daddy, how old is Matthew, Shelley's baby? Is he one year old?"

"Matthew? No, he's, I tink, a few months."

"Exactly! And, when he's eighty-two, I hope he isn't having this conversation!"

Ma and Daddy keep socking it to each other—

Daddy comes into the kitchen, two socks in hand, and starts yelling at Ma, "Don't buy me no more *dreckisha* socks like dis!" Matching one sock on top of the other, he shows her. "You bought two left socks. Dey're socks for da *left* foot."

Ma looks at me. "A *y'idiot!*" She turns to Daddy. "Here, give dem to me." Ma takes one of the socks, turns it inside out, shoves it back at him, and says, "Here. Now you have a pair."

I think it through. *Do* socks have a left and right? Is it me? The brain, an organizing organ, when unable to organize, may shut down. Melt down. Melt cheese. I'm wondering if there are any danishes left.

Now Daddy, with an entire pair of socks on, is ready to go for a walk . . .

I go too. Better walk than binge. Daddy doesn't see the curb, he trips and falls, his head comes down inches from a sharp rock. I see it happen as if in slow motion. I rush to help.

"It's *goornisht!* Don't vorry!" he says as he's bleeding.

We keep walking, silently.

After about ten minutes Daddy looks at Ma, and with angry curled lips proclaims, "It's your fault."

"It's my fault?! How can it be *my* fault?"

"You vere talking to me!"

"I talked to you yesterday, you didn't fall down." Using his whole arm, Daddy fans her remark away like he can blow it back to her.

Ma looks at me with that "see vhat I live mit?" expression.

Later, back at home, we're in the kitchen—

"So, Daddy, do you remember your mother? You were so young when she died."

"I vas maybe four years by age vhen my modder died. Can you imagine?"

"No, Daddy, not really, it must have been horrible."

"It vasn't good! I remember my friends said my modder vas mit God. I told dem, 'If God took mine modder, den God is a bandit!'" Is that why Daddy turned atheist?

"*Oy*, I remember my modder, how beautiful she vas. She vas a beauty . . . like . . . you know who she looked like?" Daddy smiles at me from across the table.

"Who, Daddy?"

"She looked *just*. . . like Sylvia."

Y'idiot.

Ma realizes she left her purse in the bathroom. There's a receipt she needs to comb over. "Da market, dey alvays make mistakes, and never to cost dem less." She's gone.

Daddy gets up from the table and goes to the sink to wash the tea glass. He's chuckling. "Suzie, do you remember vhen I told you dat you vere fat like a pig?"

"Yes, Daddy. I remember." It's become one word. *Fat-like-a-pig*. My head has the web site, fatlikeapig.com. How can I forget how disgusted Daddy was with me? I turned it into a funny story. Laugh? Yeah. Forget? No amount of alcohol or drugs, no self-help books or seminars, AA meetings or therapy could delete *fatlikeapig*. It's the you're-a-bad-girl virus.

Daddy says, "You remember in school, I paid da tutor to come to da house because you vere too lazy to learn by yourself."

"Yes, lazy." *Lazy*, a short word for a long explanation. I sit, quietly screaming inside.

Daddy's wiping the glass, his back to me. "Suzie, dis I can tell you. You deserved a better home den da one you got."

What? Is self-reflection going on?

He's rinsing the *shmatteh*. "It vas good dat you left to California—I didn't sleep for five years—but it vas very good for you dat you left. And I vant to say, if most parents ver 50 percent wrong, me and da Mummy, ver sixty."

Before I can start doubting that I heard what I heard, I grab the laptop and document it.

I take Ma and Daddy to an AA meeting—

The leader asks if there are any out-of-towners who would care to stand and identify themselves.

I elbow Ma, she almost missed her cue. She stands, "Hello, my name is Mania, and I'm from Montreal."

The room chimes, "Hi, Mania!" She's happy.

I told Daddy before the meeting started, that if he wanted, he could stand and say he's an alcoholic. "After all, Daddy, you drink every day."

The leader asks, "Are there any newcomers with less than thirty days of sobriety?"

"Now, Daddy."

Daddy stands, and to the two hundred people in the room announces, "My name is Fishel, and I'm not only an alcoholic, I'm a *professional* alcoholic!" He gets a laugh. He's happy. We're a happy little dysfunctional family.

Ma and Daddy are back in Montreal.

Kelly Lange looks concerned. This time it's not raindrops on the window, it's Ice Storm '98. "The East Coast has been put on ice." Poor Ma and Daddy, it's the worst natural disaster to hit Montreal in a century. They're prisoners in their plastic bungalow.

I call Ma from the Jacuzzi where I'm enjoying another 72 degree L.A. January.

"Oy, ve can't go outside all veek. Da sidevalk is like ice."

"Come back to California. We'll play in the pool again."

"Oh yes, it vas fun to svim. And such a pool you have, like a lake." Pete and I had designed it to look natural. With waterfalls. And then we designed drains when the waterfalls flooded the yard.

The next night Pete and I are having dinner at a swank L.A. restaurant, and halfway through my low-carb roast beef, a feeling possesses me.

"Pete. I have to call my mother." I hunt for my cellphone in the handbag I swore I'd never have to hunt through; it has compartments; but how do I remember which compartment holds which item?

Pete says, "You can't call now, it's midnight back east. You'll wake her up."

"Yeah, but, I . . . I should call." I push "7" on speed dial. The phone ID displays *Ma*.

After about six rings, Ma answers, "Hello." She starts to cough.

"Ma? What's wrong?"

"Vhat? I vas sleeping." More coughing.

"Ma, why are you coughing? What's going on?"

"Ve have no electric lights, no heat, everyting is broken now in Montreal"—cough, cough—"I'm sleeping in da TV room. So I made a little fire."

"A FIRE? From *what?*" Pete looks up from the pepper-crusted ahi arrangement.

"I vas cold. It vas dark. I took a pot and put in candles mit strings and papers, material to burn, I don't know . . ." Cough.

"Ma! Get outside!"

"It's maybe tventy-below-zero, I should go stand outside? *Oy*, vait, I'll open a vindow."

"Yes, but stay on the phone."

"Okay," cough. "*Oy*, I'm feeling like I can't svallow air."

"STICK YOUR HEAD OUT THE WINDOW AND BREATHE IN FRESH AIR—HURRY . . ."

A few minutes/lifetimes later, Ma is breathing well. Hours later, as the sun comes up, Ma sees the walls, curtains, and ceilings are black. She calls me.

"You're mine angel. If you didn't call and vake me up, I vould never vake up again."

❖   ❖   ❖

I can't explain the connection to Ma. Maybe quantum physics will one day. It's weird, I tell you. I remember the day, after finally forcing myself to see *Schindler's List* (with a towel), I called Ma—

"Ma, I saw a movie last night . . . oh boy!"

Ma says, "*You* saw a movie? *I* saw a movie, *oy!*" Ma went to a movie? Was the TV broken?

"What did you see Ma?"

"It vas a Schindle, Schnider's someting—"

"*Schindler's List?!*"

"Exactly! How did you know?"

"Because *I* saw it last night, too."

"How you like dat? Vhat a vorld. It's all like a dream. Vell, you know, da Schindle List vas only one story. Dere ver many like dis."

I'm sad to say she's right.

Ma, her black and whiteness, wrong and rightness . . . who is she?

Ma has always embarrassed me. I wanted her to watch *60 Minutes*, she'd watch *Love Boat*. I wanted her to sound like Mrs. Brady, she sounded like Dr. Ruth.

I spent years tutoring her, sounding out the word slowly, "Sand–*wich*."

Ma repeated, "Sen-a-*vich*." I used to react because I took it as "she's not *listening*!" I'd go nuts trying to get her to hear me. Again, I repeated, "Sand-wich!" And she'd say, "Sen-a-vich!"

One day I scream, "Ma, you left Poland forty years ago. After living here all this time, you can't say *sandwich* instead of *sen-a-vich*?!"

Then, the spokesperson for mental health in my head says, "Why do you still want Ma to say *sandwich*? She's not going to change. Why don't *you* change instead?"

Little Suzie says, "But I want *Ma* to change!"

"Why?" I don't have an immediate answer, which in my case, is good. My immediate answers regarding Ma tend to be automatic.

"The point isn't the sen-a-vich."

"No?"

"Think back. Were you *ever* important enough to make Ma and Daddy stop yelling?"

"Uh . . . no."

"Well, what did that tell you?"

"That what I want isn't important . . . that *I'm* not important."

"Everyone wants to feel they're important."

"So, when I think Ma's not listening to me today, I see it as, what I want doesn't matter?"

"Does she ever say, 'I know sometimes I don't have patience, and I get annoyed. I vish I could speak better, it frustrates me too'?"

"No, she usually tells me to shurrup!"

"How does that make you feel?"

"Not like Opie-fucking-Taylor! How do *you* think it makes me feel, Dr. Phil!"

"Anxious. Afraid you'll *never* be important enough. But . . . if you can get Ma to say *sandwich,* there's hope?"

"Yeah . . . . but she won't!"

"Can't."

"Huh?"

"It's not that Ma *won't* change. She *can't* change. She can't ski, but you expect her to snowboard down a black diamond run. Ma's tracks are too deeply laid. She must hold onto her view because of her fragile ego."

Who *is* this nudge-of-reason speaking? Could the critical bitch ruling my head be losing the fight over airtime? This new and improved thinking process feels much better. It's fresh, it's familiar. It's Kati. She's now heading the committee. Honey, I shrunk my shrink.

I get it! The concrete "Dis is da vay it is" stance is because Ma can't bear confusion, so she creates certainty. *"Dis ve don't have in Canada!"* Hello, Dalai Lama!

And so, I give up the *Extreme Ma Makeover.* Ma becomes Mania, the woman she is, in living black and white.

Next time, she calls and starts in, "I don't know vhy you had to take drugs and be an alcoholic! Sylvia vasn't an alcoholic, I vasn't an alcoholic! Vhy did *you* have to be an alcoholic!"

Uh-oh. Will adrenaline make me stupid and get me defending myself, or will I be able to hold onto my new view? "Because, Ma, I'm different." For the first time, it was okay to be different. Different didn't mean *bad* anymore.

Silence. And then, "Vell, I guess I'm lucky I still got you." She *got* me.

The Day Ma Died

Then this happened—

It's 6:00 a.m. Pete and I are in bed, the phone rings. I let him answer, figuring it's either his office or someone from his family calling from jail. I press my head deeper into the pillow and put my arm up in the air. "Tell them I'm not *in*."

Pete says hello, then bolts upright, "Oh, my God! Is she okay?" I have a sick feeling.

Pete hands me the phone. It's Sylvia calling from Ohio.

"Suzan, get to Montreal. Ma's had a massive stroke."

Montreal. I walk onto the eighth floor of Saint Mary's Hospital.

This place is out of the 1800s. *The Snake Pit.* Three nurses for forty-nine patients. People screaming in pain. Lying in their own excrement. Dying unnoticed. And they tell me this is one of Montreal's *better* hospitals. Unsocialized medicine. And my mother is here?

Earlier in the week, Ma had been admitted for a rapid heart rate. The doctor put her on Coumadin. She was being released, happily dressing to go home. The nurse found her on the floor, a can of AquaNet at her side. I learned later that a possible side effect of Coumadin is a brain hemorrhage.

Ma is sharing a room with two other patients. *Men.*

My-cousin-Molly hugs me as I walk in. Molly, now happily married to a good guy—a French psychiatrist—has been taking care of Ma for years, bringing her to doctors, buying her groceries, and loving her.

Sylvia is standing at the foot of Ma's bed. "She's in a coma. The doctor called it a big bleed. Her left side is paralyzed, he said she'll be bedridden for the rest of her life." Can she hear? People come out of comas and say they were able to hear, but couldn't talk.

Ma's on a feeding tube. Her eyes are closed, but she's squirming. Her hand is at her throat, tapping the tube as if to say, "I hate this." Her face looks pained.

I lean in and kiss her.

I put my finger in Ma's palm, in the hand that isn't paralyzed. "Ma, if you can hear me, squeeze my finger." She squeezes.

"Ma, if you want to say *yes*, squeeze one time. If you want to say *no*, squeeze two times. Can you hear me?" She squeezes once.

"Ma, are you in pain?" One squeeze. It squeezes my heart. I'm trying not to cry, but Ma's in pain. What can I do? It's my kitten, Pookie the dog, gas chambers. What can I do? Get a doctor. Trying not to breathe in the stench, I walk down the hall to the nurses' station.

"My mother is in pain. Can she please have something. Mania Stadwoner." The nurse checks Ma's chart. But she's ambivalent about it.

"The doctor said she could have morphine at midnight."

"But she needs it now!" I think of Shirley MacLaine in *Terms of Endearment*, banging the counter at the nurses' station. "Give my daughter her medication!"

The nurse says, "Your mother is in a coma; she's not in pain."

"She told me she is."

"How? She said, 'I'm in pain'?"

"She squeezed my finger."

"That's just reflex. Anytime you put something in someone's hand, they squeeze. It doesn't mean anything."

"Please come to her room."

"I don't have time to—"

"Look, I appreciate how busy you must be, but I'm not going anywhere until you come with me. And bring a shot of morphine. Make that two shots. And make mine a double, I just spent twelve hours getting here from Los Angeles." She almost smiles. And follows me to Ma's room.

"I'm telling you, your mother is out. What you felt was just a reflex."

Oh yeah? I put my finger in Ma's hand, "Ma! Can you hear me?" Squeeze.

The nurse remains smug. "It's just a reflex." Syl, the orderlies, and the man in the bed across the way watch.

"Ma, will you squeeze my finger three times please."

And it's unmistakable. One. Two. Three.

"Ma, if you're in pain, squeeze once." Squeeze.

The nurse leaves the room and comes back with a syringe. She looks at me, and then she gives Ma the morphine. And for a second, I'm envious.

At 2:00 a.m., Ma has stopped squeezing my finger. She's comfortable. And like in *Love Story,* I crawl into the hospital bed.

My-cousin-Molly has left. Syl is sleeping in the hall on a gurney I nabbed from another room. A few hours later we switch. I climb up on the gurney and fall asleep praying I wake up with both my kidneys.

The next day I pick up Daddy and bring him to the hospital. I'm afraid— will he be mad? At what? I dunno. I can't get past the fear of his anger. I don't want him to yell.

We walk into her room. "Daddy . . . Ma is okay."

He says, "Vhy shouldn't she be okay? She's sleeping mit two men!" It's a Fishel.

Ma's tapping her throat where the feeding tube is. It's hurting her. Daddy's stroking her arm, telling her to open her eyes, telling her not to leave him. Syl and I go into the hall with the doctor; we discusses the prognosis. Best-case scenario has Ma bedridden and in incessant pain. Syl and I make the decision. We take her off life support.

With the tube removed I kiss her. "Ma, is that better?"

Suddenly, her eyes open, they gaze into mine.

"Ma! Hi, Ma! Ma?"

No answer.

"Ma, do you recognize me?"

Her brows come together. "Don't ask stupid qvestions!" She closes her eyes again, but I know she's in there. She mumbles something like, "No more needles, give me vater, I'm so tirsty."

I go down to the hospital administration office and pay extra to get Ma a semi-private room—private rooms are for contagious/immune-impaired patients only. Ma's roommates are relieved. They're tired of all the tragic goodbyes.

Sylvia? She's been hysterical off and on since I got here, crying like I do at my worst, worst times. Oprah calls it "the ugly cry." I don't get it. Sylvia has never shown any signs of affection toward Ma. I thought she was disgusted by her. But now, the way she keeps kissing her and calling her *mommy*, I'm rethinking their relationship. Is this grief partly guilt? And sorrow for what never was? And fifty years of suppressed feelings bubbling up?

For once, I'm *not* crying. I'm too stunned by the Sylvia I'm looking at. Underneath her hard protective coating is *me*.

My niece Shelley's crying. "Gramma, we want you to get better and bake us cookies."

Ma lifts her arm and with closed eyes, announces, "Dere's an apple pie in da freezer." We think she's delirious, but later, we find the apple pie in the freezer. A Jewish mother to the end.

◆　◆　◆

A few days later, I'm kissing her, singing to her, telling her how much I love her, and Ma opens her eyes. She stares at me, deep into me. She's looking at me the way she did in my manta ray dream.

In a raspy voice she says, "I know dat you love me." And her eyes close again.

The next night at dinner—I pick a swanky restaurant downtown to take my niece—I say, "Shelley, Gramma is going to die tonight." I'd had a knot in my stomach. It's like I *knew*. After the main course and before dessert, I write the obituary to put in the paper.

I drop Shelley off in Cote St. Luc, and go to see Ma.

The hospital floor is quiet. Sylvia finally went back to the house to get a night's sleep. Except for taking the occasional break to shower, change clothes, or grab a quick smoked meat sandwich, she's refused to leave Ma's side. Most nights, she sleeps here—when she can sleep—in a chair next to Ma.

We'd hired a private nurse to be with Ma when we weren't. She's here now, watching the black and white TV we rented when we thought Ma was going to come out of her coma. I tell her she can take a break.

This is the first time in eleven days I've been alone with my mother. "Ma, do you remember when I was little, you sang the *pripitchek* song to me?" And I sing it to her,

> "*Oyfn pripitchek brent a fayerl, un in shtub is heys.*
> *Un der rebe lernt kleyne kinderlekh Dem alef-beyz.*"

Ma's lips pucker. She's blowing me a kiss. She takes my hand to her cheek and holds it there. She's hot. Fever. She's always been a fighter. Is she fighting to hang on?

"Ma, it's all right to let go. I know you think heaven is a *bubbe-myseh*, but who knows. Scientists say that energy doesn't die, it's transformed into something else. Einstein said so. *Einstein*. He was Jewish, Ma. For all you know, you might see your father and mother and sisters and brothers again. It's okay to let go. I'll come meet you later. Much later. Shirley MacLaine could be right, Ma."

I dampen her hot forehead with a washcloth, kiss her for the thousandth time, and call Pete. He'd been in Montreal for a few days, but returned to L.A. to take care of business.

I watch her chest. "Pete, there's more time between each breath." Pete continues to talk. I watch her breathe again. "Pete, her breath—" He talks. I'm trying to count the seconds between breaths. "Concentrate, count right, start with zero . . . okay, blew it. I was *concentrating* on counting rather than counting." I wait for the next breath. It doesn't come. She's dead. She heard me. She *listened* to me!

I need to tell Pete, who's talking a mile a minute about business. "Pete."

He keeps talking, not hearing me. "Pete!"

He's still talking. "Pete! My mother is dead."

Aha! I finally get through. There's a pause, and then he says, "No she's not. Check for a pulse. Call a doctor. Hold a mirror to her nose—"

"SHUT UP!" I scream, and hang up quickly, before I call him an idiot. I bend over and put my ear on Ma's chest. No heart beat. Nothing. Dead quiet. How weird is that?

Ma waited till it was just the three of us. Ma, me and Pete, like the old days.

The hired nurse comes back in the room and says, "Press the call button, quick!"

No, not too quick. What if they try to resuscitate her? No, this is what we've all been waiting for. Ma's paralyzed, with congestive heart failure, cardio-hypertension, and she's going blind. I give it a moment more and press the button.

The staff pour in the room. I ask one of the nurses to put Ma's teeth back in. I want her to look like herself. We're gathered around the bed, me holding her, the gruff orderlies have tears in their eyes. They had known Ma before the coma. They talk about how sweet she was, so bubbly and likable. Not grouchy.

I keep kissing her. Then the thought strikes, *I'm kissing a corpse.* But she's warm. And, I've never seen such a peaceful look on her face. She can finally relax. The Nazis aren't going to come get her anymore. I kiss her for the last time.

Oh, Ma. It's just like you to give me a dramatic end to the book. You were there for my first breath, and I was there for your last.

◆ ◆ ◆

I call Sylvia. "She's gone."

Sylvia says, "Oh. Okay."

"I called Paperman's. They're going to come for her tomorrow."

"Okay."

"Uh, Syl . . . How are you? Will you be able to sleep tonight?"

Sylvia says, "Su-zan, I've done *my* grieving." Okay. We decide to tell Daddy in the morning.

I'm on my own. I sign the death certificate, pick up her personal belongings, write the obituary, and go back to the hotel room.

On the nightstand is the last piece of Ma's apple pie.

The After-Ma

Ma made and paid for the funeral arrangements years before. She ordered a limo; she wanted to make sure I'd come.

A hundred people show up for the memorial. A good turnout, considering most of her friends—like Dora Biber—are dead.

Daddy wants to see Ma. He doesn't believe she died.

"Dis is a trick." The rabbi opens Ma's casket. She's wrapped in a shroud. Like Jesus, another good Jew. Ma looks pale and bony, more like Mother Teresa than Ma.

Daddy falls on her body. He holds her, kisses her. He's crying and asking over and over, "Mania, vyh did you leave me?" David and the rabbi pull him off the casket and help him to a chair.

❖ ❖ ❖

People are talking to me. I don't know how to respond. Nothing seems real, including Ma being dead. I watched her die, and I can't comprehend that she's dead. No, I didn't vote on it. Yes, I took her off life support, but . . . she's *dead*? How? Ma's bigger than life. I guess you don't know what it feels like to lose a mother until it happens. it's as if I've joined a creepy club.

Everyone sits. The rabbi speaks, then reads from the Bible. Ma would space out here. The Bible's not her thing; judging the asses on the women in the chapel, that's more her style.

Then, my cousin Jackie reads something beautiful he wrote. She'd have liked that.

Sylvia asked the rabbi to read a letter she wrote for Ma's eightieth birthday party.

My turn. I get up, no idea what to say. That's a first. I never thought to rehearse it, to prepare for it. I'm doing something I never imagined myself doing. The eulogy for my mother.

How do I talk about Ma without using the words *narcissistic, mean* or *y'idiot*? Sylvia's letter spoke of Ma's cooking and sewing. So I tell the "I got da sperm betveen my legs!" story. And then I cry.

The limo follows the hearse. It's like watching *Six Feet Under*, only I'm in it.

We bury Ma on a cold, sunny day. The rabbi speaks in Hebrew, Sylvia and I repeat. He points to a shovel. I'm supposed to throw dirt on my mother's coffin? It's customary. But how much, how many shovelfuls? I want to get it right. I don't want to mess up. Oh God, I'm still terrified of criticism. It's customary.

As we're getting back into the limo, Syl says, "What am I going to do when I go to call her."

I say, "Call me."

Syl says, "Okay."

◆ ◆ ◆

Wow, my mother died. That's the first time *that's* happened.

She's not in the house in Cote Saint Luc? Ma? How can she be dead? My whole life, she's been alive! It's not making sense. There's a hole. A Ma-shaped hole in my universe. She's nowhere I can reach her? Ma? Ma? Ma! Where are you?

We go back to Cote Saint Luc to sit shiva—

I have two hours before people start arriving for the Jewish version of a wake. Enough time to go for a run. The iPod is blasting Tom Jones' "Delilah." It's been twenty-five years since I rocked out to "Delilah" in the spider basement.

I run by Westminister Park, where Leonard first kissed me. I pass the bench where he broke up with me for the evil Lana Liebman. I run around my old high school. It seems so much smaller. This is what killed me in gym class? I wonder if Lana Liebman jogs? And now I'm jogging back home to sit *shiva* for my mother. Ma, you'd be so proud.

I shower, change into a dry pair of leggings, the only black clothing I brought—and waiting for the *shiva* to commence, I go through old photo albums. There are pictures of Ma and me, Daddy and me, or Daddy and his car. And in every picture, Daddy looks like he's being shot with a gun instead of a Kodak. Ma is usually fixing her hair. Or mine. I'm either sitting or standing stiffly next to them, arms at my sides. I'm rarely smiling.

These are pictures of us together, but we weren't together; we were next to each other. Was I the only one who knew we were a family?

I go through boxes. Ma saved every letter I ever sent her. She also saved every receipt for money she sent me. She even saved the receipt for my braces. In with the canceled checks was a fan letter I'd gotten that had obviously been folded and unfolded a hundred times. She also saved cassette tapes marked "This Tape No Good." They were the closet in a box labeled "GARBAGE."

I go to the kitchen and try to get Daddy to swallow Ensure. "Just a little, Daddy. It's strawberry, your favorite!" You'd think it was *lima beans!*

He says, "You go, go out, enjoy yourself. For me da enjoyment is over." Yes, I'll go dancing, catch a flick . . .

"Daddy, she was my mother."

Daddy says, "I know. I lost da Mummy. For sixty-seven years ve vere happy, so much in love."

Ma, you'd be *plutzing.*

"I saved dem, da whole family. I vas rich, dey vere poor. Da Mummy could go into any store and take anyting, and dey vould know my name. Later, I vould pay. And ve had a grrr-reat love. Sometimes ve had a little fight, but dat's normal." *Sometimes?*

"Da Mummy had a good life by me. I gave her everyting!"

"Yes, Daddy." Including a stroke, I'm thinking. After the minor stroke Ma had last year, her doctor said she'd recover, but it was only a matter of time before the stress of living with Daddy would kill her.

Daddy walks around the house, touching the pictures of Ma and crying, repeating, "For sixty-seven years . . . I saved dem . . . good life by me . . . ."

He hasn't eaten, shaved, or changed his clothes since Ma died. Poor Daddy. Poor Daddy. Pour Daddy a drink.

People arrive, and Daddy serves drinks. One for them, one for him. He stumbles around the living room, interrupting the prayer service, "For sixty-seven years . . ." He falls back into a chair, hits his head, and passes out. The men carry him to bed.

A *professional* alcoholic! And, like a true professional—I know, I was one—the next morning, Daddy remembers nothing. "Tell me Hanala, did somebody come to da house yesterday?"

Oh, vell. I understand, Daddy. The next thing I knew . . . it was morning.

If Ma were here, she'd be telling me about this. "Listen vhat da *y'idiot* did now!"

In AA they say, "When you sober up an asshole, you get a sober asshole." When an idiot goes through a Holocaust—you get a traumatized idiot? I looked up the word *idiot*. "ID"—as in Freud's ID—comes from the Latin, meaning self-obsessed. Idiot.

Back in L.A.—

People say the darndest things. They mean well, but are probably uncomfortable with my grief.

"She's in a better place now." No, a better place would be in the Jacuzzi with me.

"At least she lived a long life." Yes, filled with guilt.

"She's out of her misery." Duh.

"There's no such thing as death. She lives in your heart. Be grateful that you had her a long time. You must live your life." No shit, *shmendrick*. You think I'm wallowing?

And the classic, "She's with God now." Oh God.

So what do I *want* to hear? "You must miss her." "It must be awful." Yes, the more real it becomes, the more awful I feel. I'm full of awful.

It's too final. What about, "Mummy, when you die I'm going to stuff you, because I have to be able to see your sweet face every day, or I'll just die!"?

◆　◆　◆

At the end of a level-one thousand yoga class we lie on the floor, eyes closed in corpse pose, meditating. Suddenly, appearing as bright as ever, right in front of me, is Ma. Her eyes are beaming. She's smiling, she's got more confidence than she ever had in life. She looks like Ma, if Ma had gone to college.

She says, nodding her head slightly, "*Now* I understand."

Tears roll into my ears.

I understand. She has nothing to feel guilty about anymore. She's paid the price for surviving the Holocaust when her family didn't. She doesn't have to say *I'm sorry* anymore. *I'm sorry—I will never spend any money on myself*—anymore. She doesn't have to defend herself. She knows I've forgiven her for everything crummy. Of course she *gets it* now. Without guilt, she doesn't have a need to defend herself. She can just *get* it. Get *me*.

I miss you, Ma. Can't you just come back as a car? (See sixties' TV—rein*CAR*nation.)

I talk to Syl on the phone almost every day . . .

She's suffering. "It's awful. Just awful. I keep thinking, if only Ma was in a better hospital, if I went up there sooner, if I brought her here . . . That idiot doctor gave her too much Coumidan and it killed her."

"Yeah, I know. But remember, Ma had a heart condition for a long time; medicine kept her alive for years—extra years."

"True. It's just . . . I can't stand these feelings, I cry all the time. I'm depressed! God, is *this* what you've been feeling all these years?"

"Pretty much. Off and on."

"No wonder you did drugs!" Wow. She got it.

Eight weeks, and thousands of tears later—

I return to Montreal to see Daddy and to go to my thirtieth high school reunion. *Thirtieth?* How can that be possible? I go. I felt invisible back then, I feel invisible at the reunion.

The good news is, I finally lost that five pounds I've been trying to shed for twenty years. Tears must have calories. It's the *Your Mother's Dead* diet. I don't recommend it.

Daddy's happy to see me. And not just because I'm thin. He keeps forgetting I'm in Montreal, so every morning, he's happily surprised when I walk in the kitchen.

He's running the perpetual monologue: "Da Mummy vas tirteen vhen I rescued her and her whole family . . ." He repeats how he kept her alive in the forest where he was *da chief* of *da group*, which he kept alive because of his high-up connections, and came to Canada and was da head manager of the fur dressers and dyers. Oh! And what he repeats most, "I vas a very good husband, no?"

"NO! You sucked! You yelled at Ma all the time!" is what I want to say, but don't. I take a deep breath and remind myself: People who talk about how wonderful they are, have serious doubts about it. Under the bravado, Daddy is horribly insecure. He *is* afraid that he's losing his mind, and somewhere, lost in his denial, is the memory of how Ma *really* felt about him.

"Da Mummy and me, ve had a great love!"

"Uh . . . huh."

"She never had to vork a day. I told her, 'no vork!'"

"Too bad she didn't listen, Daddy."

"Vhat do you mean? She listened!"

"Well, she kept working in the bakeries."

"Vhat, are you *CRRRAZY*?"

"Why are you calling me crazy?"

"Because you speak complete nonsense!"

"Why do you say that?"

"You remember nuting! Who vas home if da Mummy vorked?"

"Nobody. Well, me."

"*Meshugeh,* you talk, complete crazy."

"Daddy, Ma worked in bakeries since I was a little girl. And when I learned how to drive, I picked her up at night."

"Crrrazy, you talk! I vorked like a horse! I cleaned! I vacuumed! I did it everyting!"

"What did Ma do?"

"Nuting! She vatched television and ate bad food. *Haserai!* Dat's vhy she left me. She vould be still alive if she listened and ate like me!"

"Okay Daddy. I'm not going to argue."

"Vhy you should argue?"

Why? Because my head is exploding. And because it's what I've always done.

"Daddy, does this window open? I'm hot."

"It's not hot."

"But I'm hot."

"You're hot? Maybe because you valk fast, you're hot."

"Yes, so I want to open a window."

"It's not hot."

"Never mind, I'll take my computer out on the porch. Where's the light switch?"

"Vhat light svitch?"

So here I sit on the porch chair with the broken leg, in the dark, balancing my laptop, understanding why I'm in therapy.

After packing to fly back to L.A. in the morning, I write him a letter—

> *Dear Daddy,*
>
> *I was here in Montreal from May 28th to June 2nd. I took you to my high school reunion, and you met my old friends. We walked to the mall and met your <u>really</u> old friends. (Ha-ha). We walked to the park and the mall every day. You walked very fast, like you were forty-eight, not eighty-eight.* We had smoked-meat sandwiches from Schwarz's. You made me latkes and I took some to eat on the plane. Thank you for showing me such a good time.*
>
> *All my love,*
> *Your little Hanala*

*He's really eighty-seven.

I leave the letter by the radio in the kitchen.

At 6:00 a.m. the taxi driver places my suitcase in the trunk as Daddy and I say goodbye—

"Tank you for coming."

"Thank *you* Daddy, I had a very good time seeing you."

Daddy says, "You know, I forget a lot of tings—da doctor told me dis vas normal considering da age—but I tell you . . . *you*, mine darling daughter, I vill never forget."

Gulp. I look out the back window as the cab drives away. It's like leaving a toddler on the sidewalk. Man, do I want a drink. But I haven't had a one in twenty-one-and-a-half years. Can't blow it. Not if I want to blow out twenty-two candles in December.

Speed dial—

I get the cell out to call Daddy and press "7." The display on the phone reads, "MA." It takes my breath away. I reprogram it to read, "Daddy."

"Hi, Daddy, it's me, your little Hanala."

"I tell you, I vouldn't take two big Hanalas for my little one."

He'd found the letter.

The phone bleeps, it's Syl. I say bye to Daddy.

"Suzan, Daddy is some piece of work. The woman who lives across the street from him called to say the basement flooded, so I had a plumber go over. The man worked all day, and Daddy yelled at me to not give him a penny, that the government would pay."

"Yes, they all know him there."

Syl laughs. "Exactly! That's what he said." Her voice softens. "You know how Daddy used to wait at the bus stop for Ma so he could carry her groceries?"

"Yeah, the one nice thing she said about him, that he'd be at the corner waiting for her to come back from the store."

"Well, he's still waiting. The neighbor said he stands there every day and watches people get off the bus, then he goes back home."

Sylvia starts to sob. Vhat can I tell you?

Finding Dog

I'm twenty-two years sober.

Ma—like Dora Biber—is still dead. It's become real, dammit. Just after she died, and for months, really, I was in some sort of shock. Except for the periodic hysterical-crying sessions, I was beside myself, watching me, but numb . . . I want my shock back. Standing at my stove I can see Ma pouring oil into the pan to fry me eggs. Whoomp, my heart sucks inside itself. I miss you, Ma. I hate that you're gone. I think of you if I get afraid to go do something and I ask myself, what's the worst that could happen? Is a Nazi going to shoot me? The worst that could happen is—not *living* while I'm still alive.

The accidental porn queen—

So, I'm jogging on the treadmill at the gym again, the man running next to me looks my way, does a double take and almost flies off the machine.

"It's *YOU!*" he says.

"Well—*now* it is."

He has something on his mind, I can see the cells cooking. "I gotta tell you . . . I hope you're not offended." I think I know what's coming. I'm wrong.

He says, "Ten years ago I wiped out on a Harley, and all the doctors said I'd never walk again. I was in bed for a year. I'd watch your TV shows and say to myself, 'One day I'm going to get out of this bed, find that woman and fuck her brains out.'"

It's nice to know that my show was inspirational. In so many ways.

Later that night at an AA meeting, a guy comes up and says, "Hey, I'd watch your show on crack!" People at meetings sometimes tell me they had watched my shows drunk; they'd laugh. And identify. Ma, do you see?

Pete and I are shopping in Pacific Palisades Village near our little villa—

The cashier recognizes me. "My husband and I loved your TV show. I was wondering what happened to you." Me too.

I try to appear cheerful, "I took time off to write a book." Five years ago.

"A book! When will it be out?" Leave me alone.

"Maybe by the end of the year." Which year, I don't say.

Pete says nothing.

Later that night, we're at Café Del Fini. A woman at the next table leans over. "I'm sorry to interrupt your dinner, but I was wondering, are you going to do your shows again?"

Again Pete says nothing.

We're home. "Hey Pete, I haven't aired a show in five years and people are still talking about it."

Pete stands silently, gazing at the contents of the fridge.

"Pete? Do you think, maybe, the universe is trying to tell me something? Pete? Maybe I should start taping again?"

He speaks. "You did your show at a time when public access was a new hot thing, times have changed." He's saying right time, right place? Wrong answer. So I shot him.

He's dead.

The cops come, a female, Caucasian, married. She understands and we stop for frozen yogurt on the way to the precinct. I'm booked by a policewoman whose husband doesn't get excited unless his team makes the playoffs. She gives me an extra blanket for the cell.

At the trial, my lawyer, *Gloria Allred,* selects the jury—"Have you ever done your hair totally different and your husband didn't notice?" The judge has been married for thirty years, she gives me the *I-know* wink.

My plea—"My husband dismissed me!"

And my case is dismissed.

At least my fantasies have morphed from suicide to homicide. I think it shows increased self-worth.

What did I want from Pete? How about, "You said important things in a unique, funny, intelligent way." Or, "I want you to succeed, and I'm also scared. When TV deals fell through in the past, you were devastated. And if do you succeed, I'm afraid of losing you." Yes, change is scary. And there have been big deals that died and I did not react well. It must have been hard for him to watch.

But what he says is nothing.

Later that night—

I'll show him what that guy on the treadmill was talking about!

I shmear on the tinted moisturizer, smooth my hair with the ionic flat iron, slip into the short white nightie and Ugg boots, and I go downstairs—

Pete's standing at the kitchen counter, with the fridge open, sucking whipped cream from an aerosol can and reading the *LA Times.*

"Pete?"

Not looking up, "Yeah? There were twenty shootings in LA this weekend. The war is *here,* in south central! Bush, that fucking criminal, we don't see *his* kids in Iraq with their chests blown open . . . Oh SHIT! It's going to rain this week!" He takes another shot of RediWhip.

"Hey Pete . . . like my new nightie?"

His eyes peep over the bifocals momentarily, "Yeah, it's nice. How much was it? Forget it, I guess I'll find out when the bill comes, and who's going to pay it—you?" His attention is back to the paper. He reads and rants and I stand there, like an idiot. I reach for my sketchbook and start doodling.

"Hey, Pete, check out the drawing . . . " I put it next to his paper.

"You showed me this."

"But I worked on it a lot since you saw it. See her hair, the swirls— "

"Well, I don't know what it means, 'suddenly her thighs didn't matter,' is that supposed to be funny?" Holy *Meshugeneh-Magoolski!* I married the Palisades Village Idiot.

So, why am I with a man who—after reading *Harry Potter*—I called a Dementor? (A creature destined to suck the spirit out of the high-spirited.) I'm into reruns. I get to feel invisible, unimportant, disgusting and alone . . . again. Of course, Pete's not all bad. He has adorable qualities. And a good heart; it's just closed to me. Divorce? Ma never divorced Daddy. If I leave I'll have to deal with lonely and scared. And with a lot less money! I've become a high-ticket fiscal princess. Yikes. If I'm on my own, I'll have to get off the couch and into action, because who's going to pay the bills—you?

I need more spirituality in my life.

I need to find DOG.

Reasons Pete and I never got a dog:

(1) Too scared it will die, (2) only *real* people have one, and, (3) Pete says,

"If I can't have a cat, you can't have a dog." He's a cat person. I'm allergic, and cats aren't dogs. (First two reasons also stopped us from having a baby.)

But lately, I've been feeling *real-er*. And I've started obsessing about dogs. I stop for dog commercials. I browse animal shelters. I peer in strollers, expecting to see a dog.

So one day, I'm PMS-ing, and I flashback to the play, in college, directed by Carl. Just before curtain one night, all the actors were in the dressing room whooping it up and Carl walked in. He was pissed. "PEOPLE! SAVE IT! USE IT ON STAGE!"

Hmmm . . . Can I use my bloated emotions to some end? And do the ends justify the means? Screw scruples, I want a dog. I make myself think of Pookie, da doggy killed by the mayor of Cote Saint Luc, a memory that always gets me crying, and I walk into the bathroom where Pete's shaving. "I'm"—sob—"over FORTY"—BIG sob—"and I . . . I . . . *never had a BABY!*" I'm on the floor. Pete, shaving cream foaming in his ears, is trying to comfort me.

"Waaa . . . I can't believe it, I'll *never* have a baby! Never!"—HUGE sob— "I can't even have . . . a *dog!*"

"Get a dog! We'll get a dog!"

"No. You don't"—sob—"like dogs; they're dirty and smelly."

"We'll get a dog."

Sniffle. "Are you sure?"

He's quiet for a moment, then asks, "Can it be an *outdoor* dog?"

"Pete, if you want an outdoor dog, get a squirrel." I promise him I'll find a medium-size, housebroken, non-drooling-nor-smelly dog.

Six million dogs are euthanized each year. Yes, *six* million. So I tour shelters and pounds around town, smelling dogs, and six weeks into the hunt, on Mother's Day, I find her in El Monte.

El Monte is a city we princesses drive by on our way to Palm Springs. It's a place of mower-transporting, mulch-filled flatbed trucks with bad transmissions. It's also home to the shelter Beagles and Buddies. About seventy small- and medium-sized dogs rush me as I enter the gate. Beagles are pouncing and pawing at me: "Take me home!" "Aren't I cute, look how I cock my head." "Forget that loser, he shits in his bed, take me!" "Brown-noser!" "Crotch sniffer!" "Like you're not?!"

And then I see the little blond—a buddy, not a beagle across the yard, sitting sideways, head turned toward me. I push through the sea of Snoopys, keeping eye contact with what looks like a wild fox. I should get this kind of eye contact from Pete. I finally get to her, she looks up with golden almond-shaped eyes and licks my knee. Once. She keeps looking up, staying politely seated. Regally. This is *the* dog. I know—like you know about a good cheese danish.

The woman in charge says, "She came from a home where she was abused by children."

"I'll take her."

We name her Hildy. Hildy and I are in the exam room with the-vet-to-the-dogs-of-the-stars. "So, Dr. Shulman, what breed is she?"

Hildy looks up at him, her head tilted, big eyes, crooked nose, all ears—she's waiting for an answer.

"Well . . ." He's contemplating. "I'd have to say . . . she's a dingo with the face of Bambi."

That seems right.

I cook for Hildy. I don't cook for Pete; then again, Hildy never said, "The chicken's dry."

By the way, the day after bringing her home, Pete, the outdoor-dog man says, "But *why* can't she sleep in the bed with us?" He takes the Hildybeast to the dog park and comes home proud. "Did you know the other dog owners nicknamed her the *aerobics instructor* because she gets all the dogs running?" I know.

I call, "Hildy!" she stops what she's doing, runs over, plops her butt at my feet and looks up. Head cocked, her kangaroo ears tuning in, the eager little fox awaits information. "We going for a walk, Mom? Is there a chewy thing? Would you like a lick? How may I please you?" And loving? Hildy makes Lassie look like a cold bitch. Hildy is the new Quaaludes.

"Want a massage, Hildy?" She lies back, belly presented, paws hinged, nose up, doing an imitation of Snoopy. Her fur is silky. It's better than stroking the velour cords I wore in highschool. She stretches as I massage her thighs.

Hildy is me. Encapsulated at my feet, doing yoga with her chew toy, is my vulnerability—in fur. Her life depends on me. I must do the right things, like not have poisonous plants in the backyard. My love for her is unconditional, although . . . I do wish she could type.

Me—A Love Story

The after-lude

I'd always hoped the perfect man—or sitcom role—would come along, and life would begin. Who knew what would come along would be *me*?

Oh, by the way, I left Pete.

Was it because he didn't fly back to Montreal for my mother's funeral? Because he can't handle his booze and RediWhip? Because he called me a pig in front of the painters? Well, there was a moment of clarity in the kitchen that night, standing alone in my hot-vixen nightie and Uggs. These boots are made for walkin'. I decided it's better to do the hard thing *once* rather than live the hard way *every day*.

I had been telling myself, for eighteen years, "Hey, what's a little verbal abuse and neglect? No relationship is perfect. It's okay." But then Ma died, and my idea of okay changed. The voice that occasionally sprang forth from the parallel universe spoke to me again. "LEAP AND THE NET WILL APPEAR." And I packed and left.

Everybody freaked. (Good thing Ma was already dead, this would've killed her.) They all keep asking, "How are you?" Ooooo . . . that question! This time I have an answer. "How was Nelson Mandela when he got out?" Free.

I wonder what's next and can I handle it? My *it's-Sunday-night-and-my-homework-isn't-done* dread, a part of the past, stays for the most part, in the past. It creeps back occasionally, but thing is, I'm not all alone anymore, trying to figure out tough answers by myself. We're in this together. Ma may have been sugar, I may be eggs, you may be flour, but together—we're the cake.

I see us all, as a big cosmic cocktail. We're drenched in one another, affecting each other in ways we don't even know. I bet one day, a software program will show us how we're points of energy, linked, riding along on God's silly string. Maybe we're here to connect the dots. I'm just a point in the universe, and I make an important point because no one sees the world from here but me. I count.

When I was little, life was limited to two TV channels in a nineteen inch box and everything was black and white. Either/Or, Good Samantha/Bad Serena. Now I can think outside that box. I can hold a complex view of situations and people, and I'm not so quick to hate, or to love. I've learned to ponder. Which is not the same as obsess.

For forty years, I drove through life with one foot on the gas, the other on the brake, stalling, going no where but crazy. Crazy is gone. Negative thoughts still come, but I don't entertain them. I don't have to invite them in and fix them a martini. I treat *I'm-a-fat-loser* thoughts like telemarketers and I hang up rather than get hung up.

I'm not gripped at the mirror anymore, trying to re-create myself so I can leave the house. I may not always love my thighs but I don't want them dead, either. Sure I feel better when my weight is down and my stocks are up, but I can still get out, even with frizzy hair and a big zit. I remember the old couch-days . . . and I appreciate how now, I can get out the front door within an hour. Faster if there's an earthquake.

So where do I go when I go? To AA meetings, to check out guys with a girl-friend, to Kati, to my trainer, to the agent, the publicist, acting class, writing sessions, botox doctor . . . I have a team. All I've ever really wanted was a team. And the perfect pair of shoes.

Jewbonics

A Glossary for the Gentile and the American Jew—

Ch is always pronounced like you're clearing your throat

babushka: Kerchief, worn on the head. It's a look.

bubbe: Grandmother; also a term of endearment, as in "Listen, *Bubbe,* if I could walk like that I wouldn't need the talcum powder."

bubbe-myseh: Old wives tale. Also used to dismiss, "Don't be stupid, that's a *bubbe-myseh.*"

challah: Egg bread.

chaynick: Kettle.

chazzer: Pig. "Don't be a *chazzer.*"

chupah: Canopy under which a bride and groom stand during marriage ceremony.

chutzpah: Guts, balls, moxie.

copviteck: Headache.

dreck/dreckisha: Vomit, piece of shit.

farchadat: Dopey, stunned .

fackackt: Shitty.

fahter: Father.

falsha: Liar, fake, phony.

farmach: To shut.

farmisht: Mixed up, to say the least. You don't know what the hell to do, it's just too much, too much I tell you!

farshtinkuneh nevileh: Not a nice person, a stinky one.

farshtunked: Stinky person.

feh!: Feh!

finagle: To manipulate someone to give you something, or allow you to do something, but not in an evil way. Mild coercion lacking maliciousness.

finstera nevileh: Dark, Machiavellian person.

fress: Eat, like a pig.

goniff: Thief.

gornisht: Nothing.

goy: Non-Jewish person (usually a man).

goyem: Plural of goy; any group that is not Jewish. (This includes those who've converted. This is generally believed, but not openly admitted.)

grobeh: Thick. A derogatory term usually referring to a part of someone's body, as in "Look at that *grobeh tuches!*"

groisseh: Big, as in "Look at that *groisseh tuches!*"

groisseh falsha: Big fat liar.

groisseh pisk: Big mouth.

haimisha balabusta: Dedicated homemaker.

haserai: Vomit.

hint: Dog.

ketzele: Kitten. A term of endearment used for children.

klutz: Klutz (yeah, it's Yiddish).

kvell/kvelling: Beaming with pride.

kvetch: To whine and complain for no apparent reason other than to let everyone know you're not happy.

latke: Potato pancake (carbs fried in oil).

malpeh: Messy loser.

meeskite: Ugly person.

mench: (Rhymes with *stench*) a man, but a woman can be one, too. An upstanding, honorable, worthy person.

meshugeh: Crazy.

meshugeneh: One who is crazy.

mishugas: Silliness, craziness, trouble, one's issues, as in, "Such *mishugas!*"

mitzvah: Blessing, favor.

narish: Absurd, silly. Another word used to cast doubt on the sanity of others.

nevileh: Not good.

pisher: A little pee-er.

pisk: A disrespectful way to say mouth.

pitskele: A tiny bit.

plutz/plutzing: Bursting, mostly with aggrevation or disbelief. "You just want to *plutz*."

punim: Face.

putz: A penis. Also a bad man.

roita kopp: Redhead.

Shabbas: Sabbath.

shicker: A drunk.

shiksa: A non-Jewish female; not exactly a derogative term, but not exactly flattering.

shlemiel: A dumb guy.

shlep/shlepping: Dragging or pulling something or oneself.

shlub: Dumb, lazy guy.

shmaltz: Fat, as in chicken fat or the reason you can't fit into your jeans.

shmatteh: Rag.

shmear: Smear, spread.

shmooze/shmoozing: Mingling, get to know.

shmuck: A penis. Also a bad man.

shmutz: Dirt.

shpritz/shpritzing: Spraying.

shrek: Scream.

(a) shrek: Someone so ugly, when you see him or her, you want to scream.

shtetl: Poor Jewish village. The 'hood—same hair, different dialects.

shturmock: A stupid man.

shvartzeh: A black person.

traipse: A good, all-purpose "walking" word. It could be walking, wandering, skipping.

tsooras: Trouble.

tuches: Rear-end.

vilda chaya: Wild animal.

zaftig: Softly fat. Good for Rubens, death for L.A.

ziseh punim: Sweet face.

Expressions:

Azameh zach!: What a thing! A phrase used for dismissing what another has said.

A mench tracht un Gott lacht: Man plans (thinks) God laughs.

Du bist meshugeh!: You're crazy!

Dine fatter hot ingeshticken a pitskele putz, und hot gotten tsrick a groisseh!: Your father put a little dick in and got back a big one!

Farmach dine groisseh pisk!: Close your big blowhole!

Gay in drerd: Literal translation: Go in ground. But it really means, "Drop dead."

Gib a kik, a chazzer, a grobeh tuches, a meeskite—feh!: Take a look, a pig, a fat ass, so ugly—get it away from me!

Hacked mir nisht in chaynick: Stop banging me in the kettle or shut up your noise.

Oy a broch!: Gee! Gosh! Oh my! Christ! Oh fuck!

Oy gevalt!: Gee! Gosh! Oh my! Christ! Oh fuck!

Oy vey!: Gee! Gosh! Oh my! Christ! Oh fuck!

Oy vey-iz-meir!: Woe is me. Gee! Gosh! Oh my! Christ! Oh fuck!

Vos host du geteen?: What have you done?

Words referring to penis and man are often the same:

petseleh: Tiny penis.

putz: Regular-size penis. Also a stupid or bad man; a jerk.

shlong: Penis (not used to describe a man, but I want to note how many Yiddish words there are for penises).

shmendrick: A penis, but a little one. See *nebish*.

shmekel: A really little penis.

shmuck: If this penis were a man, it would be J.R. on *Dallas*.

shvantz: See *shmuck*.

vyzoso: A penis and also an idiot.

Men, in other words:

dumkop: Dummy; (Literally, dumb head).

goniff: Thief.

hint: Dog.

nebish: A man who can do no right.

shlemiel: Dumb guy, fall guy. Not a guy you want to marry.

shlepper: A man who drags through life.

shlemazel: Loser.

shlub: Chubby loser.

shmegegge: Squiggy on *Laverne & Shirley*.

shmo: Dummy.

shnuk: Pathetic, but not mean.

shnorrer: A con, a chisler, petty cheapskate, no-good-nick.

shturmock: Stupid man.